5187 1449

Untangling the Mind

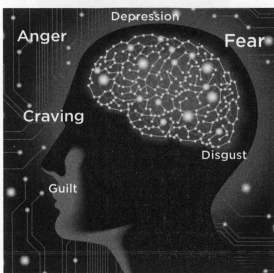

Un-tangling the Mind

WHY WE BEHAVE THE WAY WE DO

D. Ted George, M.D.

with Lisa Berger

HarperOne
An Imprint of HarperCollins*Publishers*

HarperOne

Illustrations by Jane Whitney.

FIRST EDITION

Library of Congress Cataloging-in-Publication Data

George, David T. (David Theodore).
    Untangling the mind : why we behave the way we do / D. Ted George, M.D., with Lisa Berger. — First edition.
        pages   cm
    ISBN 978-0-06-212776-1
    1. Emotions.   2. Neuropsychiatry.   3. Neuropsychology.   I. Berger, Lisa.
II. Title.
    BF531.G46   2013
    152.4—dc23   2012045928

13 14 15 16 17   RRD(H)   10 9 8 7 6 5 4 3 2 1

To W. P. W. Wilson, M.D., professor emeritus at Duke University, who taught me my love of psychiatry.

To my patients who afforded me the privilege of walking alongside them.

To my family who shared life's ups and downs with unconditional love.

Contents

Untangling the Mind

Introduction

Unsettling Questions

I am a psychiatrist and a neuroscientist. My specialty is treating people with emotional disorders and researching the neurological reasons for extreme emotions and destructive behaviors. My patients range from people with active, successful lives to individuals who have to be hospitalized. Nevertheless, each of them is troubled by strong emotions that frequently spin out of control. They are beset by anger, fear, depression, or trauma. Like countless individuals who are not seeing a psychiatrist, my patients struggle with these emotions because they do not understand them and are not able to contain the behaviors they spark.

When I began my practice almost thirty years ago, I thought my job was to diagnose what was wrong with patients and offer treatments that would make them feel better. It made sense at the time. Yet as I began listening to patients, I soon realized that I was seeing only part of the picture. Focusing purely on diagnosis and treatment was like trying to solve a complicated math problem by learning how to use a calculator. These were tools used in the healing process but were incomplete because of a missing vital third element: understanding what was happening in each patient's brain.

I remember giving a talk to a group of people at a community outreach gathering. I was one of a number of speakers talking about depression and treatments, and I was the last speaker on the program. After speaking for about thirty minutes, I answered questions. As the people were leaving the hall, I heard snatches of conversations that suggested disappointment with all the presentations. The gist of their reaction was frustration because we did not answer their basic questions. People wanted to know why they were depressed and why treatment was often not successful.

Only years later, after many hours of listening to patients, did I truly understand what that audience and my patients wanted: informative, relevant answers to unsettling questions. They wanted to know: Why am I the way I am? Why do I behave this way? Why can't I get better? They were frustrated because, for most of them, psychiatry had so far provided lists of symptoms and an assortment of drugs but little understanding. They had no idea where their symptoms came from, what the symptoms meant to their lives and why treatment was not working for them. I shared their mystification, especially in those early years. When I first began practicing, there was much about therapy and psychiatry that I did not know. Every day patients posed questions I could not answer.

A middle-aged woman who had been depressed for years asked, "Why do I always dwell on negative things?"

An older man on the brink of divorce asked, "Why can't I control my temper?"

A college student feeling overwhelmed by stress and who had become a binge drinker asked, "How do I stop drinking?"

A man who had accidentally killed a pedestrian asked, "How do I get rid of this guilt?"

A successful businessman with a drug addiction asked, "Why do I always feel inadequate?"

A teenager who was cutting herself asked, "Why don't I feel anything?"

Answers to their questions have been slow to come. Finding them is why I decided to divide my career between treatment and research. My patients' mystification about what was causing their strong emotions led me to pose a question that became the centerpiece of my research: What produces an emotion? As an extension of that, I wondered if it was possible for someone to feel an emotion for no reason. For instance, some patients said they felt angry despite not being able to identify any conflict behind it. Time and again they said that they just woke up angry and had no idea why they felt that way. And the emotion was so strong that it dictated their life. What was the difference between a legitimate emotion and a pathological one? Was there a neurological explanation, maybe a malfunction, for why my patients' lives were being hijacked by their seismic emotions?

A Panic Attack Leads down an Unfamiliar Path

My education into the mysteries of emotional distress began unexpectedly. I was conducting a study of people who experience panic attacks, attempting to pry apart the diverging symptoms of alcohol dependence, withdrawal, and panic disorder. I was interviewing each of the participants before they enrolled in the study, reassuring them that their participation was entirely voluntary. All routine stuff. Except for Paul. After we had talked about the procedure and chatted briefly about his background, I was almost at the door when his voice stopped me.

"Doc, sometimes I'm afraid I'm going to lose control and hit my son. What do I do?" he asked.

I halted. No patient had ever asked a question like that. He sounded genuinely distressed, his tone pleading for a meaningful answer. This was completely new for me—I knew next to nothing about emotions associated with violence. I wanted to be helpful but had no basis for reassuring him that such disturbing thoughts would pass. In the moment, all I could do was fall back to the psychiatrist's default response. "Tell me more," I said.

Paul didn't add much more information other than that he felt fear and unease at home and had a sense that he could quickly lose control with his family. I had no answers for him, only bland reassurances, and exited quickly. But his anguish stayed with me long after. I resolved to learn more about the neurological origins of this intersection between panic and aggressive urges. What made Paul feel as if he had no control over these emotions? Was it something in his past or in his brain that kindled his aggressive thoughts? The questions captivated me, and not just as a scientist.

As a physician trained to treat patients beset by crippling emotions, I wanted to be able to offer help. I didn't even understand what he had been going through. The more I thought about him, the more absorbed I became in probing the neurological underpinnings of emotions that could instantly push people's aggressive feelings into possibly acting them out.

That was many years ago and ever since that conversation, I've been searching for a neurological explanation to better understand behavior. Why does anger trip into rage and even violence in one person but not another? Why are some people overcome by fear even though there is no apparent danger? How does depression become so overpowering that it shuts down a life? What are the emotions that turn someone into a predator or a stalker? When do an abuse victim's healthy fears morph into post-traumatic stress disorder (PTSD)?

The emotions I encounter in my practice are not unusual. They're universal, human reactions; what makes them pathological are not the emotions themselves but the circumstances under which they flare up. Patients "lose it" when there's no rational reason—no immediate trauma, no life-and-death crisis. Their emotions are extreme, yet their daily lives and relationships often appear stable. This makes it even harder for them to understand what is happening. Something around them—a sight, sound, smell, thought, or memory—stirs their emotions to the point that their reaction is totally out of proportion to the circumstances.

Magnified Emotions

This book looks at emotions and behaviors that are out of proportion to a situation. Emotions are not the same as behavior—they fuel it. By examining the relationship between tumultuous emotions and magnified responses, you get an idea of what sets them off, who's most vulnerable, why they spin out of control, and what you can do to understand and contain them. My hope is to begin to untangle and answer the vexing questions about the *why*s, *what*s, and *how*s of emotions.

My search has helped me construct a neurological model that ties together extreme emotions with behavior, pathways, and clinical characteristics. This explanation centers on the notion that everyone possesses a neurological switch deep in the brain that can be flipped at the right time, and the wrong time. I hope to share with you my understanding and insight into how this switch works and what's going on in people's brains. As you read, I will walk you through my findings, which are illustrated by stories of individual patients. Ultimately, I hope to answer questions about your own emotional life or that of someone you know.

I also offer this caveat: I don't know everything. Far from it. Psychiatry is a daunting and humbling profession, and every day I encounter patients who continue to challenge me. My thoughts and ideas are constantly evolving, taking on new perspectives and more knowledge. Nothing is written in stone.

The book covers a wide swath of emotional landscape, yet it contains a handful of recurring themes. There is a neurological reason for emotions that seem inexplicable. These emotions arise because neurons are activated not as a single structure but as part of a process that is wired into a neurological platform. This platform encompasses not only multiple structures but also pathways and neurochemistry.

Another theme is that the purpose of human emotion is survival. Scratch the surface of any emotional state and you will find a behavior that has its roots in survival. At the heart of our survival instinct is the fight-or-flight response. This term has become part of our popular vocabulary. However, most people have only a general idea of what it means. Few realize how fight or flight is manifested in everyday behavior and how it can rule daily routines.

Finally, years of doing therapy and research have convinced me that the extreme emotions I encounter among patients are universal. While patients provide the most dramatic evidence of how and why people lose it both emotionally and in their actions, no one is immune. All people are vulnerable to having their emotions neurologically hijacked, and awareness of this is essential to learning to control them.

Many books have been written about emotion, including a small cluster about the neurological workings of emotion. But little has been written on the integration of emotional behavior and neurological pathways. The brain's machinery is hard to penetrate, and only with the advent of positron-emission tomography (PET) and functional magnetic resonance imaging (fMRI) has science been able to see what goes on inside the brain when someone feels a particular emotion. Until now, the bulk of the research has been done with animals and then extrapolated to humans. But I have had the unique experience of not only treating thousands of people derailed by out-of-control emotions but also being able to combine what I've distilled from them with years of research, both mine and that of other scientists. While studies involving chimps, cats, and mice have helped guide my investigations, my findings are drawn from complicated, passionate people. I hope this book will help people understand and navigate the origins of their troubling and often painful emotions.

Part I, "Why Emotions Spin Out of Control," begins with how I came to focus on extreme emotional disorders, survival instincts, feeling threatened, and fears that underlie emotional lives. I also try to demystify the brain's inner workings by describing how it translates sensory signals into emotions. Part II, "Losing It: Extreme Behavior," uses stories of individuals to show the inner workings of specific emotional disorders. I not only show how they derail lives but also tease apart the emotions and behaviors so you can see them in a new light. Part III, "Seeking Healthy Emotions," shows how demystifying the workings of the mind helps explain different treatments. At the same time, I offer a cautionary explanation, emphasizing that knowledge and understanding are not enough to contain people's emotional fires. It also requires taking personal responsibility.

You are going to read about patients, although their identities have been obscured for privacy and confidentiality reasons. Nevertheless, the stories represent real people, and their struggles have much to teach all of us not only about their disorders but also about their courage and fortitude in confronting them.

One last thing. Despite all the neurological realties and evidence of hardwiring for our errant emotions, I believe that in most cases, treatment works. It begins with giving patients a voice—hearing their deepest, most distressing secrets and not judging but accepting who they are. By learning about themselves, not only their psychological undercurrents but also their neurological makeup, they can shift their fears about their troubled emotions and move from the dark places of bewilderment, inner loneliness, and despair to hope. With this, they can feel the freeing effects of personal honesty and the satisfaction of taking responsibility.

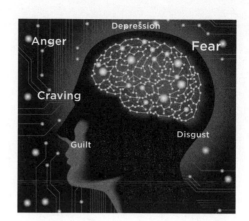

Part 1

Why Emotions Spin Out of Control

Patient Zero

A Patient Under Siege

I greeted Henry Wilson in the waiting area and escorted him to my office. It's an intimate room furnished with soft throw pillows on a well-worn couch, a couple of floral upholstered easy chairs, and a wood-paneled ceiling. I gestured to a seat and took my usual place in a chair across from him. I scanned over this new person—middle-aged, well-groomed in a charcoal suit, dress shoes, and a serious look.

We exchanged brief pleasantries, a few comments about the weather, and then got down to business.

"How can I help you, Henry? What can I do for you?" I leaned forward, making steady eye contact. I knew what my body language said about my attitude would set the course for our time together. I tried not to look too eager, although that was what I felt—an avid curiosity to hear his story and devise a way to help. My practice was relatively new, and every patient was a compelling challenge.

"I've been on depression medication, and it's not working very well. My wife thinks my thoughts are disorganized and jumbled."

"What do you think?" I asked.

"She's somewhat right. I do have a problem concentrating and don't sleep well. And, as she is quick to point out, I'm no good at planning things. She also says I've got a negative outlook. I don't know. Maybe that's the depression," he said.

He did look haggard, probably from lack of sleep.

He took a deep breath. "I have to confess, you are not the first psychiatrist I've seen. In fact, you're the fourth. And each one prescribed medication, and nothing has worked. I've been told I'm treatment resistant. Maybe I am, I don't know. But it's caveat emptor with me. I'm not an easy case, and I'll understand if you'd rather not see me." He sat back, as if waiting for me to accept his verdict.

"You're here now, so why don't we talk and you tell me later whether you want to continue." I paused, then plunged ahead. "You said your wife thinks you have a negative outlook. Can you tell me more about that? Why does she think that?"

Henry Wilson began by talking about their seventeen-year-old daughter, who was at a tough-love boarding school in Utah because of repeated episodes of cutting, lying, and drunk driving. He and his wife fought over the decision to send her there because it was costly and far away. It was now time to pay her tuition, and Henry said he couldn't afford it anymore but strongly believed she needed some kind of correctional environment. He and his wife were revisiting all the old arguments.

"The kid has problems. Okay, call me negative. We go round and round, and by now I'm just fed up with the whole thing. Helen thinks I'm the problem. I've given up trying to explain things to her. We really can't afford that school. She knows that—I was let go last month because business is so slow. And the boss and I didn't get along. I'm job hunting now, but it's not easy. She is right about one thing—we don't talk anymore. We just take swipes at each other."

"It sounds like you've got a full plate. Losing your job must have been a blow. Did you have any inkling that that was going to happen?" I asked.

He shrugged. "Yes and no. I did blow up at my boss the month before. He's a micromanager. You know the type, always double-checking, saying I wasn't paying attention to details, said clients were complaining about my style. Whatever that meant. When he got that way, I either pushed back or just made myself scarce, and left. That probably wasn't the best way to handle it."

"You mean leave work?" I asked.

"I'd go to the tavern around the corner, big watering hole for lobbyists. I'd maybe bump into someone I know, we'd have a couple of drinks, and I'd feel better. Until I got home. Helen hated it when I'd have a couple after work. She'd really lay into me, accuse me of being a drunk, which I'm not, and then keep on about how I needed help."

"What would you do then?" I probed.

"I'd lose it. Couldn't help myself. Rip into her like she was a Thanksgiving turkey. She knows what gets to me and doesn't hesitate to say things that set me off. So I lash back. I was just defending myself. In the end, I'd go into the TV room and not come out for the night. I'd sleep on the couch."

Henry paused, his eyes searching my face for a reaction. If he expected to see disapproval, he was disappointed. I had heard versions of this and was concerned about his behavior. It did not take much to send him off the rails, and I wondered why.

"Overwhelming emotions can be frightening," I said. "How do you feel when your wife gets on you?"

"Like I'm under siege. I've got no control over the situation but can't get away. Trapped, I guess."

Henry and I devoted much of that first session to his explosive temper and how it was rippling through his life. We especially examined the progression of emotions he went through, the mood swings that began with aggravation and sometimes ended in avoidance behavior that looked like depression. His range of emotions fascinated me, especially the anger. It seemed the most predominant emotion, yet it somehow was consistent with his other emotions. He was one of the first patients in my fledgling practice who had a constellation of problems that I felt were somehow related. There was a puzzle here I needed to solve, and I sensed that the first piece was Henry's rage.

Why Do People Behave the Way They Do?

I've treated hundreds of patients like Henry Wilson. I'm also a researcher, conducting studies at the edge of psychiatric science. Throughout my career, I've been absorbed with the question, why do people behave the way they do? Anger that trips into rage or violence. Fear that paralyzes someone. Depression that shuts down a life. The dead affect of a predator or stalker. Why does one person end a mild disagreement with a brutal punch while another person responds with a groveling apology or weeping? Why do they decide to act one way and not another? I've been focused on trying to understand how normal emotions get hijacked and become twisted and destructive.

Of course people are driven by a complicated mixture of genetics, environment, upbringing, and biology. Every shrink knows this. But what is it about our nervous system that differs from person to person? This is where I've been looking for answers or, more precisely, for models to explain these behaviors—biological templates that would explain what happens in our brain when certain emotions are triggered. This model would be like a switch or universal remote control—push the green button and the power always comes on, push the yellow button to mute the sound. It would provide an accurate, predictable explanation for an array of intense emotions and behaviors.

Henry presented me with pieces of a puzzle, and anger was the most predominant piece. To successfully treat him, I needed more than insight into what he was experiencing. What was happening neurologically to set him off? The better I understood his emotions and behavior, the more effective his treatment would be. It was like the adage that you feed a man not by giving him a fish but by teaching him how to fish. I could not just give Henry a drug because it would only temporarily alleviate his emotions. Medication and support would ease the immediate symptoms but not address the reasons for them. My goal was to give him the tools to manage his emotions over the long term. To do that, I had to figure out what was going on in his brain.

Now, after years of clinical research and legions of patients led by Henry Wilson, I have formulated a model for understanding extreme emotions and destructive behavior. Before I get into that, let me explain how I got here.

Surprised by Psychiatry

I did not begin my professional life intending to become a psychiatrist. In medical school, I was on track to go into internal medicine and barely noticed the few students who spent their residency not drawing blood or putting in central lines but talking to people. My heroes in medical school were the revered surgeons and internists who dealt with life-and-death issues every day. Then a friend suggested I apply for a rotation at Duke University to study with a preeminent doctor who happened to be a psychiatrist. Enticed by the man's reputation, I called him. I don't remember exactly what he said except for one question: "Are you any good?"

That intimidated yet intrigued me. Doubts are regular fare for medical students, and at the time, my plate was fuller than most. I worried constantly about whether I was choosing the right treatment or requesting the right test or knew enough to make an accurate diagnosis. The man's question was like asking a Navy Seal if he could parachute behind enemy lines, a challenge for me to plunge forward and prove I was both determined and tough enough to take on something completely foreign. My answer must have been the right one because he offered me a small stipend and an opportunity to study with one of the best.

Psychiatry came alive for me during that time. Patient stories took on personalities, and their histories became dramas. My initial misplaced skepticism about the benefits of psychiatry—what was the point when patients never got truly well?—was washed away by the realization that every illness has a natural course and an end stage regardless of whether the disease is in the mind or the body. But at that time, psychiatry from my vantage point was lodged at the bottom of the totem pole of specialties. It seemed that psychiatric residents received few patient referrals, and when they came, it was late in the day after all the other specialists had done their work. They were usually sent to some outer, dingy office to do an interview. Psychiatry was to medicine as voodoo was to healing. This presented both an obstacle and a challenge. Psychiatry would be difficult, but the field was wide open for discovery.

After getting my medical degree and completing residencies in internal medicine and psychiatry, I wrestled with what kind of psychiatrist to become. A full-time private practice seemed limited. I wanted broader psychiatric horizons, fields beyond treating one patient at a time. I cast about for room to run, an area where I could tackle mysteries and perhaps make a difference for many people. I wanted discovery and impact, not adulation and attention. It's probably natural that research excited me.

The Allure of Research

I began my career at the National Institutes of Health in Bethesda, Maryland, in a laboratory studying addiction. Around the same time, I opened a small private practice. Over the years, my patients' stories kindled ideas and theories that could be applied to many other people. Their struggles sparked in me a search for answers that I hoped would alter the way physicians and researchers thought about emotions and behavior. My motivation to help my patients dovetailed with my desire to uncover a behavioral model to guide my thinking.

Fortunately, my research into a neurological model for intense emotions didn't require redefining neuroscience. Human biology is full of models that explain physiological and neurological reactions. When you touch a hot burner in the kitchen, cut yourself with a knife, or spill bleach on yourself, your hand will become red, swollen, and painful. Every time, no matter when or where the accident happens, the body reacts this way. This is the model for inflammation.

As I pursued my research into a possible neurological model, I realized that I already had a vital piece of the puzzle. I realized that I had encountered it serendipitously during a medical school lecture describing the transection of a live cat's brain done by Philip Bard in 1928.[1] Bard was a physiologist at Harvard Medical School and a protégé of Walter Cannon, the father of the fight-or-flight response concept. Seeking to trace the source of anger in the brain, Bard had transected different sections of a cat's brain to see how the animal responded. Bard's findings were remarkable—when he transected the high midbrain, the cat responded with a fight reaction. The cat instantly arched its back, puffed up its lungs, hissed, and bared its teeth. It looked like the Halloween cat with its body enlarged by inflated lungs and fur on end. It was a classic example of defensive rage. But when Bard transected the lower midbrain, the cat did not react.

Normally, the Halloween-cat response is a natural behavior to a threat. As I learned from his experiment, all the physical actions needed for defense—an arched back and enlarged lungs to look as menacing as possible and teeth bared, ready to tear into anything— appeared to arise from the high midbrain region. By severing the connection with the cortex, which is the advanced part of the brain controlling thought, intention, and action, Bard produced an automatic reaction in the cat. He generated an emotionally charged reaction in the cat—defensive rage. There was no reason for its defensive rage other than severing the connection between the cortex and the midbrain.

Bard's findings were the foundation for the model that would explain defensive rage. What fascinated me about the animal's defensive rage was that it was uncontrollable and had no external or obvious explanation. Rage came from the midbrain. A severing of the connection between the cortex and the midbrain had generated a dramatic emotional behavior. And the cat would react this way every time this part of its brain was disturbed. It was impossible for it to learn that the threat was nonexistent and stop acting this way. When its cortex was disconnected at the high midbrain level, the cat readied for a fight.

The Face of Domestic Violence

Henry Wilson returned to my office the following week. As soon as he sat down, he sighed loudly and began talking. "This was a bad week. Helen and I . . ." he halted, perhaps searching for a starting point. "Thursday night I came home from an interview, and it was a little late. I had stopped for a drink. About seven. Not real late. The house was dark; Helen was gone. No food in the kitchen, lights off, not even a note. I thought maybe she had left me. I really do love her," he declared, looking squarely at me as if to punctuate his feelings.

I nodded and waited for him to continue. I had a feeling that Henry was tottering on a thin ledge.

"So I called her cell, and when she answered I was relieved. Meant she hadn't left me or anything. But then I got really angry. She said she was at the store, carpet shopping, and there was food in the fridge. I flipped out. How could she do that to me? Just leave me like that? She never tells me anything," he bemoaned. Then he added, almost as an afterthought, "I feel like hell. It's like my skin's crawling. I'm always agitated, always angry."

After hanging up with his wife, Henry started drinking and consumed almost a fifth of vodka.

"What happened when your wife came home? Did you talk?" I asked.

Henry shook his head. He was trembling, his eyes unfocused, as if reliving something terrifying. "She provoked me, called me a loser. I felt attacked, so I had to protect myself. I couldn't help myself. I . . ." He struggled to get out the words. "I pushed her hard into the kitchen chair. I still feel really bad about it."

Neither of us said anything for a moment. I was sorting through the combination of symptoms I was seeing—anger, impulsiveness, moodiness, depression. These were parts of a puzzle, but I could not put them together in any meaningful order. I wondered, *Why did he push his wife?* I assumed that something external was igniting his emotions, that they were event driven. Then I remembered Philip Bard and his Halloween cat, which had puffed up and bared its teeth to look fierce and get ready to defend itself, perhaps just like Henry.

More Clues to Understanding Henry Wilson

A groundbreaking experiment for me happened early in my research career. Colleagues and I were conducting experiments giving lactate infusions to panic patients.[2] Lactate infusions were popularized in the 1990s by an earlier study that linked them to exercise. If you do lots of exercise, you know its sibling, lactic acid—the glucose by-product that builds up in oxygen-starved muscles and briefly causes discomfort and cramps. In a research setting, a sodium lactate infusion, the basic form of lactic acid, was a pharmacological probe for producing a panic attack.

For me, the fascinating aspect of giving a lactate infusion to panic patients was that it induced a sense of losing control that healthy volunteers did not feel. I wondered whether this sense of being out of control was what Henry felt when he was angry with his wife. While treating Henry, I looked to the lab for more insights. To search for an answer, colleagues and I began giving lactate infusions to patients with a history of physical aggression.

Getting a Lactic Infusion

A vital tool in studying panic attacks is the sodium lactate infusion.[3] By injecting sodium lactate into a person, researchers can trigger the physical symptoms of a panic attack. Sodium lactate is a basic salt of lactic acid, which is produced by cell metabolism. Researchers have known for decades that a sodium lactate infusion produces feelings of panic, probably because it creates a chemical imbalance in the nervous system and sends signals to the area of the limbic system that controls anxiety reactions.

The injection acts within twenty minutes of the infusion, and its effects are plain to see. A person begins to breathe quickly, the heart rate increases, and the palms become sweaty. About 70 percent of panic patients have a panic attack during an infusion, while only 5 percent of healthy individuals have a panic attack. By stimulating a panic attack in the lab when a person is connected to monitors, researchers can better understand the disorder's biological markers. (There is more about panic attacks in chapter 6, "Desperate to Escape.")

Ralph, a participant in our lactate study, was a hefty bus driver who was asked to describe his feelings as we infused sodium lactate into his vein. It took only a few minutes for signs to appear. At first, there was tingling with hairs standing up on his arm. "It's like the cops are after me and I've got to run," he said. In a flash, he felt that it was too late to run and he had to stand his ground and fight. His lungs puffed up, his face became red, and he said his heart was racing. Everything around him was a blur. He sensed the researchers and technicians in the room but no longer saw them clearly. He felt out of control and wanted to strike out. It was the same feeling, he said, when he hit his wife. As soon as the lactate ceased flowing, he calmed down within ten minutes and returned to being chatty and friendly.

The findings of lactate infusion studies were huge for me. They showed that we could induce the same out-of-control feeling that people felt when they hit their spouse. Yet there was no spouse present during the study to cause this feeling. It reminded me of Bard's findings with the cat showing rage without the presence of a threat. Furthermore, non-panic patients did not experience the out-of-control sensation, and this suggested that there was something different about the nervous system of the aggressive patients that surfaced during the lactate infusion. What was it?

Thus began my research into domestic violence. Some scientists shunned it as not being worthy of rigorous examination. The medical establishment frequently regarded the loss of control that accompanied domestic violence to be a matter of personal choice, not a serious topic for science or medicine. The general belief was that domestic abusers made a conscious decision to let loose. They could act responsibly and control themselves if they wanted, but they chose not to control their temper. As a result, very little was written about the causes for domestic violence in medical literature, while there was a plethora in sociology and psychology journals, mostly written from the point of view of the victim, not the perpetrator.

I plunged ahead, and after months of notices in newspapers and talking to other health care professionals, I located enough people like Ralph who had committed domestic violence to study them. Through repeated lactate infusion studies, I began fitting together the pieces of the puzzle—the defensive rage, feelings of panic, and anger behind domestic violence. (In chapter 5, "Hair-Trigger Tempers and Anger Unleashed," I get more into the underlying causes and neurobiology of domestic violence and other kinds of anger.)

I returned to thinking about Philip Bard's Halloween cat poised to defend itself against an imagined threat. Bard had localized a region in the midbrain where defensive rage came from, but he had not identified the actual source of the rage. Now I wondered about other types of aggression. Pieces of my puzzle were still missing, but sometimes life is just following the next footstep. A literature search applying an array of search terms related to rage led me to the Departments of Psychiatry and Neuroscience at the New Jersey Medical School and neurobiologist Allan Siegel.

Siegel also dug into the neuroanatomy of defensive behavior but widened his canvassing to encompass not one but two kinds of aggression.[4] One was defensive rage, the cat reacting as if it was threatened. The other was violent behavior that appeared to have no emotion associated with the aggression. This was predatory behavior, what a well-fed cat does when it stalks a bird. As I read about Siegel's observations on how a cat slinks and then pounces, I realized that aggressive behavior, regardless of whether it was defensive or predatory, was ultimately tied to the same brain region. The brain's emotional processing system, the limbic system, was obviously part of the dynamic, but Siegel went beyond that into the midbrain to implicate a tiny structure called the periaqueductal gray, or PAG. Here, suggested Siegel, might be the source of the ferocious emotions.

After reading Siegel's research, I felt relieved and exhilarated. Relieved because his work affirmed that I was not on a wild goose chase and exhilarated because I could at last begin to sketch out the where and why of my neurobiological model. There was only one catch. Siegel's research, like Bard's, was based on cats, not humans.

Revealing Undercurrents

Henry brought his wife, Helen, with him to our next session. It is sometimes awkward asking a patient to bring a spouse to therapy; many see their spouse as the enemy or want to focus solely on their problems. But since much of Henry's misery revolved around Helen, I was eager to get her input.

They sat on the small sofa, not touching and a little stiff, as if braced for a visit to the dentist.

"Nice to meet you," she said as she shook my hand. I sensed that she was putting on her best poker face, not knowing where I was going to take our session.

We sat facing each other for a minute or two. I did not fill in the silence but waited. "I don't know why I'm here. Henry's not thinking straight. He needs meds. That's what every other shrink has told him. He just needs to find the right medication," Helen stated.

"He certainly has troubling symptoms," I said, then looked at him for a response. I had been thinking about his meds, wondering what drug to put him on. But I hesitated prescribing anything yet. The signs were going every which way. Depression, difficulty concentrating, insomnia—they're pieces of people's pain but not necessarily the reason or explanation.

"I do feel a little better," Henry said. "I'd give the depression a three. Last week, it was up to eight, almost a terrible ten."

"Glad you feel better," Helen interjected sarcastically. "I still have to deal with all your messes."

Umm, I thought, *that didn't take long.*

"I'm trying to be positive here. You're always saying that I'm negative. What messes are you referring to? Of course I have no idea since you never talk to me. Hell, you're hardly even home most of the time," Henry said.

"This isn't productive," I said. "I'm glad your depression has lifted, but as we talked about before, there are other issues here. Mrs. Wilson, you seem angry, maybe bitter despite your husband's efforts to get better. Am I reading you right?"

Helen Wilson nodded firmly. "Exactly. He's been seeing docs for months, and I'm still walking on eggshells around the house, not knowing when he's going to fly off the handle and start yelling and screaming."

Henry was shaking his head. "I can't help it. I try, I really do. But when you freeze me out, don't talk to me for days, it sets me off. My father used to do that."

"I don't talk because you always argue with me. I say something about Sarah, and you let loose on how we shouldn't have sent her to that school. I mention the car making a funny noise, and you immediately go to how we have no money. I get it. I'm as worried as you are about money. But all the yelling and arguing isn't helping." Helen was trembling slightly.

I was not surprised that Helen did not mention that her husband had become physically violent with her. Spouses are often in denial about domestic abuse, hoping it will go away. I also thought that the incipient violence revealed more about Henry Wilson than about their marriage.

"Are you often angry?" I asked Henry.

"I wake up angry, I go to bed angry. Everything annoys me. The way people drive, the way Helen chews her food, the way my neighbor puts out his trash," he said.

"You mentioned your father. That he used to set you off," I said. "How did that happen?"

Henry sat still for a moment, glancing between me and his wife as if debating how much to say.

"My father was a tyrant, pure and simple. Big on discipline. If I didn't do something his way or took too long, he'd grab me by the back of my neck and force me to my knees and push my face into whatever was close and disgusting. Dog food, dirty mop, even the toilet. I'd have to redo the job, and then he'd ignore me for the rest of the day. I'd live in fear that whatever I did, he'd be on me again. That went on until I left for college."

"You never told me this before," Helen said. The surprised expression on her face indicated that this revelation had opened her eyes.

"I had a rough childhood. Lots of people have. It's something I'd rather forget," Henry said.

His confession raised so many questions in my mind, beginning with, what connection did his past have with his behavior now? That therapy session opened a new chapter for the Wilsons and for me. I realized that Henry had become my Patient Zero, the first case in my hunt for a neurological model to explain severe emotional disorders. His distress spurred me on to do all I could to help him while also building on the neurological insights I was acquiring. The term *Patient Zero* was first used in the AIDS epidemic to refer to the earliest known patient to have the disease. Scientists now use it to refer to an index case, that is, the initial patient in a widespread outbreak. While Mr. Wilson of course was not the cause of any emotional disorders or the first to experience his symptoms, he was the first patient to show me that his extreme emotions were not unrelated. He put a human face on the pieces of the puzzle that I had been accumulating since Bard's lecture.

The story does not end there. As I continued to treat both Mr. and Mrs. Wilson and to collect neurological insights about Henry's extreme emotions, reality set in for me. I realized that these were two people who were hurting, and they were not alone. Lots of couples were going through similar distress. If I talked to such couples regularly, I realized, I could do more than understand—I could perhaps make a difference in their lives.

I know that practicing psychiatrists disagree on how to treat couples like Henry and Helen Wilson. I also know that they had hurt each other and their pain persisted. To me, they had three choices. One was to continue the way they were. The second was to declare that changing was too hard and perhaps separate. The third, which they opted for, was founded on their inherent goodness and affection—they did love each other and wanted something better. This produced the ultimate choice of committing to exploring and improving their relationship.

Summing Up

- Defensive behavior, such as rage, appears to be controlled by the cortex. If the cortex connection to the midbrain is impaired, this behavior is difficult to control. As a result, feelings of anger and fear, which may be variations of defensive rage, can erupt with no rational explanation.

- Feelings of being emotionally out of control, as happens with rage and panic, can be induced chemically.

- Stimulating select areas of the brain's PAG produces the behaviors that are characteristic of the defensive rage seen in the Halloween cat.

It's All About Survival

Survival on the Savannah

While I was treating Henry Wilson and deep into searching for a neurological model, I went on a trip to sub-Saharan Africa to speak at a symposium on grief counseling. At first the journey felt like a hiatus from psychiatry and research, but that changed almost as soon as I arrived. Far away from my patients, I quickly acquired new insights into what was possibly fanning the fire of intense emotions. My journey started in Gulu, Uganda, where civil war has raged for decades, forcing millions of people into camps where thousands have died from disease and malnutrition. Adding to the tragedy were all the young people who had been kidnapped by the most vicious combatants, members of the Lord's Resistance Army.

From what I witnessed, people didn't feel safe at night. Watching from my hotel window around dusk, I saw a long trail of women and children trudging into the city to seek refuge from marauding rebels. Every night, they would find a place to curl up, and in the morning they would return to their villages and camps.

During part of the symposium, I went into the countryside a few miles outside the city to a huge tent enclave to talk with families, orphans, and refugees. I had never seen anything like it. It was filled mostly with children, thousands of them, spindly thin, lying on blankets in the dirt. They didn't cry or chatter. Their faces were expressionless. Fearful of abductions, people had been living there for years.

I remember talking to a man, sinewy and frail. Through an interpreter, he talked about guilt and not being able to live with what he had done. Soldiers had conscripted him into the Lord's Resistance Army and forced him to kill his sisters. He had broken free but now was deadened by the memories. The trauma had rendered him numb, yet his conversation with me signaled a will to live.

Thoughts about the power of our survival instinct were still with me a week later when I left Gulu for a brief stay at a wildlife reserve on the edge of Masai Mara National Reserve. I stayed at a hotel perched atop a hill that overlooked a vast savannah of acacia trees and scrub. It was teeming with wildlife, so I found a comfortable chair and gazed out over roaming herds and feeding animals. In the distance, a line of elephants, babies in tow, plodded toward a grazing spot. A group of zebras scattered, kicking up their heels and tossing their heads. Closer by, two giraffes nibbled on branches. Antelope hung around a watering hole, drinking and alert. I sat until a guide roused me for a jeep tour around the reserve.

The sun was setting, the sky turning an inky black as the jeep wound around the edge of the plain. The driver shut off the engine, and the naturalist said we should just listen. He cautioned us about not stepping out of the jeep because, regardless of appearances, it wasn't safe. The serene silence was quickly broken by a distant roar and a flock of birds erupting from the grass, cawing noisily. It was almost dark, and I could see only shapes slinking around the periphery. The jeep moved on, crawling along a dusty road as the naturalist whispered a description of what we were seeing. Our first encounter was a pride of lions lying only a few feet from the road. They seemed almost tame, and I asked the guide why they were so docile. He pointed to a lump of something between the mother's paws. "That's because they've had a big kill and are not hungry now."

We continued on, passing closely to a family of zebras and a group of antelope. They were not grazing but in constant motion, scanning their surroundings. When one jumped, the rest followed suit and bolted into the darkness. We inched slowly past an elevated anthill occupied by a mother cheetah with two cubs. The babies were young, and the mom had just killed a gazelle, which they were gnawing on. Our guide explained that the mom had shown the youngsters how to bring down the animal by ripping into its neck, and this was an essential lesson for their future survival. For a time, the jeep paralleled a slow-moving stream that appeared empty and lifeless until the naturalist pointed out a shape on the far bank, the catchlight of two eyes near the water surface. A crocodile lying in wait.

I felt uneasy, sensing that every movement, every shape was vaguely threatening. The animals seemed expectant, braced for a sudden reaction. This wasn't the afternoon's idyllic scene but a jungle filled with predators and those searching for safety. It was as if what I had seen earlier was an amusement park with cardboard cutouts and what was now in front of me were the real animals. What daylight had obscured had become vividly obvious.

These animals were engaged in a life-and-death struggle for survival. Every act, every move was driven by instinct and aided in their survival. Their behavior had one purpose: survival. The birds shrieked to sound an alarm to warn mates. Other birds bombarded or harassed a predator to discourage it from attacking them or their young. The zebra's stripes made a single animal hard to see and enabled it to blend in with the larger herd, giving it safety in numbers. The antelope's spindly, muscled legs gave it the agility and endurance needed to outdistance hungry predators. Crocodiles were masters at melting into a stream so they could approach an unwary target. Gazelles bounced and jumped, known as stotting, to show a predator that it would be difficult to catch.

The animals' instincts were well-honed. They innately knew who to befriend, who to avoid, who was weak, and who was dangerous. Their highly developed sight, smell, and hearing were especially attuned to threats. They constantly monitored their surroundings, alert for anything abnormal or for a predator inching too close.

I realized that the afternoon's tranquil plain only hid the animals' true nature—it did not extinguish it. These creatures were designed for survival. I thought back to the people in Gulu, and something clicked in my mind. A new perspective. We, too, are designed for survival, and even layers of civilizations and technology have not erased our fundamental nature. Just as Charles Darwin described one hundred fifty years ago, we are wired to survive and endure. Every day, our instincts and actions work in concert to ensure that we protect ourselves and live to see another sunrise. Darwin's theses about survival of the fittest described the life-or-death struggle in the animal kingdom, but it shared important parallels with our lives. Even though our fight-or-flight reactions have developed into sophisticated behavioral strategies for a fast, technological world, they are rooted in Darwin's theories on survival.

In fact, we possess two kinds of survival behavior. One is attuned to react to threats and the other to pursue reward. Each makes imminent sense. We need to be able to protect ourselves and stay clear of danger, and we need to be able to feed ourselves and reproduce our kind. Each set of instincts comes with its own battery of emotions. For now, I want to talk about how we react when confronted by a threat. Farther on, I get into our reward system.

Your Primary Survival Tools

Watching the people of Uganda fight for their survival and seeing a similar drama play out on the Masai Mara made me realize that staying alive demands constant interaction between people, or animals, and the environment. This interaction involves monitoring and assessing your environment, which you do through your senses. In

Inside an fMRI

A functional magnetic resonance imaging (fMRI) machine is a large magnetic tube that a patient slides into wearing a non-metal helmet with a mirror attached. Thinking and feeling involve energy, which for the brain means consuming glucose via blood flow. The more neurons fire, the more glucose they need. The fMRI measures how blood flow changes during a mental task, like solving a math problem, making decisions, or viewing faces or scenes. The mirror enables a person in the scanner to view a computer monitor outside the scanner. In any research study on how the brain reacts to thoughts or emotions, the individual in the scanner watches a monitor via the mirror and pushes a handheld button to make choices. Complicated math formulas are then used to interpret a person's response vis-à-vis changes in the brain's blood glucose activity.

One drawback of an fMRI is that it registers activity in brain structures but does not show individual neurons firing. Sometimes significant differences in brain responses occur in a matter of millimeters and so are not detected by an fMRI. Thus fMRI offers a window into the relationship between brain activity and thought processes but not details about nerve activity.

---

everyday life, people tend to pay little attention to the routine information their senses deliver to them. So it can be a leap to connect these seemingly innocuous impressions with survival. That is, until you visit a country where people are constantly fighting for their survival or a savannah teeming with life-and-death struggles. These offer vivid examples of the vitality of one's senses. Missing the slightest detail or not recognizing a sound can become a fatal mistake. Our survival senses are as valuable in negotiating the streets of Everyplace, America, as in surviving the plains of Gulu, Uganda.

Your senses are your primary survival tools. Behavior is essential, too, but the survival response begins with information from your senses. Your senses inform you about danger long before you have time to think. They deliver instant messages demanding action. They bypass the slow process of thinking and immediately tell your brain and body if you are in danger. You can overhear an argument in the grocery store between two people speaking in a foreign language and even if you don't understand the language, you can recognize anger and aggression.

Survival can be understood as a kind of chain reaction: senses take information from the environment, this information excites emotions, and emotions impel action. So to understand behavior and emotions, I turned to their origins—how our brain processes sensory information.

Several brain structures are vital to sensory processing for survival. Precisely how the brain processes sensory information into emotions and behaviors is immensely complicated, involving numerous brain regions and millions of neurons. For the sake of simplicity, I am going to focus on certain key brain structures. The dominant ones are the thalamus, amygdala, hippocampus, and cortex. The diagram below gives you an idea of how they are situated. Phil's story will give you an idea of how sensory information travels through these structures to influence behavior.

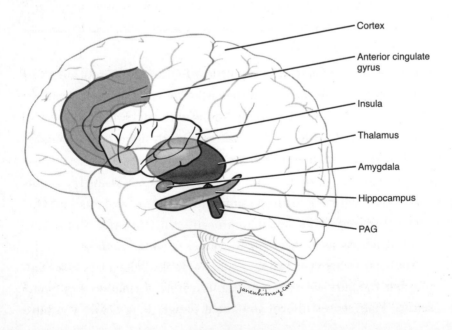

A Threatening Situation

Phil came to me because a judge instructed him to get treatment for anger management. He had a history as an aggressive driver and knew if he received one more ticket, he would lose his license. He was a reluctant patient and did not believe he had a problem because his outbursts were sporadic and unpredictable. Furthermore, he felt his actions were legitimate responses to others' behavior and not of his making. Little did he realize that survival responses in his brain played a huge role in his experiences. Although his drastic behavior brought him to me, I am going to tell his story not only in terms of what he did but also from the perspective of what was going on inside his head at the time.

The incident began as a routine commute from his job in a government printing office to his home in the suburbs. This particular day was stressful for him because he'd promised his wife he would be home early, but bad weather had slowed traffic to a crawl and gridlocked intersections all over the city.

He was almost across the bridge leading to Virginia when he had to halt suddenly for a stream of pedestrians in a crosswalk. His car was in the crosswalk, so people walked around it, everyone trudging ahead tucked under umbrellas except for one man. The man wore a dark suit and horn-rimmed glasses that reminded Phil of his boss. As he passed Phil's car, he pounded his fist on the hood, called him an asshole and yelled at him for blocking the box. Phil remembers the man's eyes magnified by the glasses, glaring at him.

Your Sensory Net

Your survival response begins with the senses. When you see, hear, or feel something that could be harmful, a signal goes via specialized sensory receptors to the thalamus. The thalamus functions as a gateway for sensory information passing to other parts of the brain. It handles messages from both your environment as well as your body. It processes signals indicating internal pain from a physical blow just as it processes signals from around you, whether from situations or other people. It manages a barrage of activity, sending sensory information to the cortex and to the amygdala.

When Phil was stuck in the crosswalk as pedestrians streamed by, two of his senses picked up threatening information. There was the sound of the man pounding on his hood and berating him and, even more powerful, the look in the man's eyes. The eyes are a rich source of information about potential danger. In this instance, the thalamus processed the man's glare and sent an alarm to a brain structure that reacts to possible danger: the amygdala.

A Lightning-Fast, Unconscious Reaction

Once the crosswalk cleared, Phil proceeded across the bridge to the George Washington Memorial Parkway, his blood boiling with the image of the man's look of contempt. He remembers feeling sweaty and jittery. Traffic sped up, and Phil switched lanes repeatedly to get ahead of the pack. He was already late and feeling pressured to make up for lost time. At one point, he cut especially close to a Lexus SUV. As soon as he pulled ahead, the SUV came so close to Phil's bumper that he braced for a collision.

The instant Phil saw the car tailgating him, he took his foot off the gas and flipped the bird. Suddenly slowing down appeared to aggravate the SUV driver even more. The driver honked repeatedly at Phil and then zipped out of the lane and raced ahead. Phil was so furious he was shaking, and he couldn't help but notice that the driver also wore thick, dark-framed glasses, like the pedestrian in the crosswalk. He gunned his car and gave chase, weaving in and out of traffic to catch up with the SUV. *The guy needs to be taught a lesson,* he thought. He barely saw other cars pulling over or slowing down to avoid him.

When Phil caught up with the SUV, he rolled down his window, screamed obscenities at the driver and then veered his vehicle beside the SUV to force it onto the shoulder. Both drivers were going over eighty miles per hour as they shouted and gestured at each other. Phil had almost pushed the SUV into a ditch when it accelerated up the shoulder to an off-ramp. The SUV disappeared as Phil barreled on. He arrived home thirty minutes late and was unable to stop shaking.

The Amazing Amygdala

The amygdala is critical to handling sensory information, especially signals that convey a threat or danger. It is your principal survival weapon. It is like a bodyguard, helping ensure your survival by protecting you. It is so well attuned to reading threatening signs that when it is electrically stimulated in a research setting, it generates feelings of foreboding or imminent danger.[1] It has been programmed over time in certain people to cause them to instinctively react to snakes, spiders, heights, enclosed spaces, loud noises, and sudden movements.

The pathways between the thalamus and the amygdala are like a superhighway—much faster than other connections, such as those linking the thalamus with the cerebral cortex. Any sensory message that contains an element of fear goes via the express lane. The signal zips through the thalamus and lands in the amygdala so it can launch the body's defenses.

The SUV driver's actions—pulling so close to Phil's car that they almost collided, honking, and yelling at Phil—were threatening. As a result, Phil's thalamus alerted the amygdala, which processed the signal to indicate imminent danger. The amygdala was now fully engaged.

Phil's immediate reaction to the SUV—gesturing and taking his foot off the accelerator—were amygdala driven. Instincts were in charge at this point, not rational thought.

The amygdala functions so fast that it registers possible danger before you are aware of anything threatening. It's like an early warning system that sounds an alarm even before you know what set it off. It is particularly sensitive to reading emotional facial expressions and can do this without a person realizing it.[2] Cognitive science researchers have found hard evidence for the amygdala's subconscious detection system.[3] They conducted a study involving volunteers looking at facial expressions. The volunteers were shown faces on a computer screen while their brain activity was monitored by PET scanning. They were instructed to press a button if or when they saw an angry expression. Unknown to the volunteers, an image of an angry face sometimes flashed on a screen for less than forty milliseconds (too short a time for the brain to consciously recognize the angry face). Then the image was replaced by a neutral face, which stayed on the screen longer. Volunteers only reported seeing the neutral face, yet their amygdala reacted the same as when they saw an angry face for a longer time.

Once the amygdala detects strong emotion that indicates a threat, it launches a response. It is so forceful and essential that it can override signals from the larger, more developed cortex. The amygdala dictates survival reflexes and, at the same time, suppresses input from the cortex. In the face of danger, the amygdala takes charge of the body's entire survival system. It can galvanize the brain and the body into reactions such as fighting or running away. It prompts the autonomic nervous system to prepare the body for action. When it comes to danger and fear processing, the amygdala is the boss.

The power of the amygdala over the cortex in a threatening situation has been eloquently demonstrated by neuroscience researchers in France.[4] Led by Rene Garcia, the researchers used electric footshocks to expose lab mice to painful situations. Once the mice were conditioned to recognize a coming footshock, researchers monitored nerve activity in the amygdala and cortex. In the instances when an electric shock was certain, the rats' amygdalae became active and controlled their physical responses, namely their fear reactions. At the same time, neural activity in the cortex slowed.

I use the word *eloquently* because Garcia's team employed a lab experiment to reveal an essential fact about our body. It must be able to react quickly and not think. This is basic to our survival. It makes sense that our body can disconnect thinking from reacting in order to do what's needed to survive.

The same happens with people, as Phil's actions show. All the sensory information traveling to his amygdala—the sights and sounds associated with the threatening SUV—dictated his behavior. Especially amazing is that his extreme emotions and behaviors took place in a car—*amazing* because the car provided an environment packed with a variety of sensory stimuli that indicated he was being threatened. The notion of being threatened is a common theme in this book, and you will be reading a lot about it. For now, and to explain Phil's behavior, I apply the term to the broad concept of anything that challenges either your physical or mental sense of well-being.

The first threat and trigger to Phil's behavior was being stuck in his car in traffic, which was making him late. He had promised his wife that he would be home on time, and now he wasn't living up to her expectations. The man pounding on his hood and glaring at him in the intersection signaled a threat of dislike and disapproval. The SUV that tailgated him presented another threat. It said, "You don't know how to drive—get out of my way." On top of this, the man's glasses were possibly associated with the threatening man from the intersection and his boss.

Phil's reaction to these threats—his disregard for his own safety as well as that of others—illustrates that his amygdala was in control and he wasn't thinking. This is precisely what Garcia's study shows, that threat disconnects the cortex so that there is no thought, only reaction.

The fact that all this happened in a car reveals how the hippocampus interacted with the amygdala to add a context to Phil's instant reactions. The hippocampus provides the amygdala with vital extra information—it shares memories and experiences so that a threat can be given a context to determine how dangerous it really is.

Despite a car's license plate, cars offer a place where people's emotions and behaviors can be anonymous. We are all just faces in a window. (This cloak of anonymity is also present with domestic violence, which happens behind a home's closed doors where social inhibition may be minimal.) Phil felt a sense of righteousness, namely that he would teach the other driver a lesson, which was coupled with an activated nervous system, making him sweat and his heart pound. Together, these gave him the power to do things he would not normally do.

And the car, with its speed and metal enclosure, gave him a feeling of protection and security that he would not have felt if he encountered the SUV driver at work. The brake and accelerator made Phil feel external control even though he felt out of control internally. People tell me they feel this same sense of control when holding a gun as they walk through a dangerous neighborhood.

On Second Thought

The only reason Phil was talking to me about the road rage duel was because a third driver had taken a picture of his license plate and forwarded it to the Virginia State Police. He was not remorseful about the incident, feeling he had been provoked by traffic conditions, particularly the pedestrian, who had glared at him, and by the SUV driver, whom he called the instigator. These rationalizations did not occur to him at the time, but only after he had calmed down and his amygdala had loosened control of his survival reflexes. When it did, his thoughtful cortex reasserted itself.

While the amygdala is deep in the brain and more closely associated with primitive functions, the cortex is your upper brain. The cortex generates thought, language, and consciousness, among other

Darwin Tries to Outwit His Amygdala

At one point in his career, Darwin wanted to test his survival re-actions and see if he could control them in the face of danger.[5] He undoubtedly asked himself, "Just how strong are my sur-vival instincts? Can my modern brain take charge?" He went to the reptile house at the London Zoo and put his face against the glass cage that contained a puff adder, a highly venom-ous African snake, intending to provoke the snake into trying to bite him. He was determined, he wrote in his diary, not to flinch or move. Suddenly the snake lunged at him, hitting the glass barrier. Darwin describes his reaction: " . . . as soon as the blow was struck, my resolution went for nothing, and I jumped a yard or two backwards with astonishing rapidity."

It made no difference, he wrote, knowing that the snake could not reach him through the glass. His thoughts were pow-erless; instinct propelled him with " . . . an imagination of a danger which [he] had never . . . experienced."

The snake's attempt to bite Darwin launched a primitive reaction beginning with visual stimuli registering the snake's movement and ending with a message to the brain's amygdala. The result was Darwin jumping or, put another way, survival behavior. The cortex had no role in the reaction. Darwin could not control the reflex, even though the glass between him and the snake meant the danger was not genuine. His instinctive jump backward was automatic, happening without thought or awareness of what he was doing.

---

functions. In contrast to the amygdala, the cortex operates more slowly, generating conscious thoughts rather than subconscious reflexes.

The amygdala and cortex have a dynamic relationship and send information back and forth. They are connected, so it is possible for the cortex to assert control. The cortex can contribute to sur-vival too, but it needs to be taught how to respond in a threatening situation. It does not react automatically but deliberates and then initiates action. When law enforcement personnel or soldiers practice reacting in dangerous or emergency situations, they are learning to impose thought and assessment, namely cortical control, over their amygdala's survival reflex. In essence, it is learning to look before you leap.

Research confirms that the cortex can take control of instinctive emotional reactions.[6] Ahmad Hariri, an ingenious neuroscientist, undertook a study of the neural mechanics that control the amygdala's reactions. He and his colleagues showed study participants a series of faces with either angry or fearful expressions. They applied fMRI to record participants' brain behavior as they viewed and then matched a range of expressions, such as angry faces with other angry faces. This was a perceptual task. Then he added a twist to see whether an individual's thought processing affected the brain's emotional reaction. As volunteers viewed the faces, Hariri asked them to press a button the moment they could label the expression. They were to push the fearful or angry button as soon as they picked out the expression of a target face. This was a cognitive task.

Their fMRI scans revealed a remarkable finding: matching the emotional faces was associated with increased blood flow to the amygdala, the primary fear center. However, when volunteers labeled the expressions they were seeing, the cortex became active and the amygdala activity quieted. When participants paused to consider which emotion they were looking at, the thoughtful brain took over and decreased activity in the instinctive amygdala. The few seconds taken to put a label on an expression was all the cortex needed to take control. This labeling study confirms that even though the survival-driven amygdala is the first structure to react to a threat and generate fear, the cortex can seize control. In doing this, the cortex suppresses a fearful reaction and interjects rational thought.

For example, imagine you are home in bed asleep and are awakened by a crashing sound in the living room downstairs. Instantly you are alert with your heart pounding and your breath shallow and fast. You tiptoe downstairs, flip on the light, and halt, braced for action while you scan the room. Your amygdala is on the edge of initiating a threat-response reaction. Then you see a broken vase and Zippy the cat peeking from behind a chair. As rapidly as your survival brain geared up, it slows down and you feel normal again. Putting a label, "Zippy the cat," on the source of the crashing noise gave your brain time to activate the cortex and calm the amygdala.

If you had charged into the living room without pausing, your amygdala would have ramped up your entire body so that it could confront what it felt was a dangerous situation. On the other hand, by pausing and assessing what happened, your brain was able to decide not to react as if an intruder had broken in. Many, like Phil, find it difficult, if not impossible, to check their instinctive emotions. They don't pause, they plunge headlong.

Taking Control

As I have seen with patients, learning how to suppress fear and consciously judge what's really happening in a situation is difficult. Complicating the task is that your brain does not always give you accurate information. The senses and thalamus can misread, the amygdala can overreact, and the cortex can misjudge. Your survival system can temporarily malfunction. This may happen when you feel stressed by demands and expectations of coworkers or family and too overwhelmed to handle all that is coming at you. At times like this, the connection between the cortex and the amygdala weakens, and the cortex loses its influence.

The amygdala is always alert to signs of a threat. In times of stress, it sends out strong signals because the cortex has less influence. Let me give you three examples of how this might play out in the workplace. For instance, say your company is doing well, it's making money, and management clearly values you. At a time like this, if you get an e-mail from your boss asking to see you ASAP, you probably don't think much of it and go see him right away. This is a normal reaction—you do not feel threatened, and your amygdala isn't activated.

However, if your company is struggling and losing money, and there is talk of layoffs, every day is stressful for you. Now if you receive an e-mail from your boss saying to come see him ASAP, you may get extremely defensive and angry. You may suddenly go home sick or become passive and expect to be fired. These reactions—versions of fight or flight, or passivity or depression—are also normal. You legitimately feel threatened. Given your company's condition, you could lose your job. So, in response, your amygdala sparks some type of survival reaction, overriding the influence of your cortex.

A third scenario is that your company is healthy and doing well with no talk of layoffs. This time, when you get an e-mail from your boss, you react with some form of fight, flight, or shutdown. This is not normal—you feel threatened, but there is no rational reason to feel that way. Nothing in your environment is truly threatening. Nevertheless, your brain launches a survival response with the amygdala taking control and the cortex having no say in your actions.

This third response is what some people go through. Their mind registers a threat around them even though none actually exists, and their emotions and behaviors initiate survival reactions. Their feelings and actions are not appropriate to the situation and external facts, but they have little control over them.

Summing Up

- You engage in survival behavior all the time, and it is usually a reaction to a threat or overwhelming fear.

- Essential survival tools are your senses, which transmit messages about danger to key structures in the brain via the thalamus.

- The amygdala is the brain's principal survival structure and is noted for working very quickly, below conscious awareness, and for being able to override thoughts from the cortex.

- The cortex is essential for thoughtful deliberation and aids survival by presenting choices for ways of reacting in a dangerous situation.

3

What Ignites
Your Emotions

Patients Lose Control

Carl, an engineering consultant, had just completed weeklong contract negotiations with a client. The deal was vital to his business, and he hadn't slept or eaten well throughout the week, worrying about what would happen if it went south. It was still unresolved when he arrived home on Friday evening. He had spoken with his wife earlier in the day, telling her that he planned to be home by six P.M. Knowing of his stress at work, his wife, Bethany, had prepared a favorite dish, homemade lasagna. It had taken her a couple of hours, so she was both annoyed and worried when his car didn't pull up the driveway until around nine o'clock.

As soon as Carl came through the back door, Bethany was on him. "Are you okay? Where have you been?" she demanded. "I've been waiting for hours. Dinner is cold."

"Jacob needed help. Figures for the new contract. You know, the Ridgeway project," he explained apologetically.

"You could have at least called!" she shot back, her voice rising.

"Don't talk to me like that! Damn it, Bethany, you think I like being at the office? While you get to stay home and do your nails . . ."

When Carl talked about the incident, he said he understood Bethany's anger and had intended to apologize profusely and offer to take her out to dinner. But then the tone of her voice made him "flip out."

Another patient, Mary, was a college student living at home. One of three siblings and the baby of the family, she was on track to graduate early. Both her older brothers had graduated with honors from prestigious universities and had landed well-paying jobs in computer science. She knew her parents expected equal success from her, and she, too, was eager to finish school, get a job, and move out. Studying at home was difficult. She felt isolated from her classmates and missed dorm-style chat sessions with other kids in her classes. And her parents nagged her, asking about every paper she turned in and giving her advice on how to manage her time.

Mary was fragile and had been seeing me for panic attacks and bouts of depression. She always felt the weight of the world on her shoulders, struggling to meet expectations and prove herself smart and capable enough to live on her own. One particular evening, she felt especially beaten down. She was facing deadlines for three separate classes—quizzes looming in two of them and a big paper due for another. As she stared at her computer, jumping between studying Confederate warfare and writing calculus theorems, she flicked to her Facebook page. A girlfriend had posted a link to a YouTube video.

The video showed her friend with a bunch of boys who had congregated in a flash mob and were dancing in the stacks of the university library. It looked like such fun, with everyone laughing and jumping about, then running from security guards. Mary watched the clip a dozen or so times, and with each viewing, she grew more desolate. She could have been there, having fun like a normal college kid. After watching the video, she clicked back to Facebook and cruised her friends' postings.

Hours passed until around one A.M., when she curled up and went to sleep. The next morning when her mother came to wake her, she pleaded illness and stayed in bed. When she eventually got up to eat, she told her mother that she thought she had mono and was going to drop out of school. Watching that video had sent Mary on a downward spiral. She never returned to her classes, and though she tested negative for mononucleosis, she still felt an overwhelming desire to sleep all day. Mary was in shutdown mode.

Both Carl and Mary were reacting to what they saw and heard. The facial expressions and tones of voice used by their family and friends were registered as threats and set off strong emotions in both of them, prompting them to react. Yet neither of them realized what set them off. They had no idea why they reacted so strongly. Carl became aggressive, and Mary retreated into herself. What they didn't know was that both of these reactions arose from their brain and body interpreting the messages from their senses. The message Carl inferred was that no matter what he did, he couldn't keep his wife happy and that she didn't appreciate his hard work. The message Mary inferred was one of inadequacy and worthlessness. She felt like an insignificant spectator on life.

Other than overreacting to what they were seeing and hearing, Carl and Mary are not very different from most people. Everyone's senses can trigger an emotional reaction. Some sensory stimuli have more influence depending on where they come from. A scene that triggers a strong childhood memory or a condemning look from your spouse affect you more than a scene without a memory attached or a look from a stranger would. Yet people are not always aware of the signals that set them off. So many things can push people's buttons and prompt them to react emotionally.

You may realize that you are sensitive to your husband's look of disapproval but not that you are also picking up on his body language, like crossed arms, that also may signal disapproval. To someone with hair-trigger emotions, such seemingly trivial events become the final straw—the ultimate proof that they are being challenged in some way. The challenge, and the implied threat, could be disrespect, inconsideration for their feelings, or being ignored.

Lighting the Fuse

The fact that Carl and Mary had difficulty controlling their emotions in response to perceived threats suggests that survival instincts were activated. As Darwin first recognized, your senses are for survival.[1] In his book, *The Expression of the Emotions in Man and Animals*, published in 1872, he explained the survival value of individual expressions. He gave the example of an angry person. The upper lip is raised to expose canine teeth, or cuspids, indicating readiness to defend. Darwin concentrated on facial expressions, yet he also considered the emotional impacts of voice, tears, and posture. Even certain body movements communicate emotion, like a step backward with the hands raised and the head turned slightly aside, revealing fear.

Particular emotions make people feel threatened. Of course anger and fear are at the top of the list, but there are many other challenging feelings, such as disrespect and loathing. Adding to the mix is that some people are more sensitive to certain stimuli and emotions. For instance, Mary the college student wasn't bothered when she was confronted by a hot temper, but if she heard arrogance or disdain in a voice, she flipped out. I never asked her but suspect that bursts of temper were common in her household and perceived as not a big deal. On the other hand, growing up as the little sister of two high-achieving older brothers, she acquired a sensitivity to not being taken seriously.

People react especially to stimuli that, according to their personal danger thermometer, deliver a strong threat. Consciously or subconsciously, we scan our environment for danger. We may see it in an angry face on a passerby, hear it in the sad tone of voice of a partner, or smell it in the smoky air. Information picked up by one sense can be influenced by additional information from another. A fearful tone of voice may amplify the fear you see in someone's face. You are more likely to conclude that someone looks afraid if you also hear trembling in his voice.

As I explained in the previous chapter, when your senses detect something in your environment, a signal goes to the thalamus for processing. From here, the signal splits into two pathways, one to the cortex and another to the amygdala. The signal to the amygdala goes fast, while the one to the cortex takes a lot longer. As a result, the amygdala reacts long before the cortex if the sensory information includes signs of danger. The amygdala does this by using memories and knowledge stored in the nearby hippocampus about what's harmful or dangerous. Moments later, the cortex adds more information about what the senses detected.

There are universal expressions of emotion that affect most people. Facial expressions have a huge impact—the look of anger, sadness, or fear is the same in every culture. You can tell what ignites your emotions by noticing what in your surroundings, your circumstances, or other people grabs your attention when you lose it. Which of your senses is most engaged? An abundance of research indicates that facial expressions, the eyes, the pitch and tone of a voice, and sometimes smell can carry some of the strongest messages. Even though much of our communication happens electronically nowadays, we still engage our senses. While reading a Facebook post, we "hear" a tone of voice; while seeing a person on Skype, we detect a certain facial expression; while looking at an online photo, we imagine a smell. The fact that these sensory experiences are largely imaginary does not matter. They are real enough to the person having them.

What's in a Face?

Your face conveys essential information about you, particularly your mental state. The eyes may be the window to people's souls but the

Noise Can Make You Crazy

Specific sounds and decibel levels are known to provoke people's emotions. A common example is nails on a blackboard, but music and voices can also set you off. For some people, swear words produce an immediate reaction from mild anxiety to rage. Unpredictable noise has been found to be more frustrating than predictable noise. Most often, people react to noise with annoyance, which can be a valuable survival emotion. Annoyance can be a kind of warning that something around you is unpleasant or even harmful. Experts estimate that 4–6 percent of the population is noise sensitive, meaning that these people do not adapt to new sounds.[2] They experience noise overload and are more susceptible to being overwhelmed and then reacting.

---

face is the door, and it's often wide open. For most people, facial expressions are one of the primary fuses for igniting extreme emotions.

The pioneer in researching how facial expressions are linked to emotions is Paul Ekman.[3] While his most well-known work involves reading faces in order to tell when someone is lying, he has dug much deeper into facial musculature and emotional networks to reveal the underpinnings of fear, anger, and sadness. A facial expression can spark an emotion in two ways: someone else can observe it and react, or the act of moving certain facial muscles can produce an emotion in the person doing it. Put another way, you can pull your own emotional trigger by creating an emotion in your face. (Smile and you feel better—it does work.)

Ekman has identified clusters of facial expression that signal a single emotion. He reports that people have sixty facial expressions that show anger, the range taking into account intensity (from annoyance to rage), the level of control, how authentic the emotion is, and the circumstances surrounding it. Types of anger he has analyzed include resentment, indignation, outrage, vengeance, and berserk—which he describes as an uncontrolled, out-of-control response to a provocation. He has also deciphered fear expressions and clusters of related emotions, including fright, worry, terror, phobia, and panic, each with degrees of intensity, a sense of timing from urgent to pending, and an element of control or not. These appear slightly different on each human face. And a mere muscle twitch can alter an expression from concern to panic.

Facial expressions associated with specific emotions are innate and cross cultures. When people are sad with grief, whether in New Delhi, New Zealand, or New Jersey, their facial muscles move the same way. The same is true for other basic emotions Ekman has teased apart—surprise, fear, disgust, contempt, and happiness. What is equally true is that everyone recognizes these emotions. Your ability to read emotions is as hardwired into you as your ability to express them. As Ekman succinctly puts it, "Emotions are not private."[4]

Emotions are woven into survival at the most fundamental level. People's faces speak volumes about their feelings, plans, and motivations—whether they mean us harm, are willing to help us, or want sex. Is he going to hurt me or hug me?

A comparison of brain activity in people viewing a fearful face and then a scene of mayhem produces markedly different patterns.[5] A fearful face, more than almost any other sight, be it a crime scene or a beautiful landscape, sets off more reactions in more parts of the brain. Both stimulate the amygdala and surrounding region, but a fearful face also lights up regions that handle emotional processing and awareness.[6] As a result, a fearful expression triggers a larger and stronger barrage of emotions.

When you see an angry face, your thalamus delivers it almost instantly to the amygdala while sending it on a slower route to the cortex. Researchers believe that dopamine reinforces news of an angry face to the amygdala.[7] Also, the amygdala contains visual perception receptors that specialize in interpreting facial expressions. It makes sense that the amygdala is equipped for interpreting faces. Without a well-functioning amygdala, you would not see fear in another's face, so you would not be able to determine that a threat is present.

The amygdala's ability to recognize a fearful expression can function like a second sense of sight. Again, scanning studies are invaluable sources of information about what people focus on in an expression. In a study by the Psychiatric Neuroimaging Research Group at Massachusetts General Hospital, volunteers looked quickly at two images, a fearful face and a happy face.[8] The faces were shown so quickly that the viewers did not know what they were seeing. The faces appeared for thirty-three milliseconds, enough time for the amygdala to process images, and then the screen showed a neutral face for a longer period of time so that the cortex could process it. Afterward, the scans of the volunteers' amygdalae showed that they became active when the fearful faces flashed by but not when the happy faces did. The participants reported seeing only neutral expressions.

Another factor in this second sight is the brain's acuity for emotional valence, that is, the degree of positive or negative feeling apparent in a face. The brain attaches more significance to a negative or fearful sight because seeing it is important for survival. Valence is sometimes described as pleasantness. Whether consciously or unconsciously, you immediately know if someone looks unpleasant. Our brain has a propensity to focus more on negative sensory signals than on positive ones.

A damaged amygdala can cause a person to misread facial expressions. Not being able to read a face accurately or distinguish hostile intentions from harmless ones eliminates an important survival weapon. A case study by Ralph Adolphs and colleagues at the University of Iowa described such a person, a woman referred to as SM.[9] If you met SM, you would probably think she was a normal, cheerful young woman. But she suffers from a rare syndrome, Urbach-Wiethe disease, which destroyed her amygdala. As a result, when she is shown typical expressions of fear, anger, and surprise, she rates them as much less intense than people with mild brain damage. Even more strange, when she looks at faces evincing subtle fear, she does not see the same fear that normal people do. And she is largely blind to complex degrees of fear. However, she can identify people's faces even years after not seeing them. Her story has filled in some of the blanks for researchers by demonstrating that the amygdala's fear-recognition wiring is highly specialized. The amygdala-destroying disease did not impact her ability to recognize and remember faces, just her ability to see various emotional expressions. As a result, she is trusting and friendly with everybody.

Researchers have since concluded that SM cannot detect fear specifically because of an inability to use information from the eye region of people's faces. Unlike people with a normal amygdala, SM does not lock on to people's eyes when looking at their faces. This emotional blindness impairs her ability to read fear, since fear is expressed mainly in the eyes.

The whole face is most revealing for basic emotions such as happiness, sadness, and anger. However, researchers at the University of Cambridge, England, found that the eyes are a better place to focus to detect complex emotional states, such as scheming, admiration, interest, and thoughtfulness.[10]

Eyes are enormously expressive. One of the more significant messages the eyes can reveal is social disapproval. A lowering of the inner corners of the eyebrows, as if confused, can express judgment or disapproval, especially if the dipping brows are accompanied by raising one side of the upper lip and slightly tilting the head or pulling it backward. A disapproving look can signal a threat. Researchers who have put such expressions into an fMRI scanner have found that disapproval expresses more than a negative feeling.[11] It declares that someone has done or said something socially undesirable. The person being judged this way faces possible social rejection. Adding to the emotional impact is that people highly sensitive to rejection may also be highly sensitive to facial expressions that show rejection. For these people, a look of rejection may be a distinct social threat. Feeling such a threat can have potent consequences, like a strong emotional reaction.

Interpreting a Voice

For many people, what gets their blood boiling is a tone of voice. Emotions can be launched by an array of nuanced tones, including sarcasm, surprise, disgust, disrespect, dismissal, approval, anger, or condescension. Each of these can fuel a dramatic emotional reaction. Time and again, people refer to someone's tone of voice as the final straw that pushed them over the edge, as happened with Carl.

Being able to recognize the sound of danger is vital. People who do not hear a threatening tone are ill-equipped to protect themselves in a dangerous situation. And hearing a threat when none is intended can also lead to overreacting and even physical violence. Normally, someone speaking in a fearful tone of voice warns listeners of some kind of danger. It does not matter whether the danger is genuine or not, or whether it applies to the listeners as well as the speaker— the listeners receive the warning. People need to be able to recognize the sound of fear before being able to assess it.

The case of DR illustrates the extreme disadvantage of not being able to recognize fear in a voice.[12] Although not studied until she was in her fifties, DR had developed epilepsy at age twenty-eight. When drugs failed to help her, she underwent surgery on her amygdala. The result was profound.

After the surgery, she still recognized faces she had known for a long time and remembered ones she just met, but she had difficulty processing social cues in faces. As researchers expected, her damaged amygdala made it impossible for her to see fear in a face. They also decided to test how well she recognized emotion in a voice. First they made sure that she heard well enough and could discriminate between similar words, like *house* and *mouse*. They also made sure she understood the meaning of words that conveyed emotion, like *sadness* and *anger*.

DR had little difficulty understanding individual emotional words, but she could not interpret an emotional tone of voice. Asked to identify whether someone reading a sentence sounded happy, sad, or angry, she got the correct answer only a fraction of the time. She also struggled with determining what kind of emotion was behind a laugh or a growl. Without being able to recognize an emotion-charged voice that might signal danger, DR was severely impaired.

Your auditory system is designed to pick up sound frequencies and intensities vital to survival.[13] The response orients your head and eyes to the sound to ready you for potential action. It's how a mother knows if her baby is crying long before anyone else hears it. Why else would you be able to hear when you are asleep? A loud noise immediately alerts your defense mechanisms, causing you to startle and freeze. Interestingly, auditory development has not kept up with social progress. Even though people spend lifetimes in loud, noisy cities and should have grown accustomed to the cacophony, some still jump when a truck door slams.

Voices are an especially powerful instigator of emotions because it is difficult to disguise a feeling in a person's voice. If someone is angry or sad, you hear it in her voice. Fortunately, our auditory channel for alarming sounds is not made of concrete and, like most areas of the brain, possesses a certain amount of plasticity. You can mold your auditory alarm center by teaching it, through experience and repetition, precisely which noises mean danger and which don't. Repeated exposure to a sound, making it almost commonplace no matter how frightening it was when you first heard it, desensitizes your internal alarm. Even though survival instincts have made you sensitive to loud noises, you can train your system so that you don't run for cover when you hear explosions on the Fourth of July or yelling at a football game.

Because you can sense positive or negative notes in a voice, you instantly know the difference between a scream of joy and a scream of terror. While it is normal for your amygdala to be attuned to sounds of danger, not everyone's auditory system reacts normally. Just as DR misses the sound of a dangerous growl, other people hear danger when none is meant. Because people are more sensitive to valence than intensity in a voice, it is likely that the pitch of a voice is a more accurate sign of trouble.

Noises other than voices can also ignite an emotional reaction.[14] The sound of a barking dog, a baby crying, or your phone ringing at three A.M. can launch survival reflexes. Some people break out in tears at the sound of a particular piece of music. And even supposedly neutral sounds, like people whispering or the honk of a horn, can stir emotions. Everyone has emotional flash points that are lit up by sounds. People struggling to understand their out-of-control emotions should consider their auditory flash points. What tones of voice set them off? Is it the tone or person it's coming from? Being able to recognize and articulate the sounds that set you off is the beginning to controlling these reactions.

A Nose for Fear

A sense of smell can also contribute to an emotional outburst. Smell does not play as big a part as visual or auditory stimuli, but for a small percentage of people, smells set them off. It does not have to be a noxious odor or a pleasant one. It just has to have an emotional connotation acquired sometime in the past.

An exception to this is carbon dioxide, which few people have much experience with or recognize but which nevertheless can be a potent catalyst for producing a panic attack.[15] Rising concentrations of carbon dioxide in the brain can happen either by inhaling it or in suffocation. Animal studies show that the amygdala has specialized acid-sensing receptors that are activated by carbon dioxide and lower the brain's pH. The result is a feeling of panic or anxiety. Whichever way it gets into the bloodstream, a strong dose of CO_2 can produce a feeling of dread or intense fear.

The notion that someone could have a nose for fear is not outlandish. The smell of a person's sweat can indicate fear. This was shown in a study involving sweat samples from two groups of people.[16] One group had just exercised on a treadmill, and the other group had just completed its first free-fall skydive. The length of time for each activity was the same. After the activity, the researchers removed any bacterial odor from sweat samples and then gave participants samples to smell while hooked to fMRI scanners that monitored brain activity. The study was double-blind, so neither the researchers nor the volunteers knew whose sweat they were smelling. Nevertheless, their brain knew. When a volunteer smelled a sample taken from a skydiver, the amygdala reacted. It did not react to a treadmill runner's sweat. The participants' amygdala instantly detected fear and excitement from skydiving while barely reacting to sweat that was generated from a safe treadmill.

Another smell that can be linked to an emotional reaction is that of a woman's tears. Researchers at Weizmann Institute conducted a study to test how a woman's tears affect men.[17] The first three experiments looked at whether the smell of tears affected a man's empathy, sadness, or negative emotions. They did not. However, almost by chance, the researchers noticed that after the men smelled tears, their sex drive and testosterone levels plummeted. Brain scans confirmed that the structures involved in sexual arousal were less active after a smell of tears. This reaction was subliminal but was a fascinating example of how smell acts as a pheromone to influence behavior associated with emotional arousal.

Here's a more overt example: I know a man who says he feels his blood boiling at the smell of linseed oil paint. Every summer when he was a teenager, his tyrannical father made him paint their house with it. Each time, they had a battle royal, with my friend consistently furious at his father's treatment of him.

A Physical Stimulus of Emotion: Two Theories

What pushes someone's buttons does not always come from environmental sensory information. Internal sensations can generate

The Meaning of a Look

Eye contact is an essential communication tool, and researchers have focused on the gaze as an especially powerful sensory stimulus. The direction of a gaze, direct or averted, sends signals as to a person's intentions, thoughts, and desires. "Direct gaze or gaze contact can have a variety of meanings ranging from the expression of hostility to that of intimacy, which makes it an essential cue that has to be detected and decoded early for adaptive behavior," concluded scientists at Pierre-and-Marie-Curie University in Paris.[18] Another scientist has suggested that we may possess unique neural wiring dedicated to processing a gaze. So a gaze not only captures our attention but can prompt us to think about its meaning. This makes sense, given how important interpreting someone else's look is in your relationships and even survival.

---

turmoil that spins emotions out of control. For centuries, thinkers have explored where in the body emotions come from. The investigation advanced from the realm of philosophy to science in the 1880s when William James published the essay, "What Is an Emotion?"[19]

James was a medical doctor who never practiced but wrote and taught psychology at Harvard. His essay on emotions was groundbreaking because he proposed a novel scientific explanation for why people feel them. The body, not the brain, he declared, launches the emotions. Emotions are the final product of a series of events beginning with the senses, usually eyes, detecting something exciting or interesting, and then the body, namely the viscera and nervous system, sending signals to the brain.

"We feel sorry because we cry, angry because we strike, afraid because we tremble," James wrote. "Common sense says, we lose our fortune, we are sorry and weep; we meet a bear, are frightened and run; we are insulted by a rival, are angry and strike . . . this order of sequence is incorrect." It's the other way around, he insisted. We do not run from the bear because we feel fear. Instead, we feel fear because we are running from it. In running, we breathe heavily and our heart pounds. These physical sensations travel to the brain via the autonomic nervous system and, only then, spark an emotion.

Around the same time James was writing about emotions, a Danish physician named Carl Lange was delving into emotions and arriving at similar conclusions.[20] Also a physician, he too thought emotions first arose in the body. Although instead of pointing to the entire physiology, he thought emotions were a vasomotor reaction—the final product of nerves and muscles that cause blood vessels to dilate or constrict. Nevertheless, Dr. Lange's ideas were forever linked with Dr. James's in the James-Lange theory.

The biggest challenge to James-Lange came about forty years later from another pair of physiologists, Walter Cannon and Philip Bard (the same Philip Bard I studied in medical school). They thought James-Lange had it backward. Their theory sprung from the idea that your senses pick up something emotionally charged, the sensory signal goes into the brain, emotions are generated, and the body reacts. Here's how you would react: I see a man outside my window. I am afraid. I begin to perspire.

Cannon and Bard said that people react to a situation physically—sweating, crying, running away—after they have felt the emotion.[21] For them, the brain wasn't the last to know, but the first. Walter Cannon conducted numerous experiments into the physiology of strong emotions. He often used dogs and cats and their natural antipathy to each other as a testing ground for how the body and brain process excitement and fear. In a key experiment, he severed the connection between a cat's sensory detection structures and its basal ganglia, which handled physical movement. This is similar to what Bard had done. Next, the cat was provoked and predictably, it reacted like an angry cat—its hair stood on end, it growled, and it bared its teeth, even though there was no neural connection linking the cat's senses and its movement controls. The cat showed emotion despite the fact that its brain was not connected to its viscera.

For Cannon, this was proof that emotions arise from the brain's sensory processing and then stimulate a physical response. The cat's defensive rage started in the brain and was not the result of a motor response or physiological reaction. The two scientists even narrowed the likely region where emotions were formed—an area around the thalamus, which is part of the lower brain stem.

This diagram illustrates two theories about where emotions come from. Both agree that emotion starts with a sensory stimulus, like seeing a bear. But they immediately part ways. As the illustration shows, James-Lange believes the sight of the bear sets off a physical reaction, the arrow to the man's face and the "somatic, visceral response." From the physical reaction, the signal travels to the brain and results in a person feeling fear. On the other hand, Cannon-Bard, shown by the lower arrow, thinks the signal first goes to the brain and produces fear. This fear then travels to the body, the face, somatic and visceral responses, to produce a physical reaction.

I suspect that the truth lies somewhere between the two theories. I do not think the truth is either-or but instead a complex interaction of the two, with the autonomic nervous system and the brain's emotional structures constantly looping information back and forth. In this way, physical reactions and neurological responses stimulate and inhibit each other to produce a multidimensional emotion.

A good example of this mind-body emotional reaction is the stress response. You can feel stress from your environment—urgent cries

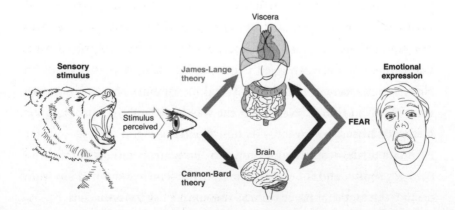

for help, the sound of honking in a traffic jam—or for internal reasons, like pressure to succeed. When you are feeling pressure either physically or psychologically, your body and brain set in motion the autonomic nervous system. This prompts a series of reactions by vital organs and motor nerves by what's called the hypothalamic-pituitary-adrenal, or HPA, axis. When these systems rev up, you go into a classic fight-or-flight response. A steady flow of stress chemicals plays havoc with your emotions and can make you more apt to overreact.

It is undeniable that some people are more vulnerable to the stress response. Their brain chemistry may be different, causing them to suffer from a chemical imbalance.[22] A possible reason may be a deficiency of neuropeptide Y. This neurochemical circulates throughout the brain and helps the amygdala counteract effects of stress hormones and reduce anxiety. Studies involving active-duty soldiers who have proven highly resilient on the battlefield and able to function superbly in the face of threats of being killed reveal that they have high neuropeptide Y levels. In contrast, patients with depression or anxiety disorder have much lower levels.

City Living: An Assault on the Senses

Certainly we can all relate to facial expressions and tones of voice and how they can affect us. But I strongly suspect that they are only the tip of the iceberg of what sets people off. I hear many people, and not just patients, say, "I'm really stressed." We all know the obvious causes, such as deadlines, getting the kids to school, answering all of the e-mails, paying the bills, fending off telemarketers, and money worries. But I don't think that's the whole picture. What about the things that are below our conscious awareness?

Anyone who spends time in a city encounters a daily barrage of sounds, sights, and smells. Traffic, of course, can be a huge assault on the senses, but there are also the sounds of alarms and planes, the smells of food carts and stale office air, and jarring sights, from the bizarre to the hilarious.

A recent fascinating study looked at how city living affects the brain, particularly what urban stress might do to the brain and our emotional health.[23] The German scientists doing the study noted that more than half the world's population today lives in urban areas, and this figure is steadily rising. Urban stress can come from overcrowding as well as from sensory overload, and city living increases people's risk for depression and anxiety.

To study the effects of urban life, the researchers looked at three groups of healthy people—those who were raised or living in rural areas, those from towns with more than ten thousand residents, and those from cities with more than one hundred thousand residents. To simulate social stress, the researchers gave the participants math problems under time pressure along with negative feedback from the study experimenter. During the test, the participants' brain activity was measured by fMRI. The results revealed a significant difference in amygdala and cortex activation in the brains of city people compared with rural folks. The city dwellers had the most active amygdalae. Even more remarkable, those participants who were raised in a city also showed a disconnect between their cortex and amygdala. In contrast, those who were living in the city but had not been raised in one showed no disconnect. This suggests that early city living can alter a person's emotional control. City living is not stressful for everybody. Some people thrive on the energy and diversity, and I know more than one person who prefers the cacophony of the city to the soft sounds of crickets in the countryside. Sensory overload can happen anywhere, yet as the German scientists found, years of exposure to city living can have a pronounced effect on the brain's emotion-processing regions.

The next chapter delves more into this disconnect between the cortex and the amygdala and shows how it may be contributing to people's anger and violent behavior.

Summing Up

- Certain sensory stimuli have more influence over you depending on where they are coming from. Sometimes you are not aware of what is setting you off.

- The strongest emotions are sparked by facial expressions, the eyes, the pitch and tone of a voice, and sometimes smell.

- The brain's emotional processing system is especially attuned to signs of anger and fear because these are most threatening to your survival.

- Some scientists believe that emotions arise from external sensory stimuli, and others believe they arise from internal physiological reactions.

4

An Answer in
the PAG

A Patient Begins to Solve the Mystery

Every so often I encounter a novel perspective that challenges the
foundations of my thinking about psychiatry and leads me in a new
direction. Janice is a perfect example of this phenomenon. For me,
she shattered the widely held belief that emotions and behaviors arise
from specific events. This is the idea that there is always a reason for
your feelings and actions, whether it be a distant childhood experience, a current relationship, or something around you.

Psychiatry is built on the assumption that with enough explora-
tion, a therapist and patient can find what's causing the patient's distorted emotions or behavior. I have spent countless hours with upset
patients trying to find the cause of their distress. Janice exploded
this assumption. Her emotions and behaviors defied this idea, not
fitting into the neat little package of cause and effect. Instead, like
wayward orphans, they stormed in and out of her life without any
rational explanation.

Janice came to me with an assortment of issues. In her early twenties, she had led a tumultuous life. The pivotal event was at sixteen when her parents divorced. It was an ugly split preceded by months of yelling, fights, and visits from the police. Her mother was an alcoholic and her father had a violent temper, and Janice was often caught in the middle. When the divorce became final, she was forced to live with her mother, whom she hated, while her charming father moved from the area. The trauma of the divorce and the threat of losing her father cracked her fragile temperament.

Soon after moving in with her mother, she felt herself coming apart. Always at odds, their arguments became vicious. If her mother asked Janice where she was going and with whom, Janice would fly into a tirade. She'd throw things, slam doors and, on at least one occasion, became so angry that she punched a wall and broke her hand. Janice was angry at everyone. She fought viciously with her friends, especially when they disagreed with her. Other girls or boyfriends were either the most wonderful person she had ever known or liars, and her loyalties and loathing frequently switched back and forth. Many had ended their friendship, which made her even angrier.

What brought her to me was that she was cutting herself and this frightened her. At one point she showed me a line of scars that looked like railroad tracks along the inside of her upper arm. The cutting was preceded by a pervasive feeling of numbness. She repeatedly declared, "I don't feel anything, I don't know who I am."

Janice's emotions were all over the map. Even during an hour-long session, she could arrive furious, withdraw into herself, then end it by coyly trying to manipulate me into flattering her or agreeing to something. In the course of an hour, I saw a wide range of expressions flit across her face. One moment she saw things in our setting that ticked her off; then minutes later something else made her flirty. Occasionally, when I pointed out something contrary to her reality, like how her mother's questions were not unreasonable, she'd stomp out of our session. The following week, she would return as if nothing had happened.

Janice was a mystery. Beyond knowing that her symptoms were typical of borderline personality disorder, I did not understand them. They were irrational, without rhyme or reason. Her anger was unmistakable in her expressions, the glare in her eyes, her aggressive pacing about the office, and the loud, imposing voice she used to try to intimidate me. At other times, she was fearful and anxious to leave. Or she could be overcome by depression and numbness, sitting listlessly and not making eye contact. Yet another side of her was what I can best describe as coyness. Her voice would turn light and girly, with suggestive insinuations.

During our therapy sessions, she talked about people and experiences, and most of her descriptions painted these as black or white. Her friends were either the most wonderful, loyal girls she ever knew or they were lying tramps. I recognized such thinking as her way of making judgments or decisions. There was nothing deep or nuanced about her thinking—it was largely instinctive. It was a form of survival thinking, enabling her to react immediately to a person and determine, at least in the moment, whether that person was friend or foe. She made the same instant judgment about her actions, from eating in a new restaurant to seeing a movie. It was either fabulous or disgusting. Listening to her, I could not decipher whether her emotions were driving her behavior or her behavior was causing her to feel certain ways. It was all disjointed.

Perhaps the biggest mystery for me was the cutting. I could not fathom how she could take a knife to herself. The scars indicated deep cuts that would draw blood and, in an average person, hurt badly. How could she deliberately subject herself to that kind of pain?

Something was terribly askew in Janice. It wasn't that her emotions and behaviors were wrong—everyone goes through times when they are angry, fearful, depressed, or disjointed. But healthy people feel these things when there is a reason, some type of threat to their physical or mental well-being. There were no obvious threats in Janice's life, at least none that were severe enough to warrant such intense reactions. She argued with her mother and missed her father, but her emotions and behaviors were way out of proportion to these situations.

These thoughts led me to consider for the first time the possibility that maybe there was no understandable reason for her emotions and behaviors. Maybe there was no psychological or psychiatric reason for what she was going through. Other patients, whose symptoms were even more volatile than Janice's, reinforced my thinking that this was possible. I had treated people who always felt angry and would tip toward violence even though nothing had provoked them. Other patients talked about being so terrified of everything around them that they stopped going to work and spent their days in the safety of their homes. Again, I could find no cause for their fear. They had normal lives with no major issues. I could not explain their individual feelings and reactions, and I certainly could not explain Janice's.

The only explanation that made sense was that there was no obvious psychological reason for their emotions and behaviors, but maybe there was a neurological one.

Anger Opens the Door

Some of my earliest insights into neurological causes come from my interest in domestic violence. Here I struggled to understand why a large man would hit someone much smaller, such as his wife. My education was gradual, beginning with research studies involving lactate infusions in domestic violence perpetrators. Evidence from these studies, especially listening to participants describe their feelings of fear and threat being the same as those they felt before they hit someone, gradually changed my thinking. I began to understand that their violent behavior was defensive, not offensive.[1]

A researcher who specializes in understanding defensive rage made a big impact on me. Allan Siegel, whom I mentioned earlier, has been studying defensive rage since the 1970s, exploring how and where in the brain it is generated.[2] Although Siegel uses cats, not people, for his studies, much of what he has discovered can be applied to people. He prodded cats into the kinds of defensive behavior I saw in patients. One way he did this was by provoking a cat with a stick or by putting another animal near it. Another method he used, which grabbed my attention, was stimulating a part of the brain called the periaqueductal gray (PAG).

The PAG is in a strategic area of the brain surrounding the fourth ventricle, a narrow tubular structure in the midbrain. It receives neurological signals from numerous structures, but for my study, most important are its connections to the amygdala and the cortex. This strongly suggests it is involved in survival behavior. It is also close to the brain stem, which contains cranial nerves. They are responsible for facial movements, head turning, swallowing, and vocalization and house the vagus nerve, which controls many internal body functions. It struck me as significant that the PAG is near nerves essential for emotional expression.

Janice revealed defensive rage when her mother asked her questions. Like the cat in Siegel's studies, she took an aggressive posture and tone of voice but did not attack. If her mother became insistent or somehow cornered her, I am sure Janice would have lashed out. The fight part of her fight-or-flight survival mechanism was ready almost all the time, especially around her mother. As happens with most of us, the people closest to us, like family or best friends, can present the biggest threat. Their words and behaviors have more emotional impact on us than a stranger's would. Janice felt this firsthand, and probably every day.

Siegel's studies on another kind of aggressive behavior, predatory stalking, helped explain another facet of Janice's actions. Sometimes her aggression was not defensive but more subtle and circumspect. It was not unlike Siegel's cat when it became alert, scanned its cage, and began to circle a nearby rat, then pounced and bit it. This type of aggression was different than defensive rage, yet it was still fight behavior. Among animals, the presence of a weaker, vulnerable animal in its field of vision can set off a predatory attack. A stalk-

Ways to Calm Your Nervous System

When you feel jittery and hyped up, as if your body and mind are spring-loaded, here are ways to quiet your nerves.

- Lower or eliminate alcohol and caffeine consumption.
- Identify what is revving you up.
- Talk about what makes you nervous and how this feeling affects your behavior.
- Try breathing exercises.
- Do vigorous exercise.
- Engage in an activity you find especially relaxing.

---

ing cat moves slowly, methodically, not hissing, and rather than teeth bared, its mouth is closed, it doesn't make a sound. In people, not only like Janice but also ordinary folks with an aggressive streak, predatory behavior can be circumspect but can have aggressive intentions. Janice's coy manipulative behavior during our sessions, I believe, was a kind of predatory action, perhaps an attempt to gain some control over me.

Although predatory behavior does not look like anger, it is closely related. Like defensive rage, it is a form of adaptive aggression. It is a way an animal defends itself. A threatening or hostile situation may require defensive rage, then stalking, and finally defending again. The switch back and forth happens very quickly, but these forms of aggression do not overlap in an animal or person. You can see this kind of behavior in an ex-boyfriend who is constantly showing up at his former girlfriend's home, sometimes with flowers, begging to be taken back, and sometimes pounding on the door, declaring, "I'm going to get you!" and demanding that she return gifts he gave her.

Siegel's research into anger and the PAG explained much about Janice. For one, the anger she displayed whenever she was criticized and her quiet but not-so-subtle manipulation came from parts of the

PAG that were close to each other. Janice appeared to flip back and forth between anger and coyness, two forms of fight behavior. But what about the other behaviors, the numbness and withdrawal? In what ways were they survival behavior?

Understanding Numbness

While I gradually recognized Janice's defensive rage and predatory behavior, I wondered whether depression was the emotion that was driving her numbness and if it could possibly have a survival value.

I knew that cutting was a response to feelings of numbness and that she would make repeated slices on her thigh because only pain pulled her out of an emotional stupor and made her feel alive. She often returned home from work depressed, particularly on days after a gossip session with coworkers. On her way home, she'd replay the phrases and words and become fixated on them, looking for hidden meanings. By the time she got home, she was sure they had been making fun of her. Each time, it was a devastating thought, and she'd retreat to her computer and play mindless video games until she fell asleep. The cutting usually happened in the mornings, after she awoke and still felt disconnected from her emotions.

I couldn't connect this behavior with her anger because, so far in my experience, patients' emotions did not seesaw back and forth across a broad spectrum. And they certainly didn't switch on and off as if changing TV channels. Clearly I needed to know more about the PAG. This led me to another neuroscientist, Richard Bandler.[3] A neuroanatomist at the University of Sydney, he delved into the PAG's internal wiring and how it meshes emotions and behavior. One area of focus was emotional coping. He identified two types. Active coping is familiar: it is how an animal or person behaves if a threat is escapable—fight or flight. Passive coping is a more novel concept.

To see how an animal reacted to a threat, he injected a stimulant into one of three areas of a cat's PAG and then watched what happened when he put a rat in the cage. An injection to the first PAG region caused the cat to back up into a defensive posture. Its fur stood on end, it hissed, it turned sideways, and its pupils dilated. An injection to a second region made the cat lunge forward and jump around. It was trying to flee by running around its cage and looking for an escape hole. Its pupils also widened, its fur bristled, and it made desperate mewing sounds. These two reactions were fight or flight.

It was the cat's reaction to an injection in a third area that surprised me. The animal became immobile. There was no movement, no posturing, no sniffing around. The animal was still and quiet. It sank into coma-like behavior, with no spontaneous movement and reacting to nothing around it. Was this synonymous with the concept of human depression?

Bandler concluded that the cat looked as if it were responding to a severe injury or defeat in a social encounter. It showed distinct visceral changes too. Its heart slowed, and its blood pressure dropped to an abnormally low level. Another noteworthy reaction was that the animal's passive response accompanied a release of opioid analgesia chemicals in the PAG, which stayed in the cat's system a long time. Opioid analgesia helps recovery and healing, and it deadens pain.

The purpose of the animal's passive behavior looked clear. It allowed the cat to recover from the trauma of being threatened; it was a survival response. Going limp and not interacting with its environment meant that it could devote biological resources to speed recovery after an injury or while in the deadly grip of a predator. This was a way of coping with, and beginning to heal in the midst of, an inescapable threat or trauma.

It was not a large leap to apply this concept to people. Whether in a cat or a human patient, this behavior provides time and internal resources for recuperation. The nature of the trauma could be anything that had threatened it—from the intrusion of another animal to a severe injury, hemorrhaging, deep visceral or muscle pain, or an emotional and social catastrophe.

Bandler's findings explained much. For instance, he had produced what appeared to be three distinct emotions associated with behaviors—anger into fight, fear into flight, and numbness into passivity, or in human terms, sadness into shutdown. He accomplished this by stimulating areas of the PAG that were only millimeters apart. Thinking about Siegel's research, which pinpointed predatory and stalking behaviors, I realized these two researchers had identified four types of behavior coming from the PAG. And they showed that each of these behaviors had a corresponding emotion.

Reading about Bandler's cats, I realized his description fit Janice. She showed similar passivity, limpness, and disengagement from her environment. Especially tantalizing was his finding that the PAG releases opioid chemicals when an animal is in its passive coping mode. The PAG has an abundance of opioid receptors, which are pain modulators. In fact, the PAG's role in pain regulation is one of its better-known functions.

The opioid release could explain how Janice could inflict such pain on herself without apparent sensation. The cutting was not painful, perhaps because her emotional numbness was also accompanied by an opioid release in her PAG. Perpetrators of domestic violence tell me that when they are physically aggressive, their arms and hands are like feathers and they are not aware of any sensation in them.

The numbness people feel after a battle or illness reflects this physiological condition. It is a time of healing. However, feeling numb when your body is not recovering from an injury is not a pleasant feeling. Patients say that it is an oppressive sensation and makes them feel out of control, disconnected from their body. Cutting comes in, I believe, as an attempt to create new sensory stimuli in an attempt to reset their nervous system back to normal.

A while back I was treating another young woman who arrived at my office agitated and enraged. She sat for a bit and then paced about, waving her hands as she talked. Then, in a matter of seconds, she reached into her purse, took out a razor, and sliced it down her arm. She filleted herself, making a long gash that spilled blood—so much that I sent her to the ER. The instant she cut, her expression

Inside the PAG

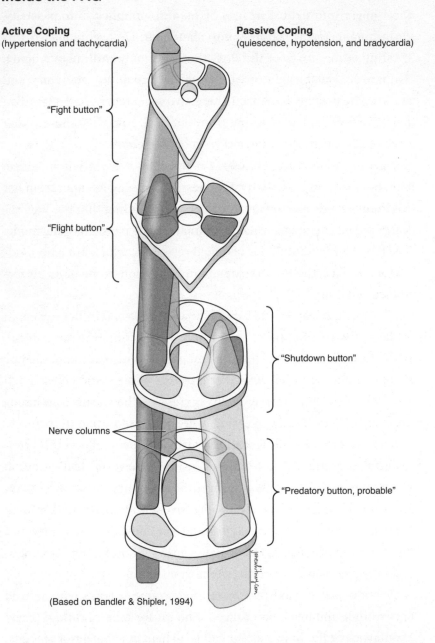

Active Coping
(hypertension and tachycardia)

Passive Coping
(quiescence, hypotension, and bradycardia)

"Fight button"

"Flight button"

"Shutdown button"

Nerve columns

"Predatory button, probable"

(Based on Bandler & Shipler, 1994)

changed. Her face relaxed, her body became still, and she was calm. She announced that she felt much better, and she sat. I believe that the cutting quieted her nervous system.

This diagram shows Bandler's PAG, how its functions are divided into four columns and how each column connects to nerves that activate active and passive coping behaviors. The active coping strategies are flight and confrontational defense, namely defensive rage, and the passive one is going still and quiet. Each of these behaviors, I believe, has a corresponding emotion that sets them off. Anger launches fight, fear to flight, and depression to quiescence. The fact that they are only millimeters apart in the PAG means that the nerves that stimulate them can ignite multiple emotions and behaviors. In people, switching between anger and depression looks like a huge change. But in the PAG, such a switch can happen with a microscopic shift in nervous system activity.

Exploring Emotions

Imagine an intricate spider's web. At the center is the PAG, and extending from it are countless threads or pathways leading to the clumps along the edges, each representing a separate brain structure. The PAG's connections with numerous other brain structures have a big impact on how it turns emotion into behavior. Signals from these other structures can amplify or inhibit survival behavior from the PAG.

Scientists have long known that the PAG is central to behaviors associated with survival. These behaviors include physical actions as well as an array of physiological reactions that enable you to act. Through its connection with the autonomic nervous system, the PAG instructs the body to prepare to defend itself or recover from battle. It gets your body ready to react and recruits internal organs and systems like the lungs, heart, liver, stomach, and intestines, and tells your body to either gear up for action or go quiet and conserve energy. It also sets off clotting factors to lessen hemorrhaging from wounds and activates the immune system to help with healing.

The essential spark for these behaviors is emotions. One reason many people do not understand their emotions is that they feel so personal and individual. The deeper, more primitive function of emotions—to help us survive—may not be immediately apparent. People like to own their emotions, and it can be hard to understand that what they are feeling is a universal, human reaction to something that is threatening them. And furthermore, they do not understand that reacting the way they do to a potentially harmful situation is normal. What's not normal is when survival emotions erupt when there is no danger.

A pioneer in explaining the how and why of your emotions was Walter Cannon, whom I talked about in the previous chapter.[4] His 1915 book, *Bodily Changes in Pain, Hunger, Fear and Rage: An Account of Recent Researches into the Function of Emotional Excitement,* identified one of human behavior's most fundamental principles: the survival instinct of fight or flight. His studies into the survival drive also connected survival actions with specific emotions. The emotions he described were not those normally associated with the struggle to survive. How could anxiety and depression be a survival response? Cannon's investigations into the dynamics of physiology and emotion signaled a new era in psychology. Using scientific methods to dissect the components of emotion, he laid solid groundwork for later researchers to uncover the neurological wiring that powers emotions.

From here, it was just a short step to the next landmark in the evolution of the science of emotions—the limbic system theory. This concept has been around a long time and, like the ideas put forth by James-Lange and Cannon-Bard, it has added volumes to understanding how emotions work. As with its antecedents, scientists have found that it includes insightful revelations as well as questionable elements. The term *limbic lobe* was first used in 1878 by French physician Paul Broca to refer to an area of the brain that borders the brain stem (the word *limbic* means "edge" or "margin"). Dr. James Papez was the next popularizer of the term, using it in the 1930s to describe what he called the "anatomy" of emotions. The notion of a system that produces emotions came from Paul MacLean in 1952. His idea was that the limbic system was the emotional center of the brain, while the neocortex arcing above it was in charge of thinking.

Sometimes people ask, "Where exactly is the limbic system?" The best answer I can give is an analogy. The limbic system is like Silicon Valley, which is a network of towns and highways dedicated to an industry but not a single place. If you've ever traveled to that part of Northern California, you know that there is no town, city, or county called Silicon Valley. The same is true if you look at an anatomy book illustrating the human brain. You will see structures and connections but no banner that reads, *limbic system*. Just as Silicon Valley encompasses places like San Jose and Los Altos, connected by the I-280 freeway, the limbic system encompasses structures like the amygdala, hypothalamus, and hippocampus connected by neuropathways.

The limbic system theory has the same shortcoming as the Silicon Valley label: there is no general agreement on what it composes and precisely what it does. Joseph LeDoux, a leading scientist who has written extensively on fear and the emotional brain, has done studies that highlight the drawback of the limbic system theory.[5] He has pointed out, for instance, that many variations of fear—fear of failing, fear of being afraid, fear of falling in love—are conceived in the amygdala but then scatter signals beyond the limbic arc. As a result, fear from the amygdala may trigger a survival reaction or be processed further, generating other kinds of reactions, like regret or shyness.

There is still much about emotions that science does not know. Where in the brain emotions are processed—given meaning in our conscious mind—and how the PAG converts into behaviors is not fully known. Other brain structures feed into it. A study of how the brain processes anger involved eight healthy young men who were asked to imagine a time when they were "the most angry you've been in your life."[6] Researchers monitoring their brain activity during the exercise noted that several cortical structures were activated. Remarkably, many of these structures have direct connections to the PAG.[7] At the same time, they noticed that the amygdala did not become active.

I suspect that survival emotions like anger coalesce and acquire meaning in the PAG so that it reacts with an appropriate behavior. The signals between the PAG and other regions work two ways. They not only activate or magnify an emotion but can also suppress it, preventing the PAG from setting off a particular response. The PAG does not initiate simultaneous behaviors, for instance fight and flight. That would be counterproductive to survival. However, it does appear to be able to switch very quickly between responses so that people may flee at one point and soon after engage in predatory behavior, like lying in wait. Rapid switching can give people flexibility in deciding how to react. Experiments with cats show that typically if one kind of aggression is stimulated, other kinds are suppressed.[8] People in fight mode will resist the urge to flee. Researchers were unable to activate defensive rage and a predatory attack at the same time. When one set of neurons was stimulated, a corresponding cluster was dampened. In this way, if an animal was in predatory mode, it would not growl to ruin the stalking.

A study out of Duke University shows how the PAG appears to match an emotion with a behavior.[9] By stimulating a certain area of the PAG in awake patients, researchers were able to produce painful sensations, emotional reactions, and survival reflexes. These were associated with feelings of fear and pending death. At the same time, participants' bodies reacted with hair standing on end, sweating, increased pulse and heart rate, and flushing. Their bodies at first produced primitive survival sensations, and then their emotions and behaviors followed. The study provided evidence that the PAG was where emotions were integrated.

How Your Brain Reacts to Sensory Stimuli

Often when I am trying to explain to patients what happens in their brain once their senses have picked up something, I sketch this diagram. My goal is to help them understand how their brain processes emotions. Of course this processing is enormously complicated (there is much about it I still do not understand), so I stick to the basics.

In my explanation, I begin on the left side and describe possible sensory inputs, like tones of voice or certain sights. The next step is the thalamus, which acts as a gateway for sensory information, sending it to both the cortex and the amygdala. The final step leads to the PAG, with the emotions of anger, fear, depression, or flat emotion being turned into what I call output behavior, namely fight, flight, shutdown, or predatory.

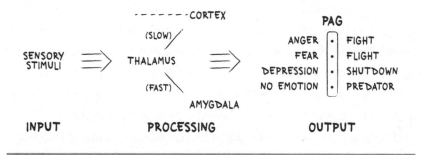

When the System Malfunctions: A Broken Rheostat

Your PAG triggers essential coping behavior. It is how you get through hard times. Someone who just received a cancer diagnosis may need a period of shutdown to find emotional stability. Intense anger and striking out at someone is an appropriate response if that person has hurt your child. Fleeing your house in the middle of the night is the right thing to do if it's on fire. Predatory behavior is critical for law enforcement people who stalk criminals.

Think of your PAG as a rheostat controlling the lights in a room in your house. This rheostat is tended by a dutiful servant. This servant adjusts the rheostat up and down according to your needs, usually making the lights brighter after the sun sets and dimmer during the day. For most people, the PAG rheostat goes on and off at the appropriate time.

A study by Dean Mobbs at University College, London, showed how a normal PAG functions in processing an emotion like fear and prompting someone to react and protect themselves.[10] Fourteen participants attached to fMRI machines negotiated a computer maze that contained a virtual predator. The virtual predator could chase, capture, and deliver painful shocks to the participants. In the beginning, the participants avoided the predator, and their PAG was quiet. Even being chased did not activate it. But as the predator moved near the participants and they could not avoid it, their PAG became active. The participants felt dread and fear over the near certainty of an electric shock. Accompanying this emotion was a strong urge to escape the predator. The maze players' PAGs reacted normally, activating an appropriate emotion, fear, and survival behavior, an urge to flee, because they were threatened with a painful shock.

I believe that most of my patients, as well as countless individuals whose emotions and behaviors race out of control, do not have normal control over the functioning of their PAGs. Their rheostat is not working properly. The servant is not dependable, coming and going at odd times, disappearing on long vacations. The servant is the keeper of the switch. The neurological equivalent of the servant is the brain's neural processing, which determines what signals go to the PAG.

What makes the servant notch up the rheostat—that is, your brain processing signals into the PAG—can be obvious sensory stimuli or some unknown reason. The servant may turn up the rheostat for a good reason or none at all. People with uncontrollable emotions and behaviors probably have rheostats or PAGs that are set off for no clear reason. All science knows is that something has gone wrong with their survival behavior processing system. Emotions and behaviors designed to help keep them safe are somehow hijacked, and they overreact. Nothing in their personality or experiences is setting off their emotions and behaviors. I believe that there is a reason for these strong feelings and inappropriate behaviors, but it is not what most people think of when trying to explain them. I think the cause is neurological, a malfunction in the brain.

The problem lies, I think, with the connections between brain structures. The amygdala may send a dire alarm to the PAG despite the danger being only mild. The cortex may contribute to this faulty signal. The cortex normally acts as a brake on strong emotions by applying reason, explanations, and definitions.[11] But if its link to the amygdala is corrupted, a false alarm goes through to the PAG. As a result, someone could feel extremely threatened and not be able to rationally think through the situation. There would be no cortical input to the thought process. The person would experience only a strong survival drive stimulated by the amygdala.

When connections into the PAG are not functioning normally, a person's behavior spins out of control. The slightest hint of a threat can send them into full survival mode, which could be fight, flight, shutdown, or stalking. The reaction is totally inappropriate. An employee who receives a poor job performance evaluation launches a virulent internet attack on his boss. A woman screams obscenities at a neighbor who has asked her to move her car. A person perceives a slight when she doesn't get a birthday card from her brother. A man in a sports bar starts a fistfight with an opposing team's fan. These overreactions indicate a flaw in the signals to PAGs.

Malfunctioning survival wiring also produces collateral physical damage. Out-of-control emotions can make people sick. People with a PAG button constantly activated also have an autonomic nervous system stuck in the *on* position. The nervous system is active because the PAG has mistakenly informed it that physiological defenses are needed immediately. Various scientists have found direct links between extreme survival emotions, like anger, and chronic health issues.[12] In American and European men, researchers have noticed that high levels of anger and hostility are predictive symptoms for coronary artery disease. Conversely, men who learned to control anger, depression, or anxiety with the help of therapy, drugs, and effort lowered their risk for coronary heart disease. Women, too, can have a higher risk of cardiovascular disease as a result of an angry or hostile temperament.

Another area of the body affected by anger and aggression is the immune system. Many people who have scored high in tests for hostility and hostile marriage conflicts also have higher than normal levels of cytokines. Cytokines are proteins that the body makes to generate inflammation and speed healing. More cytokines mean more inflammation, and chronic inflammation can cause a host of ailments, including allergies, arthritis, asthma, eczema, hypertension, chronic pain, and kidney stones.

A Bingo Moment: Finding a Neurological Model

Bandler's work, at last, gave me a model for severe emotional reactions. While Siegel's research pointed to three types of behavior—defensive rage or anger, predatory behavior, and flight, Bandler added the missing piece. This was an explanation for the survival value of numbness I encountered in depressed patients. His explanation had an elegant clarity—numbness, or what would look like the emotion of depression and shutdown behavior in an individual, was beneficial because it provided time and energy for recovery and healing.

This was a neurological model that explained the emotions and behaviors I saw in my patients. I thought of the PAG columns as nerve bundles that acted like a button. Stimulate or push one button and you get defensive rage coupled with fighting behavior. Push another and the result is fear and flight. A third button controlled predatory behavior. Its triggering emotion was the patients feeling emotionally flat and devoid of empathy. Finally, pushing a fourth button stimulated depression and shutdown behavior. These buttons could be stimulated for an appropriate reason or an inappropriate reason.

I picture the model as a panel of *on-off* buttons that generate the behavior needed to handle a survival situation. When a threat stimulates a person's button, the PAG produces reactions to help the person survive. The threat could be real or imagined, but it would be enough to engage this survival center. Fear started the flight button. A distinctive lack of emotion appeared to be connected to the predator button. A fourth button, what Bandler found, was the button for depression and shutdown. Using Bandler's illustration as a guide, I sketched my PAG model:

Anger	○	○	Fight
Fear	○	○	Flight
Depression	○	○	Shutdown
Absence of Emotion	○	○	Predatory

For many people—not just patients but also anyone who's experienced the effects of a fiery temper—there is no more mystifying or upsetting emotion than anger. I regularly hear a distraught *why* from friends and family as well as patients. So I hope the next chapter will begin to untangle the mystery.

Summing Up

- Patients and psychiatrists assume that there is a psychological reason to explain why emotions and behaviors spin out of control. A more accurate reason may have nothing to do with personality or individual experiences but may be neurological.

- Research has identified a little-known brain structure called the periaqueductal gray, or PAG, as central to stimulating survival behaviors like defensive rage and escape.

- Numbness or going quiet, behavior very similar to depression and shutdown, can serve a vital survival purpose by providing time and energy for recovery and healing following a battle or an overwhelming mental assault.

- The PAG activates normal, necessary survival actions. It serves as a platform for the expression of anger, fear, depression, and flat emotion to produce behaviors of fight, flight, shutdown, and predatory actions.

- In some people, the PAG malfunctions so their emotions and behaviors are in constant survival mode.

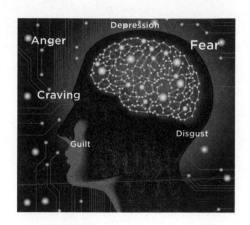

Part 11

Losing It:
Extreme
Behavior

5

Hair-Trigger Tempers and Anger Unleashed

Understanding Explosive Tempers

This is a hard chapter to write. Angry people do awful things. They destroy lives and damage property. Their hair-trigger tempers have ruined countless family gatherings and have estranged generations of children. It's hard to sympathize with people who go into furious rages without any apparent provocation. One moment they're talking and interacting normally, and the next they're fuming and lashing out. I have enormous sympathy for their victims.

Anger	●	●	**Fight**
Fear	○	○	Flight
Depression	○	○	Shutdown
Absence of Emotion	○	○	Predatory

However, years of research and therapy with people with explosive tempers has expanded my perspective. When patients tell me about their violent acts, I think not only about the victims but also about the turmoil the offenders are going through. It is not for me to judge them but to explore with them whatever is happening in their life and brain to cause their anger—and then try to help them.

Patients with a history of aggression report that when they are angry, their emotions can feel overwhelming and lead to impulsive actions. Their emotions often feel strange, as if they do not belong to them. They become enraged over trivial or nonexistent slights and have difficulty controlling their overreaction. They behave irrationally, like dropping an atomic bomb on an anthill.

They have little insight into their mental state. However, as time passes after the violence, they add a qualifier: "I know I shouldn't have hit her, but if she had done X, then I wouldn't have had to." They typically blame others for provoking them. They may acknowledge the damage they created yet don't take responsibility for their actions. From the perspective of a victim or witness, such blame shifting seems ludicrous.

My perspective as a psychiatrist focuses on their emotional and thought processing. I understand that violent people often don't feel at fault, because they have little grasp of how their emotions can spin out of control. They look for reasons and often cannot find any. My goal is to share my insights into neurobiology so they better understand their emotions and uncontrollable behavior.

When you think about anger, it's useful to remember that, in itself, anger is not all bad. It serves a purpose for everyone. In many instances, it tells us when something is wrong and needs fixing. Anger fuels action, which may be self-protective. Here's a simple example: You hear through the grapevine that a coworker is bad-mouthing you, declaring that you are incompetent and lazy. It is normal to be angry about this—anger prompts you to try to fix the situation. But it is not normal to trash the coworker's office. Normal anger is appropriate to the situation and serves a genuine purpose. It alerts you that something is wrong, from the mild anger you feel at being slighted by your spouse to the extreme anger you feel upon seeing your child bullied on the playground.

Too often, people try to ignore their anger because such a strong emotion can be frightening and make people uncomfortable. So they bury it under more acceptable emotions, like sadness, disappointment, or anxiety. The upshot is that the underlying problem persists, perhaps to fester and grow worse. Compounding the obstacles is that anger has many forms, such as irritability, aggression, hostility, agitation, and restlessness, the degrees of which can vary wildly. Nevertheless, it needs to be addressed—but appropriately and not out of proportion to what made you feel it.

People whose anger turns to violence possess distinctive traits. For instance, twin studies have found a genetic component for aggression and impulsiveness.[1] Other studies have focused on neurotransmitters, finding that chemical concentrations differ in the brain of violent people.[2] A third group of studies has examined brain structure, noticing differences in volume, glucose metabolism, and communication signals between critical areas.[3] Scientific explanations of the origins and causes of violent behavior are not intended as excuses. But the studies contribute enormously to a fuller understanding of the neurological roots of violence.

The spectrum of anger and violent behavior I see in therapy includes not only domestic violence but also anger attacks, such as bullying, road rage, and emotional battering. Even though women are as frequently violent and aggressive as men, I have found that men tend to do more physical damage and so receive more attention. Here are three stories of such patients, told from my unique point of view. Each story contains clues as to what was fueling the anger and offers a perspective on the behavior in terms of the PAG model. I have italicized phrases in the first story that broadened my knowledge of the model's anger-fight button.

Do You Have Intermittent Explosive Disorder?

IED is classified in the psychiatric manual as follows:

A. Discrete episodes of failure to resist aggressive impulses that result in serious assaultive acts or destruction of property. Examples of serious assaultive attacks include striking or otherwise hurting another person or verbally threatening to physically assault another individual. Destruction of property entails purposeful breaking of an object of value.

B. The degree of aggressiveness during an episode is grossly out of proportion to any provocation or precipitating psychosocial stressor.

C. The aggressive episodes are not due to the direct physiological effects of a substance (e.g., a drug of abuse, a medication) or a general medical condition (e.g., head trauma, Alzheimer's disease).

D. The individual may describe the aggressive episodes as "spells" or "attacks" in which the explosive behavior is preceded by a sense of tension or arousal and is followed immediately by a sense of relief.

E. The individual may feel upset, remorseful, regretful, or embarrassed about the aggressive behavior.

F. Individuals . . . sometimes describe intense impulses to be aggressive prior to their aggressive acts.

G. Explosive episodes may be associated with affective symptoms (irritability or rage, increased energy, racing thoughts) . . . and rapid onset of depressed mood and fatigue after the acts.

H. Some individuals . . . report that their aggressive episodes are often preceded or accompanied by symptoms such as tingling, tremor, palpitations, chest tightness, head pressure, or hearing an echo.

I. Individuals may describe their aggressive impulses as extremely distressing.[4]

Note: It is not an everyday feeling or one that pops up regularly or easily.

Why the 210-Pound Man Hit His 120-Pound Wife

"Doc, sometimes I'm afraid I'm going to *lose control* and hit my son. What do I do?"

I met Paul, as I mentioned in the introduction, when he volunteered for a study using a lactate infusion to examine the relationship between panic attacks and alcoholism. His question opened the door to a possible connection between panic and domestic abuse, and it sent me on a career-defining quest into the neurobiology of domestic abuse.

Six months after the study, Paul told me that the arguments with his wife had been getting worse and that after the latest, he had choked and hit her. I knew he had a problem with alcohol and that his feelings of panic could swing into violence. I asked for details, wanting to know more about what he was thinking and feeling at the time. What would compel a man like him to physically assault someone who was not only much smaller than he but was also someone he loved?

"I got home early. Work wasn't going well—a job had just fallen through. Emma was watching TV, which I didn't like. Watching TV during the day is a total waste of time. *It's what lazy, aimless people do.* She could have been fixing dinner or reading or something. But I didn't say anything, just opened *a bottle of wine* and went outside for a cigarette."

Paul and Emma had been married twenty-nine years, and they'd had a son when they were in their thirties. I suspected that they hoped the child would be a comforting patch to their frayed relationship. Paul was an engineer with an international construction company, and he traveled regularly to distant sites. Emma had never worked, but she had hopes of becoming a novelist and had been working on a book for many years.

"Was Jared around?" I asked about their son.

"No, he was doing after-school sports. He got home later."

"Was anything different for you this particular night?"

"At first, no. I finished the wine and was *getting another bottle* when Emma yelled to me. Something about ordering out for dinner. *I ignored her.* I had no interest in carryout; I wasn't even hungry. I went back outside and *she came after me,* harping about dinner.

"She stood in front of me with that look, you know, looking at the bottle and *looking at me like I was some kind of cockroach.* I told her to leave me alone, that I'd had a bad day. But *she wouldn't leave me alone.* She just stood there, *in my face,* yammering on. I couldn't listen to her, so I got up to go into the study, and she stood in my way."

"Do you remember how you felt right then?" I asked.

"Not really. *It's all a blur.* I do remember that my *heart was really pounding* and I was shaking. Her voice was like a buzz saw in my brain—I had to get away from it. So I pushed her to get by. And she pushed back. That was it."

Paul's description of their fight was sketchy but vivid enough. After Emma pushed him, he slammed her into a wall. She fought back, flailing with her arms, so he went for her throat, choking her to the point that she collapsed gagging.

I could see that Paul was *hesitant to tell me everything,* which is not unusual for domestic abusers. They know their behavior is abhorrent.

"She started it," he continued. "I warned her, I told her to leave me alone. But no, she had to go on and on. She shoved me. *I had to protect myself.*"

"What do you mean 'protect yourself'? You're a big guy," I probed.

Paul shook his head as if he didn't understand. "Yeah, that's obvious now, but at the time, her voice and the shove. She was so in my face and wouldn't let me get around her. I felt exposed, vulnerable."

We kept talking, with Paul adding more about what was going through him during the fight. He could dredge up specific sensations because, he confessed, he and Emma had a battle royal every six months or so. I explained to him that the feelings of panic and the domestic violence were wrapped together and that to defuse them, he had to make a commitment.

"It's a lost cause if you keep drinking. I know you don't think you're an alcoholic, and I'm not going to argue with you about the exact label. It doesn't matter. What matters is that if you keep drinking, I can't help you," I said.

Domestic violence is largely a hidden crime, with victims as well as offenders reluctant to talk about it. Experts believe that only one-quarter of domestic violence incidents are reported to the police.[5] Nevertheless, *The Journal of the American Medical Association* estimates that in the United States, that there are approximately 5 million assaults each year.

Paul's account told me volumes about how anger spills over into violence. Beginning with the first clue, indicating overt violence, I noted specific features of his anger-fight reaction. His wine consumption strongly suggested an alcohol problem. His drinking problem was not surprising, as domestic violence and alcoholism go together like a lock and a key, with a large overlap between the two disorders. Still, it's important to recognize that heavy drinking and violence are not necessarily bound together.

Abusive individuals frequently say that they feel out of control much of the time. Their thoughts race, and they feel bombarded by sensory stimuli, especially when they experience stress at work or chaos at home. One person said to me, "If you knew how jumbled my thinking is sometimes, you'd lock me up." Another said that he often felt like Fred Flintstone madly paddling his feet but going nowhere.

Unable to control their internal state, they try to control their external world. But when they can't, their anger escalates. They hate feeling out of control, and alcohol takes this feeling away. But this is not a solution, for two reasons. They cannot drink enough to stay ahead of the game. The more they drink, the more they need to drink to quell the chaos in their head. They develop a tolerance, resulting in a need for ever-increasing amounts of alcohol. The drinker also has increasing episodes of withdrawal, which spurs even more drinking. The alcoholic becomes trapped in a cycle of feeling out of control, drinking, and experiencing withdrawal symptoms of shakes and heaves, all of which lead to more mental chaos and more drinking.

Another reason that drinking harms abusers rather than helping them is neurological. Domestic violence can occur in a split second. People with a history of volatile, angry tempers are not like nonviolent people when they drink. There appears to be a unique interaction between alcohol and the brain's threat pathway, which is activated in the perpetrator. Alcohol makes the pathway activate faster. As researcher Kristie Schubert demonstrated in experiments stimulating cats to induce rage, ethanol decreased the time it took for the animal to show defensive rage.[6]

The clues indicating what Paul was sensing from his wife—the look she gave him, her tone of voice—suggested that she was upset. Anyone who is married or has had a close relationship can identify with Paul's emotional reactions to these provocative gestures and looks. But it happened so fast, he could not put his feelings into words. Nevertheless, her actions made him feel threatened. This began with him feeling she would not leave him alone and progressed to her shoving him, though she was much smaller than him. These imagined threats activated his survival reactions—he felt he needed to protect himself, and his blurred vision and pounding heart confirmed this. Paul's reaction was instant, automatic, and defensive. Both his brain and his nervous system responded to the challenge from Emma.

It was also revealing that Paul believed that Emma was partly responsible for his hurting her. This is a common refrain among domestic abusers. While it is a self-serving justification, it does contain some validity. A spouse may fuel a violent assault by doing or saying things that are unintentionally provocative. With Emma, her nasty look and shove set Paul off. Adding fuel to the fire was her blocking his path, preventing him from escaping. As I explained in the chapter on sensory stimuli, some people overreact to facial expressions, tones of voices, or behavior because they see or hear a threat.[7] In the moment, Emma was also threatened by Paul's bullying behavior. When he tried to walk away, she felt like he was discounting her.

Their two angers came together to spark violence. Both stepped over the line to irrationality.

A normal, healthy person whose PAG anger button is not continuously on would immediately realize that Emma's actions were attempts to get his attention and were not genuine threats. She wanted to be heard, and Paul wasn't listening. But Paul's button was on, making him see signs of danger and respond accordingly. He wasn't thinking, only reacting. He was deaf to reasoning. Feeling threatened by his wife, Paul's brain and body launched their survival reflexes. At this point, it became nearly impossible for him to pause and consider whether the danger was real. There was a disconnect between his brain's survival system and its thought processing.

Colleagues and I have explored this structural flaw using PET scans to study groups of men with a history of domestic violence and healthy, nonviolent men.[8] By tracing glucose metabolism in different areas of their brain, we could make inferences about the communication between the cortical structure, which generates thought and reason, and the amygdala, which seems to control survival instincts.

The scans of the domestic violence offenders showed a decrease in the strength of the connections between the cortex and the amygdala based on glucose metabolism. Their cortex was not sending strong enough signals to inhibit survival reactions. This suggests that the wiring was flawed. I am not quite sure why this critical link between these two brain regions was not functioning normally. However, the result is that perpetrators are hypersensitive to stimuli—they have hair-trigger reactions. This happened with Paul. He felt an immediate and uncontrollable need to protect himself and fight.

The Mother Who Flipped Out at the Mall

Gail and her husband, Thomas, were divorced. The custody arrangements for their six-year-old daughter, Hillary, were a constant source of irritation for Gail. She was given equal time with her daughter, rather than more time than her ex-husband, as she thought she deserved. She frequently talked about how her husband lied about her at the custody hearings, calling her "emotionally unstable." Nevertheless, she and Thomas had alternate weeks and weekends with Hillary. The split was Thomas's idea after he became involved with Gail's best friend, which further angered Gail. She felt betrayed by her friend and discarded by her husband, and she was furious with the court system for not giving her sole custody.

Gail had a history of outbursts. If something disrupted her normal routine or she felt someone was defying or criticizing her, she'd react with cutting remarks, sarcasm, or verbal confrontations. Once when a store clerk could not find a special order, Gail heaped loud scorn on the woman and then marched out of the place, knocking over a vase on the way. At the supermarket, she would stand in the express line counting items in other people's carts and demand they leave the line if they were one item over the express-line limit. At least two stores had ejected her and told her never to shop there again because of her arguments.

These confrontations gave her no satisfaction. In fact, after a confrontation, she was usually so upset that she'd shake for hours. At night, she had difficulty sleeping as she relived the exchanges and imagined other outcomes.

She came to me because of an incident with her ex-husband. It happened on a Saturday afternoon when Gail was shopping at a local mall. She turned a corner and literally bumped into Thomas, Hillary, and his girlfriend, Angela. Both Thomas and Angela were carrying multiple shopping bags from expensive shops. The collision sent the bags flying, and as soon as Gail realized that they represented big spending, she went ballistic. She had battled her ex for every dollar of alimony and child support, and seeing luxury logos made her lose it. Regaining her balance, she repeatedly kicked the bags, sending the new purchases flying, all the while screaming about money. She stopped only when mall security intervened.

As Gail recounted the story to me, she said she had felt justified

The Many Faces of Domestic Abuse

Experts have identified a variety of ways spouses react to someone they feel a need to dominate, control, or protect themselves against.[9] This behavior includes:

- Aggression (injury to spouse or pets, damaging furniture or possessions)
- Control (withholding money, car)
- Isolation (not letting spouse come and go freely)
- Harassment (telephone calls, visits, stalking, embarrassing spouse in public)
- Physical aggression (slapping, hitting, kicking, pinching, biting, choking)
- Intimidation with physical threats (use of weapons, cornering victim, shouting, swearing, driving recklessly)
- Threatening (threats related to custody, kidnapping children, killing self or spouse)

---

in her anger but also realized that it had gotten out of control. Her anger had never been so physical until that encounter. Until now, her weapon had been her tongue. She knew this eruption had gone over the edge. Before, she thought she could control and direct her temper to suit her purposes. Now she was no longer sure.

"My husband, that woman, are trying to erase me from Hillary's life by making me so poor I can't afford anything. It was like an out-of-body experience. I don't know what happened to me. Why did I do that? I'm not a violent person."

As I listened, I imagined Hillary shopping with her dad seemingly forgetting her mother. The scene represented a threat to all Gail valued in her life: her child's affection and her role as a provider. She felt that everything important to her was being threatened and that she could lose control of her emotions because of it. Lashing out was her way of defending herself, her life. Gail's angry reaction was normal because her role as a mother was being threatened. The abnormal part was how she handled it.

Gail's extreme sensitivity to criticism and defiance is common for someone on the anger button. Her environment is not a safe place but instead presents constant threats to her psychological well-being. The shaking she felt after confrontations was her nervous system, which had been activated by survival reflexes, trying to restore normalcy. There was less thoughtful, cortical input to her survival system, making it almost impossible for her to calm down.[10] Her floating, disconnected feelings also highlighted the lack of cortical input to her emotions. Her emotions were not only out of control but also unreal and impossible for her to understand. Similarly, her mystification about why she acted the way she did emphasizes that absence of any thoughtful input to her behavior.

As Gail and I talked about her feeling that her identity and motherhood role were being usurped, we revisited other confrontations of hers. Was it possible, I asked, that the shop clerks, restaurant staff, and other strangers she'd fought with also represented some form of threat?

Complicating her insight into the source of her anger was, I believed, a personality quality called trait anger.[11] Most emotions can be categorized as either trait or state. Trait means that the anger is a permanent part of her temperament, while state anger comes and goes in the moment. Trait anger is always there on a low simmer, ready to explode at any time. It's a persistent feeling not connected with any single goal or situation. It's chronically pushing the anger button.

Gail's behavior could also be described as intermittent explosive disorder (IED).[12] This is a relative newcomer to the psychiatrists' diagnostic manual, first included in a 2004 edition. Gail certainly had some of the signs: frequent bouts of verbal aggression as well as impulsive rage that was uncontrollable, unplanned, and without any apparent purpose or goal. Typically, someone with IED goes through brief outbursts, experiences physical symptoms like sweating or heart palpitations, and afterward feels remorse.

The Bullying Boss

Roger came to my practice at the recommendation of a friend who told him I treated a number of business people. We had barely sat down to our first session when he announced what he wanted.

"Gavin says you're a savvy guy. That's what I need. Not a lot of touchy-feely stuff. I need someone with the guts to tell me what I should do. The HR director in our company has told me to change my management style. I get results, but people don't like the way I do it. Can you help me?"

Roger's aggressiveness put me on alert. I sensed an erratic temper lurking beneath his surface. He was jumpy and kept shifting in his chair. Roger showed no signs of insight into how he was perceived. I didn't respond right away, hoping he would expand on what he wanted from therapy.

"I'm sorry, that didn't come out right," he said in a different tone. This comment was slow and sincere, not the pressured speech I first heard. "I really could use your help. My job's on the line, and my wife thinks I need to learn to control my temper. Can you help me?" He smiled like a supplicant.

He was an executive for a defense contractor, directing a group of consultants and former military officers in securing contracts and then implementing the successful ones. The firm was midsize, and he was upper management with ambitions to go higher. Many of his days were devoted to marathon meetings to hammer out contract terms or massage proposals. Meetings can be a petri dish of personal styles. I asked him to describe a typical one.

"They're usually in the morning, though sometimes I gather people late in the day, to check their progress, head off any problems, give them a pep talk. I've picked up grumbling about those meetings, people whining about not getting home on time. Please, this is a business. We've got competitors nipping at our heels—we need to be on it, 24/7."

"Do you do most of the talking at these meetings?" I asked

"It depends. I ask a lot of questions, try to drill down into their answers, find out what's really happening. People will gloss over a problem, not say anything. I want to hear it all."

"What if you don't like what you hear?"

"Then . . ." he paused. "Again, it depends if they're making excuses for themselves or it's a legitimate beef."

"Do you ever get angry at these meetings?"

"Occasionally and only if I have to, if they're behind schedule or going off on a tangent. I try to be firm and may yell a little. You know, to motivate them. Keep them on their toes. I only get really angry if I see someone ignoring what I'm saying, showing disrespect. Rolling their eyes, that really sets me off. But that doesn't happen much. My people are pretty professional."

I continued to push Roger into describing his interactions at work. "What do you do to motivate people?"

"Good question. I believe in the carrot, not the stick. I try to instruct them through example. I might tell them about how something worked out for me. The gym teacher story seems to rev them up," he said.

When Roger was in high school, he and a couple of pals decided to get rid of the new gym teacher. He would throw things at him when his back was turned, pepper him with senseless questions, make comments about his small size, and lead the other boys in making odd noises. At times, he switched up the attack, acting helpful and eager to learn.

"We destroyed him. He barely lasted a month, and I tell people that's what you do with competitors. Relentless pursuit, be unpredictable," he said proudly.

We ended the session with me asking what precise circumstances at work made him lose his temper. He answered with another story.

A man on his team, a relatively new hire, had asked him at a large meeting for advice in handling a difficult client. The client wasn't providing timely information or returning phone calls. Roger went ballistic. What infuriated him was that the employee was bringing up something Roger thought was trivial in a big meeting, and further, the employee had obviously not made much of an effort to solve the problem himself before complaining. Roger lit into the man.

"Were you able to give him some useful advice?" I asked.

"Yeah, I told him to get some guts. It wasn't my problem, it was his," Roger declared.

Many of the early sessions with Roger were like that. He would reveal himself in stories he thought reflected well on him, and I would dig deeper. The same pattern was apparent when we talked about his family life. Small things set him off, especially if his wife asked for help making a decision about something he didn't know much about. When that happened, he would fly into a rage and then not speak to her for hours, sometimes days.

Roger had begun to recognize how his volatile mood swings were affecting his mental health and that of the people around him. He was restless, had trouble sleeping, drank too much, and woke up many mornings with a dull headache. His confrontational, bullying style had thrown his physical health into a downward spiral.

Like the other patients whose PAG anger button is always on, Roger saw threats everywhere. His justification of his anger—"only if I have to"—suggested that he felt he had to show anger often. He felt this way because he could not withstand any hint of criticism. It was threatening. The same was true if people rolled their eyes around him. It was like a slap in the face. More than eye rolling triggered his anger. Seeing anger or fear in another person's face, hearing a note of criticism in a tone of voice, or innocuous cues like a misplaced report could launch him. People on the anger button often misread facial expressions and see threats all around.[13] Their cortex is unable to reduce the intensified threat signals going to the amygdala. As a result, Roger was unable to dampen or control his reactions. This became a vicious cycle, with people reacting to his anger with their own temper, escalating the anger as it went back and forth.

Studies into aggression have shed light on the wiring of anger. Researchers have theorized for a long time that some types of aggression reflect neurological malfunctioning. A fruitful focus of study has been a form of aggression known as impulsive antisocial behavior.[14] This kind of aggression is characterized by being emotionally driven and reacting out of proportion to any provocation. Scientists have found that people who act this way have a flawed sensory filter, especially their ability to judge the faces of others. They tend to see hostility in a neutral or harmless expression.

A study demonstrating this involved twenty people, half with a history of intermittent explosive disorder and half healthy.[15] Each person was hooked to an fMRI scanner as the researchers watched how a brain responded when a volunteer looked at a series of faces.

When the aggressive volunteers saw a threatening face, their amygdala showed greater activation than that of the nonaggressive individuals. An overactive amygdala stirs up stronger emotions than the facial expression warrants. In this way, the sensory information going into their brain's emotion-processing circuit somehow becomes corrupted. Researchers believe it's likely that the malfunction occurs in the pathways between the cortex and the amygdala, and sensory messages are mistakenly amplified. They see hostility where none is intended and may lash out or become aggressive in their body language or words.

The ultimate threat to Roger was the employee at the meeting asking a question about how to handle a client. It was in front of other people, and he felt on the spot because he didn't have a good answer. This threatened his public image, his reputation. The last clue, Roger's response to a confrontational situation at home by not talking to his wife for long periods, was a survival response. His behaviors were either fight or shutdown.

In each of these patients, anger and aggressive behavior sprang from feeling threatened. Each sensed a threat, regardless of how real or not real it was, and that is what stirred their anger and made them act. The trigger might have included a hint of physical danger or a danger of being disrespected, demeaned, ridiculed, or simply ignored. Any challenge to their well-being, self-image, or self-worth became a tangible threat. Thinking about my model of the PAG, I understood that anger and its matching behavior, fighting or aggression, became pathological when it was too intense for a situation or went on too long. The servant that managed their PAG rheostat had turned it up to high and left the house.

Reducing Anger, Adding Thought

In talking about treating aggressive behavior, I want to emphasize that these patients exhibited a particular kind of aggression. It was defensive, even though the external cause did not justify their over-the-top behavior. The cause was neurological—pathways controlling their behavior had been disrupted.

My treatment approach to anger is based on the same principle you would apply to an animal that has been backed into a corner. As you know, you do not lunge at a trapped animal; that just makes the situation worse. I find it helpful at the beginning of treatment to take a detailed history: *Did the explosive behavior happen once or reoccur? Have you noticed a pattern of when it happens? How do others react?* With this approach, I not only avoid making snap decisions before I have all the facts but it also makes the patient feel listened to and valued.

Once I have a full history, I typically take out a pencil and paper and draw my PAG model. I highlight the anger-fight button, and explain the lack of connection between the cortex and the amygdala. I rarely say much more before the patient declares, "That's me." With the help of the PAG model, we acknowledge the anger and violent behavior without confrontations or my eliciting defensiveness.

The PAG model also helps show that without good cortical control, the amygdala processes sensory information lightning fast, in less than thirty-five milliseconds. For example, a husband may see his wife talking to another man and immediately conclude that they are having an affair and do something about it. This is the amygdala's instant reaction and the root of jealousy and passion. The quick amygdala also explains why traditional anger management alone may not be effective. By the time people are able to verbalize a threat, they have already reacted. A nervous system geared for survival needs to act instantly. Speed is of the essence, or you do not survive. The problem is that an activated nervous system does not know the difference between a war zone and the living room with a loving spouse.

At this point, I frequently introduce the possibility of treatment with antidepressant medication. I emphasize that this recommendation is not because I think the patient is depressed but because antidepressants, particularly classes of antidepressants like Prozac, can treat a fast trigger.

Prozac (generic name: fluoxetine) belongs to the selective serotonin reuptake inhibitors (SSRI) class, meaning it increases the amount of serotonin in certain areas of the central nervous system. Serotonin, a neurotransmitter, helps regulate moods. While used most often to treat depression, Prozac also diminishes anxiety and panic attacks, mood swings and irritability, and anger and physical aggression.

Recently, I led a study that showed good results in curbing violent behavior with Prozac.[16] The study involved men and women with histories of repeated domestic violence and alcoholism. It was a double-blind, controlled study, so some participants were in a group that received a placebo, not the drug, and the others took fluoxetine. We did not know which group received which drug.

At the beginning of the study, we tested the participants to rate them on the Modified Overt Aggression Scale. Participants who took the fluoxetine and did not drink alcohol showed a significant reduction in anger and aggressive behavior compared with the placebo group. The drug group had less anger, irritability, and feelings of annoyance as well as fewer instances of argumentativeness, shouting, loss of temper, and physical aggression.

The drug decreased the participants' overall sense of anger. By their accounts, they were less sensitive to sensory stimuli that previously set them off. They had more time to react to what they saw and heard. This slower sensory reaction theoretically allowed time for cortical signals to dampen instinctive reflexes. They said the drug gave them "more time to think." However, the drug was less helpful for participants who continued to drink.

A number of years ago, I was treating a young man with a history of repeatedly hitting his girlfriend. Violent, aggressive behavior was not his only problem. He also drank heavily. Following alcohol rehab, he began taking Prozac. Prozac takes weeks to reach therapeutic levels in the blood, so I did not expect an immediate change in him. I knew it was working, though, when he came to therapy about four weeks later with a story about his roommate.

The young man was living in a sober house and had a male roommate. Normally, my patient showered and went to work around seven thirty, before the roommate got up. But on one particular morning, the roommate got to the bathroom first and was still in there at seven thirty. My patient yelled through the bathroom door, saying he needed to shower before work, but the roommate didn't answer and stayed in the bathroom. Time ticked by with my patient becoming increasingly enraged at the thought that he was going to be late for work. All this created a collision of forces, pushing the young man into a threat response.

A fight response consistent with the PAG model would have been knocking down the door and attacking the roommate because of the disrespect. A flight response would have been angrily packing up his things and leaving the sober house. Yet another response, shutdown, might have been going back to bed and skipping work. Plotting to get even with the roommate to make him pay would have been a predatory response. And he could have resumed drinking to numb his negative emotions.

Yet he did none of these. Instead, he went into the kitchen, made a pot of coffee, and waited. He was still angry, which was appropriate, but he didn't engage in inappropriate behavior. As he and I talked about this incident, we surveyed the possible peaceable solutions to the situation. I emphasized that his measured anger was not a sign of weakness but could be used as a starting point for talking to his roommate about their issues.

At this point, therapy was invaluable. The drug had slowed his instant anger reactions and given him time to think about the situation. Therapy gave him the tools to work out his differences with his roommate without aggressive reactions. With his brain functioning more thoughtfully and slowly, he could work out solutions to real-world problems.

Perhaps you are wondering whether you should be on medication. My answer is this: maybe. It really depends on an honest appraisal by you and those close to you of how you handle conflict. If the judgment is that you have a pattern of angry outbursts and overreactions, you need to consider a range of solutions. You may need to reduce the stress in your life and set aside time to think about the irritants in your life. Maybe you need to pay more attention to your routine and physical health, like sleep habits, diet, alcohol consumption, and amount of exercise. Or, finally, you may need to seek professional help.

Summing Up

- People with a hair-trigger temper tend to be extra sensitive to their environment and sensory cues that feel threatening enough to necessitate a fight-or-flight reaction.

- Angry people often feel like victims. A victim mentality enables people to justify irrational behavior and ignore any consequences of their behavior. Irrationally angry people believe they are totally right and justified.

- People with extreme anger problems are unable to quiet their survival emotions or control their behavior. At the time of violence, their thinking has become irrational and disorganized. They are focused solely on the target of their anger and cannot see or consider anything else, including other people and consequences.

Desperate to Escape: Panic

Talking About Fear

Fear can pervade the most normal of lives. It may come and go, or it might move in. Living in fear, feeling that everything around you, whether at home or at work, is frightening, can create a new normal so destructive that it cripples you. Even in small doses, fear can be unnerving. I hear about people's fears every day, not only from patients but also from friends and colleagues and in the news. We all have experienced its upsetting effects, especially if we've ever heard someone make one of these declarations:

Anger	○	○	Fight
Fear	●	●	**Flight**
Depression	○	○	Shutdown
Absence of Emotion	○	○	Predatory

"I want a divorce. I don't love you anymore."

"I'm sorry, but the test results aren't good."

"You can't think about retiring—you haven't saved enough."

"Did you hear our neighbor was mugged last night right in front of his house?"

"We just got a call from the credit card company. Our card is maxed out."

People are afraid of losing their job or not finding one, of being a victim of crime, whether on the street or in the home, of terrorism, or of anyone different, be it protestor, political firebrand, the homeless, or people of different religions and races. The news is riddled with mentions of threats: the terrorist threat, the cyber threat, the recession threat, the global warming threat.

At times, our world reminds me of my trip to Uganda a few years ago when the Lord's Resistance Army, notorious for kidnapping and torturing, was terrorizing the population. The streets of Gulu at night were empty and silent because its residents were huddled in their homes. Restaurants and retailers were dark and shuttered. Outside the city, women and children had abandoned their farms to move to tented settlements because of fear of attacks and kidnappers. I realize that the streets of Uganda are not the same as the streets of American cities. Nevertheless, fear possesses a power that can alter people's lives in any American city just as it does in Gulu.

Fear is essential to survival. It triggers the flight part of the fight-or-flight defense system. A person caught in a burning house feels fear before jumping to safety. Someone trapped in the bleachers of a frenzied soccer match feels it before clawing her way to open space. A pedestrian feels it before running away from a mugger. Fear that drives the urge to escape is healthy.

On the other hand, fear can be so intense, persistent, and inappropriate that it is pathological. It does not come and go according to a situation but moves in for a long-term stay. This fear causes people to react in ways that undermine their physical health and damage their relationships. I treat many people beset by overwhelming fear and its common companion, panic. When I ask about my patients' fears, they frequently can't explain them or point to any one thing. The same is true for people with panic attacks—they often have no idea what sets them off, only that the feeling is horrendous. For some unknown reason, they have become wired for excessive fear and panic. Their PAG rheostat button for fear-flight is stuck on high.

Learning to Be Afraid

Fear can be innate or learned. Innate fears are those we are born with. The usual targets are snakes, spiders, heights, and enclosed spaces, to name a few. Scientists believe that these fears have strong survival value and have been coded into some people's genetic makeup. A single encounter with a black mamba snake will kill you, so it's vital to avoid them even the first time you see one. Innate fear does not require your thoughts, or even your attention, to spark action. It's linked directly to the amygdala and instantly launches a defense. It travels on what neuroscientist Joseph LeDoux calls a "low road" in the brain, which is a straight shot from the thalamus to the amygdala.[1] It bypasses the cortex, traveling from the sensory-processing center to the fear-processing center without pausing for conscious thought. Your innate fear system is so refined that you do not even have to be aware of something fearful for your body to automatically defend itself.

If you are about to cross a street and you suddenly see a car barreling toward you, you jump back to the curb.[2] You don't think, *This car could kill me. I'm in danger, so I must move out of the way.* You jump because your brain and body take action without you thinking. The part of your brain that generates conscious thought moves too slowly to protect you in emergency situations, so another part registers the fear and acts. Unlearned fear is fast. It comes on rapidly, and once you have escaped the threat and feel safer, it dissipates.

Researchers have probed people's fear-sensory systems. One study watched the reactions of two groups of people, each with a different innate fear.[3] One group had an intense fear of snakes, and the other an intense fear of spiders. Both groups watched pictures of snakes and spiders, but the images were buried in pictures of mushrooms and flowers. During the viewing, the participants were connected to monitors that registered skin conductance, which measures moisture in the skin from sweat, linking it to fear. The researchers discovered that participants' bodies had noticeable fear responses before the individuals were aware of seeing something they feared. And the snake-fearing people did not react to spider images, and vice versa. Their sensory network, brain, and autonomic nervous system did not react indiscriminately but only to the creature that each person feared.

Ivan Pavlov popularized the concept of learned, or conditioned, fear.[4] If you've ever sat through a basic psychology class, you know about his famous dog demonstration. He rang a bell (a conditioned stimulus) while feeding the dog meat powder (an unconditioned stimulus) to make the dog salivate (the response). After repeating this a number of times, Pavlov's dog would salivate at the mere sound of the bell without any meat powder present. This was classic conditioning. Then he added a fear element.

Using rats, Pavlov applied a footshock for the unconditioned stimulus and a loud tone as the conditioned stimulus.[5] The end result, the response, was a conditioned fear reaction—at the sound of the tone, the rats went into defensive behavior, like freezing or running away, and also experienced a spike in blood pressure and heart rate and a cascade of stress hormones. The loud tone was a threat—it signaled the coming of something painful. When he stopped giving rats the footshock and only sounded the tone, they still went into fear mode. This is the way you learn to react to a threat.

Are You Having a Panic Attack?

The psychiatrists' manual *(Diagnostic and Statistical Manual of Mental Disorders, Fourth Edition)* states that a panic attack is a discrete period of intense fear or discomfort in which four (or more) of the following symptoms develop abruptly and reach a peak within ten minutes:

- Palpitations, pounding heart, or accelerated heart rate
- Sweating
- Trembling or shaking
- Sensations of shortness of breath or smothering
- Feeling of choking
- Chest pain or discomfort
- Nausea or abdominal distress
- Feeling dizzy, unsteady, light-headed, or faint
- Feelings of unreality or disconnectedness
- Fear of losing control or going crazy
- Fear of dying
- Numbness or tingling sensations
- Chills or hot flashes[6]

You can be conditioned to fear anything at any age. A researcher at Johns Hopkins University in 1920 conducted a study to see if he could teach an infant to fear something it would not normally fear.[7] The famous behaviorist John Watson showed "Little Albert," who was eight months old, an assortment of small, furry animals, like a rat, a rabbit, and a dog as well as objects such as a newspaper and a Santa Claus mask. Albert played with these things, none of which frightened him. In separate tests, Albert did show that he was afraid of loud noises. Next, Watson gave Albert the same small animal he had been playing with and loudly banged a steel pipe with a hammer. He did this repeatedly behind the child so Albert couldn't see it. After only seven pairings of holding the animal and hearing the banging noise, Albert became so fearful when presented with the animal, he cried and crawled away.

Sometimes you are fearful without knowing why. The body may remember fear that the mind does not. A famous experiment by a French physician involved a patient with brain damage that had destroyed her short-term memory.[8] She was unable to form any new memories and would forget from minute to minute the people she had met or the things she had done. Every morning when the doctor visited her, he had to reintroduce himself. One morning he decided to test what memories she could retain. As he introduced himself, he extended his hand to shake hers and in it was concealed a small tack. When they shook hands, the tack pricked her. The next day he returned to her room to introduce himself. Although she still did not remember him, she refused to shake his hand. Some corner of her fear system remembered that shaking hands with the doctor was painful.

Everyone possesses a deep reservoir of conditioned or learned fears that help them navigate their life but at times become dysfunctional. I have a patient, a woman in her late thirties, who hates hospitals. She especially hates spending the night because nurses are constantly coming into her room. When someone comes in during the middle of the night, she jerks awake in a fearful sweat. Her heart is racing, and her breathing is short and quick. She believes her reaction comes from her sleep being disrupted. However, her physical reactions are fear based. I know from treating her that, as a child, she was often awakened in the middle of the night by the sound of her parents' fighting. She was terrified that she would wake up the next morning and Mommy or Daddy would be gone. Fears that have not been defused even though the threat has passed underlie PTSD as well as other trauma-related disorders.

When Fear Strikes out of Nowhere

So far I have been talking about understandable fears—fears that pose a genuine threat. But what about the fear that has no threat and makes no sense? This fear is immensely perplexing. You don't know which way to run. This kind of fear makes some people stay home from work on any Friday the 13th or an airline passenger load up on Xanax whenever he flies, or a person obsess about getting hit by an asteroid or space junk. This fear is similar to pathological fear, although physicians refer to this condition as generalized anxiety— there is no identifiable threat, as there would be with a fear reaction.

Pathological fear skews everything you feel and do. Everyone knows fear in small doses and for a reason, but a few feel this way all the time. Gunther is a middle-aged man who came to me with drug and alcohol problems. After almost losing his job, he went into rehab and was sober for almost a year. In spite of all of this, he always felt uneasy, especially when going anywhere new, meeting someone he didn't know, or in any meeting with his boss. It was like he was infected with a fear virus, he said.

Other sensations intruded into his days. He couldn't finish anything, flitting from task to task. His thoughts often raced, and he fixated on what-if disaster scenarios. He imagined a catastrophe at every turn, from being assaulted on the street to being hit by a car. Facing the day was frequently overwhelming, and he felt exhausted most of the time. It took all his energy to get out of bed and tackle the deadlines and uncertainties of dealing with demanding clients. Listening to his accounts, I struggled to discern valid reasons for his concerns but could find few. It did not make sense.

Thinking about Gunther's angst, I realized that we had spent hours talking about bosses, deadlines, and difficult clients but never grasped the larger picture. There was a common theme throughout his life—a pervasive sense of fear. He never mentioned it, and it did not fit with what I knew about him. He was an intelligent, motivated, well-liked person who had a successful career. There was no reason to think he would be afraid. And as I later learned, he was embarrassed to talk about his fears because they were so out of proportion to his circumstances. They didn't make sense to him, and worse yet, they made him feel weak and inadequate. His fear button had been pushed, and it colored the way he saw the world. Fear had become as much a part of him as his high blood pressure.

People on the fear button see threats everywhere. Their attention naturally turns toward anything possibly fearful or ambiguous.[9] This is more than street smarts and being aware of your surroundings. The anxious person adds more meaning to facial expressions and frequently interprets them as hostile. Furthermore, once an anxious person sees something she thinks is threatening, she has difficulty turning away. The amygdala is alert and ready to help her survive. She stares at the individual whose expression looks angry, fixating. Her fixation, however, is selective. She would not be so absorbed in a sad or worried expression—only an angry look. It's as if she has special antennae designed to pick up facial expressions that tell her there is a possible personal threat.

People with panic disorder are also more inclined to dwell on threatening or fearful thoughts.[10] A study of two groups of people, one healthy and the other with diagnosed panic disorder, gave them a series of words to remember. The words related to a physical threat, a social threat, or a neutral situation. Hours later, when asked to randomly recall the words or use them in a sentence, the panic disorder individuals remembered words related to panic, while the healthy participants did not.

A panic disorder patient's amygdala is always alert and always overreacts. It's as if the motion sensor in a house sounds the alarm with just a slight breeze. For example, people who are prone to anxiety or have been diagnosed with an anxiety disorder have been shown through brain scans to have a hyperactive amygdala. The slightest suggestion of danger can produce fear in them.

A British research group found this with a group of twenty-three volunteers with varying degrees of anxiety.[11] Researchers were trying to answer a fundamental and intriguing question: Why do some people handle fear and anxiety better than others? To find an answer, they asked the participants to view video images of three rooms. Each room was intended to portray different anxiety-producing conditions. In the first room, there was a person who put his hands over his ears for six seconds. At the same time, there was a loud scream. This room showed a conditioned fear response—hands over ears became associated with a fearful scream. In the second room, the person put his hands over his ears for six seconds but the scream came at a different time. It was not associated with the gesture. This room showed contextual fear—the fearful scream was not connected to the gesture but to the room itself. Finally, in the third room, the person put his hands over his ears, but there was no scream. This was a safe, non-fearful room that served as a control environment from which to gauge participants' responses when they viewed the other rooms.

The researchers made several findings about fearful and non-fearful participants. When viewing the first room, people with higher levels of trait anxiety had a more active amygdala than people with lower levels of trait anxiety. When the trait-anxiety people looked at the second room, their amygdala still reacted. This suggested that they had been conditioned even by a neutral, fear-free situation. The context affected them, which could mean that their trait anxiety put them at greater risk of developing a fear disorder. Those people with low trait anxiety had a more active prefrontal cortex when viewing either of the fear rooms than the high trait anxiety people did. The researchers suggest that the ability of these participants to engage their cortex helps explain a resilience to pathological fear and anxiety. This study emphasizes, as do the others in this chapter, that a strong connection between the cortex and the amygdala is needed for people to be able to regulate feelings of fear.

A threat that once made you fearful can lose its power or no longer pose a danger. An empty lot where you were mugged when

Why More Women?

At least two times more women than men suffer panic attacks.[12] Here's a sketch of some of the possible reasons why:

- Reproductive hormones: Scientists have found that anxiety disorders strike women especially during reproductive years and when hormones are in flux. Estrogen can have a significant effect on areas of the limbic system and has been found to decrease panic and anxiety. Progesterone, however, can add to the signs of panic. As a result, researchers have noticed fewer symptoms of panic among pregnant women and more panic disorder among postpartum women. Even among women who are not pregnant, anxiety symptoms may rise and fall with phases of the menstrual cycle.

- Brain structure: Women's brains may be more sensitive to certain types of threats. Imaging studies show the amygdala and prefrontal cortex function differently in women, resulting in heightened sensitivity to social threats. Also, women's autonomic nervous system reacts stronger to anxiety than men's, making them perhaps more susceptible to panic systems arising from physical signs of anxiety.

- Diet and culture: Women with children are more likely to have disrupted sleep and to diet. Diet especially can influence serotonin processing and increase likelihood of anxiety.

you first moved to a city may now be a safe park. Normally you learn to separate a past threat from feeling afraid through what is known as extinction. You extinguish a conditioned fear by separating the dangerous aspects of an experience, like the mugging, from the surrounding circumstances, like the park itself. You repeatedly confront the once-dangerous, now-harmless surroundings, and over time the fear is gradually extinguished by forming new memories as you keep going back to the park and enjoying it instead of being mugged.

Someone with PTSD or an anxiety disorder has difficulty extinguishing the fear response even though a threat has passed. For example, soldiers who suffer from PTSD experience persistent conditioned fear responses long after their war zone service. Such a case was a soldier who served in Iraq who had learned to be watchful around roadside debris because that was where explosives were usually hidden. But after his tour, when he came home, he still broke into a sweat at the sight of trash along the road. A not uncommon example is the woman who, because of a volatile and hurtful relationship with her father when she was growing up, is fearful or anxious in most close relationships with men.

When Fear Is Near: Panic Attacks

Fear that sparks a fight-or-flight response from the PAG is intense and centered on an imminent threat. Fear goes through stages, with each stimulating a different brain area. Imagine you are driving home late at night and as you pull into your driveway, you see a hooded figure down the alley but not near your garage. The person has something in his hand and is not moving. You stop the car to study him—you freeze to gauge the threat. A neighborhood kid taking out the garbage or someone up to no good? At this point, the threat is not sufficient to make you feel you must defend yourself. You get out of the car and see the figure moving closer. Now your fear rises because the threat is moving closer to you, and you run for the back door. The proximity of the threat elevates your fear to the point that it triggers a response from the PAG.

Here the fight-or-flight response is a two-stage reaction, not an either-or. When the object of your fear is near but you have time and space enough to escape, the first reaction is to search for an escape and flee. Only when you are trapped and attacked or you know you're going to be hurt does the fight instinct kick in. Panic is how someone reacts when fear has risen beyond the freeze-and-assess stage and before the point of needing to fight. It is fleeing behavior. If a threat is genuine, panic can be an expedient way of finding an escape and fleeing to safety. But if the panic arises without a threat or lasts beyond the need to escape, it becomes incapacitating.

Anna began suffering panic attacks when she was in college. The cycle started freshman year with mountains of classwork making her feel crushed under a pile of deadlines, assignments, and class projects. The feeling of being overwhelmed would paralyze her until the night before something was due, when she would stay awake all night to complete it. Then she would escape to bed for days. Although she made good grades, she felt that failure was just around the corner and any day she would flunk out. The attacks would strike when Anna was sitting in class, walking across the campus, or studying in her room. They had no pattern and always produced waves of dread, choking sensations, skin crawling and tingling, and extreme nausea. Each time, she felt a sense of doom and a certainty that she was going to die. Despite experiencing dozens of panic attacks, each time brought the same terror that she felt with the first attack. She knew during an attack that she would get over it, but that knowledge did not lessen the intensity.

Afterward, Anna would feel like she was in a trance. She didn't seem in control of her body. Her legs, heavy and sluggish, moved of their own accord as if not attached to her. Depression settled in, and she stared into space for long periods. Studying, going to class, and even talking to someone were impossible. Hours would pass, and gradually physical sensation would come back as she broke from her trance. She said it was as if she had been desperately treading water to avoid drowning. Even when she did recover, she was so exhausted by the effort that she would sleep for days.

Anna finished college, but it took her six years with numerous starts and stops. She continues to have panic attacks, but they are less frequent. Medication and support groups have helped, along with a carefully crafted career that imposes no deadlines and allows her the freedom to set her own hours and working environment.

Some people who occasionally experience panic have developed their own ways to cope, such as breathing exercises and talking their fears out with a friend.

Panic disorder is getting ready to flee when a threat is not near, is nowhere in sight or is imagined. A person's threat defense system malfunctions and regularly flashes "Danger! Danger!" when no threat is nearby.

Research indicates that panic disorder stems from malfunctioning or abnormal activity in neural pathways. A telltale sign is that the body reacts to fear and goes into panic mode long before an individual is conscious of any threat or sees any sign of danger. In a study by the psychology department of Southern Methodist University, researchers recruited forty-three people, ages twenty-three to sixty-two with history of panic disorder.[13] Each person was wired with an electric monitor that tracked panic attack signs like heart rate, respiration, and skin conductance. They wore the monitor during normal activities throughout the day and night. They were to notify the researchers when an attack occurred by pressing a button on the monitor to record when it started.

When the researchers compiled the results, they found that physiological changes associated with breathing, smell, and CO_2 in the blood (you might remember from chapter 3 that the amygdala is especially sensitive to changes in CO_2) arose almost an hour before the person felt panicked. The attack itself lasted around eight minutes. These attacks occurred at all times and in various situations. One occurred when the person was sleeping, two came on suddenly when the people were at home, and another while the individual was driving.

Controlling Symptoms: Treatment

People frequently go to a hospital emergency room during a panic attack. Having one can feel life threatening, and patients often tell

ER staff that they have severe chest pain and dizziness. They think they're having a heart attack. Some of my patients have gone to an ER and been examined and tested, only to hear the doctor say there's nothing wrong. Although their tests typically show no abnormalities, to say nothing is wrong could not be farther from the truth.

Some doctors do not consider panic disorder to be a medical condition. Instead, they assign it to a loose category of psychological problems, with the patient being the most likely cause. As a result, people with panic attacks do not always receive serious medical attention. They are often on their own, struggling to understand a disorder with causes that are deep in the brain and symptoms that can dismantle a life. They are beset with feelings of inadequacy and a constant dread of the next panic attack. They are embarrassed to tell others and don't know where to turn.

Panic patients sometimes devise their own strategies for coping. One such strategy to reduce feelings of fear and dread during a panic attack is to find or imagine a safe place. A patient who experienced an attack at work immediately left her office and retreated to a comfortable couch in the ladies' lounge. It was a small, dark, and quiet place, and she was able to relax.

Sometimes I tell patients that controlling panic is like being in an emergency situation. First, take a deep breath. A common symptom of panic attacks is hyperventilation, and research has shown that hyperventilating can aggravate the other symptoms of an attack too.[14] If you can control your breathing so you don't hyperventilate, your symptoms will recede. One way to do this is change your breathing from short and shallow to long deep breaths, slowly blowing out air through pursed lips. This small change seems insignificant, but it can change your sensory input by shifting your attention away from your rapid breathing.

Then engage the cortex and try to control your emotions. Sometimes, getting angry at the circumstances surrounding this emergency will lessen the fear. Encouraging anger during a panic attack sounds counterintuitive, I know, but being able to focus your emotions helps control them. Another important step is to enlist help, friends and family who can evaluate your panic-inducing situation and provide objective perspective. The act of verbalizing your fears can also be helpful. Talking about what you are going through engages your cortex, helping you to think more rationally and to organize your thoughts. You need to avoid over- or underreacting. Controlling other symptoms, like jumping to conclusions about what your physical reactions mean, may also diminish panic attacks. The dramatic physical signs of panic, often a wildly pounding heart and feelings of suffocation, precede any conscious thought of what's happening. Your body reacts before your mind does. People having a panic attack tend to jump to conclusions about what's happening. Mistaken assumptions add fuel to their condition.

An enemy of rational thinking during a panic attack is catastrophic thinking.[15] Assuming you are doomed the instant you feel the pounding of your heart and feelings of suffocation plunges you further into trouble. In the same way, misinterpreting physical sensations can be disastrous. Thoughts like, *It scares me when my heart beats fast*, may automatically lead to panic.

A goal of therapy is to help patients replace the default thinking that leads them to fearful outcomes with more balanced thoughts. Therapy can help patients read their body better and adopt thinking that helps them realize they are not dealing with a health crisis. Being able to feel your heart pound or your breathing accelerate and not assume you are having a medical emergency can be a huge step in controlling panic. Remind yourself that you have survived panic attacks before and you will get through this one.

Part of the process of moving past a panic attack involves simply talking about your fears. This may sound like a therapeutic platitude but verbalizing fears and talking through disjointed thoughts can have a huge impact on calming panic. At the same time, assess your lifestyle to see if you are somehow contributing to your condition with excessive alcohol or caffeine. Perhaps your life has gotten beyond your control with too many deadlines, expectations, or problems threatening your mental well-being. You may need to distance yourself from a situation to sort out what is real fear and what is irrational. Write these out—the process of writing each can be helpful for beginning to address them. Next, outline steps for handling each one. Sometimes organizing your outside world, particularly deciding how you are going to respond in a certain situation, helps quell inner turmoil.

Lastly, see a doctor. Not only will a professional opinion be reassuring, but a physician can also rule out potential medical conditions, such as thyroid disease or cardiac conditions, that can contribute to panic. There are also prescription drugs that can help with panic. For recurrent attacks, an antidepressant such as an SSRI (even if you are not depressed), can effectively control symptoms.

Some Final Thoughts About Fear

Two years after I first visited Gulu, I returned for a second visit. In the intervening years, there had been a weakening in the power of the Lord's Resistance Army, and this made an amazing difference. Without fear penetrating every element of the society, new buildings had sprung up, cell towers dotted the landscape, and people moved freely and with energy, milling about the streets, eating in restaurants, shopping, and carrying on normal routines. At night, the streets were vibrant.

Looking back, several things stick in my mind. When I first went to Gulu, official sources estimated that there were only a few thousand members of the LRA, yet they held millions of people hostage to fear. The people's fear had more than one dimension. Beyond fear of kidnapping, they were also afraid to confront all the horrors that had taken place and, in some cases, their part in the carnage.

Even though many overt signs of fear had disappeared from street life, I found a disconnect between people's calm external appearances and the turmoil going on inside them. A vivid example was the man who had killed a family member, and he surely was not the only person with this kind of disconnect. I'm convinced that most of the people of Uganda did not want to kill, but once they were involved with the LRA, they did not know how to get out of the organization for fear of losing their own lives. Which in itself is another example of fear. If they had the courage to examine their behavior, it would have unleashed feelings they would not know how to handle. In a distorted way, believing in the LRA provided distance from these feelings and gave them a sense of purpose and belonging when their lives seemed to lack direction.

Gulu, its citizens, and the Lord's Resistance Army are extreme examples of the power and destructiveness of fear. Yet, while these fears are unique, they also reflect what happens in the world every day. Wars are everywhere, and people are hurting each other. Fear of facing ourselves and fear of facing consequences for our actions hold us captive. Someone may be fearful of facing the guilt of getting a girlfriend pregnant or breaking up a marriage or of not being a good parent. Our actions affect people all around us, and it can be enormously difficult to take responsibility for damage we have caused. In the chapter on responsibility (chapter 12), I delve into this.

Summing Up

- Panic disorder is the body's survival reflex and is a form of the flight, or escape, phase of the fight-or-flight response.

- Abnormal fear is at the root of many emotional disorders, particularly panic.

- Panic attacks can make a person physically as well as psychological ill.

Going into Shutdown

A Good Reason to Be Depressed

Bernard, who I'd known for years, didn't seem like himself. When our families got together for a meal, he was quiet and withdrawn. He didn't participate in the conversation and picked at his food. Usually a gregarious fellow with a great sense of humor—he loved nonsensical, absurd stories—his expression had become dour, almost sad. Once or twice, I thought he might burst into tears. His wife told me he'd been this way for almost a month, and it was affecting their life together as well as his work. He was calling in sick more than he ever had. I offered to talk to him.

Anger	○	○	Fight
Fear	○	○	Flight
Depression	●	●	**Shutdown**
Absence of Emotion	○	○	Predatory

The conversation was awkward at first, with Bernard saying he was just tired and nothing was wrong. I persisted, saying that others had noticed he wasn't himself. For a moment, his eyes welled up.

"It's Donna. It's so awful I can't get over it."

"What happened? Is she okay?" Donna was their only child, a twelve-year-old daughter who'd had developmental problems as a baby. Now she was also struggling with obesity.

"Something's going on at school. She comes home glum, and sometimes her face looks tear streaked. She doesn't say much, so I decided to start picking her up. I waited for her outside the school to see if I could see what was going on. About a month ago as I was sitting in the car, I saw her come out of the building and behind her were two girls who she was sort of waving at. Like you wave at a fly. The girls had puffed out their cheeks and were walking like sumo wrestlers. And other kids coming out were laughing at the scene. Donna's face was screwed up, like she was trying not to cry. It absolutely broke my heart. I've seen this happen a couple of times."

Bernard and I talked for twenty minutes, with me mostly listening to what he was going through. His depression and shutdown made sense once I learned what had caused it. Seeing other children taunt and ridicule your child would send any parent into despair. Knowing Bernard and that even the healthiest among us can go into shutdown after a terrible experience, I suspected he would come out of it and resume a normal life.

Depression can strike anyone, and it does. It's all around us—people who feel beat up by everyday life, people who feel numb as they grapple with personal crises, people paralyzed and unable to function because of worry and sadness. For most people, it is a natural consequence of something happening in their life that makes them sad, unhappy, uninterested in pleasure, and numb to sensation. It can be the result of mourning a death, experiencing a disease, or being dumped. It's part of life.

Out of the Blue

But not everyone who is depressed can point to a reason for what they're going through. For some people, like many of my patients, their depression and shutdown strikes them like a bolt out of the blue. Their life seems fine with no crisis or trauma or overwhelming worry, yet depression derails them.

This happened to Diane and Dave, a couple whose frustration and misery were palpable. Diane was depressed, but Dave was suffering too. They initially came to therapy together, with Dave doing most of the talking while Diane sat mute, eyes downcast. When she spoke, her speech was slow and there were long pauses between her sentences.

They ran a successful business together, a design-construction firm. Dave said the first sign was that Diane was sleeping later and later, accompanied by an increasingly gloomy outlook on their life. Normally she was athletic and active. The business was doing well, both were healthy and had strong friendships and family connections, yet Diane repeatedly talked about feeling like a failure. She felt defeated and unable to cope with simple tasks like preparing company payroll checks. "Why can't I handle life?" she said more than once.

They waited to see if her mood would pass, but it did not, and over months it became worse. Diane tried antidepressants, but they did not help. Dave grew frustrated as Diane withdrew into herself. He tried to cajole, to argue, and to reason with her to "snap out of it." Her usual response to his "buck-up" pleas was to shrug and escape to the bedroom to stare at the TV. When they did talk, she dwelled on catastrophe scenarios of their business going under and them losing everything. She saw everything going down the tubes and their future destroyed.

Dave was in an equally bad place because he did not understand Diane's tailspin. There was no precipitating event, and nothing in their personal or professional lives warranted such a bleak outlook. He was angry, frustrated, and beside himself with helplessness.

Symptoms That Signal Someone Needs Help

Certain symptoms show that people have succumbed to shutdown mode and need help. These are symptoms that cannot be ignored. Typically, these people have more than one of these symptoms and also indicate severe depression. If your spouse or good friend is exhibiting these behaviors, you may need to organize an intervention to insist the person see a doctor:

- Staying in bed all day or regular insomnia

- Not going to work

- Not eating or constant overeating; related behaviors, like not bathing or taking care of personal hygiene

- Ignoring personal obligations like paying bills

- Cutting off contact with friends or family

- Constant fatigue or lack of energy

- Pain, headaches, cramps, or digestive problems that do not ease with treatment

- Mental agitation or jumbled thinking

- Feelings of worthlessness, guilt, or helplessness

Important caveat: If depressed people mention suicide or say anything that suggests they might hurt themselves or anyone else, this is an emergency. They need to get professional help immediately.

Diane's extreme reaction to her depression is what I call shutdown and is probably the most common complaint among my patients. While some patients are like Bernard, whose shutdown was temporary and an understandable reaction to seeing his child in pain, many are like Diane. Their shutdown is not a temporary state but seems unending. They feel trapped in a room with no doors and no windows. They come for therapy not because they're having a bad day or a vague malaise but because of an unending pain and sense of failure.

What's the Point?

Listening to people like Bernard and Diane made me wonder about their symptoms. They had felt the same emotions and reacted the same way even though Bernard's depression stemmed from a specific situation and Diane's struck her from nowhere. They experienced numbness, hopelessness, a sense of defeat and failure, and a loss of energy and interest in the external world. In a way, their behavior represented a form of psychological and physical escape.

I recalled Richard Bandler's research into "passive coping."[1] He's the neuroscientist I mentioned in a previous chapter who explored the behaviors elicited by stimulating parts of the PAG. He generated fight and flight as well as another behavior that he called passive coping. The animals showing this behavior became quiet, immobile, and ignored their surroundings. This behavior can help recovery and healing after a fight response.

Bandler's research was an eye-opener. Before it, I did not understand the purpose of depression. It seemed like a useless emotion that just made people feel miserable, weak, and unable to cope with life. He pushed me to adjust my thinking, beginning with the word *depression* itself. The term *depression* is usually used to describe a behavior, and this is misleading. It is more helpful when I think of it as an emotion synonymous with sadness. The actual behavior that results from this sadness is what I call shutdown and has its own clinical definition, just like fight and flight do. Its characteristics include lack of energy, disinterest in the outside world, and a bleak view of reality and the future.

Bandler's research also showed me that shutdown has survival value. It promotes survival by allowing people time to regain their health. This purpose can be difficult to recognize. I had to explain to Bernard that his shutdown gave him a mental respite from his sadness over his daughter being bullied by her classmates. A patient named Bethany provides a more dramatic illustration of how shutdown can help healing.

Bethany came from a large family, one of six children who were ruled by a patrician father. Her mother, a mean alcoholic, stayed on the edge of family dynamics. Bethany adored her dad, so it was natural and automatic that when chronic obstructive pulmonary disease (COPD) threatened his life, she was there for him. Night and day she took care of him, while her siblings were much less attentive, much less helpful. In the course of his dying, Bethany came to resent her siblings and would talk only with her younger sister, and only if it was an emergency.

When her father died, Bethany was devastated, experiencing a depression so profound that just maintaining a conversation was impossible. She retreated into herself, feeling that her grief gave her the right to mourn in her own way. She avoided her mother, siblings, and friends, and thus any emotional demands. Shutdown as a model of survival explained Bethany's behavior. Here you have the death of a loved one, which most people can relate to. There is a sense of numbness, of just going through the motions. You feel like you are in a fog and have this nauseous pit in your stomach. Life looks bleak—how can I go on without the loved one? In some ways, as bad as shutdown feels, it can act like the shot of Novocain you get when a tooth is pulled. It's no fun, but it gets you through it.

In shutdown, you expend less energy, you do not engage other people who may drain you, and you limit your sensory stimuli so that your nervous system can calm down. Some people would never slow down long enough to heal unless a behavioral reaction made them. Scans of people with a foremost symptom of depression, the inability to feel pleasure, reveal that their brain had a reduced response in regions associated with reward, such as an area called the nucleus accumbens.[2] This is their brain forcing them to slow down. While this decreased response to reward may contribute to their condition, it also may put a brake on their mental and emotional activity so that recovery is possible.

But what if the Novocain does not wear off? Numbing depression often lingers following the loss of a loved one, the loss of a job, a divorce, or another life trauma in which feelings of numbness initially provide a respite from daily demands but then become a prolonged state of destructive depression.

Unfortunately for Bethany, her time of shutdown and emotional isolation had stretched into months, long past a reasonable recovery time. Although there is no standard recovery period for grief, shutdown for close to a year strains arguments about healing. Her survival system had initially been activated for a good reason, but now it was stuck in the *on* position and out of her control. Her brain and body reacted as if the survival mode were necessary even though the time needed to heal had long ago passed.

The Many Faces of Shutdown

Sadness and shutdown have many purposes. The first is to numb emotional pain, but there are others. They also facilitate healing. If you have ever had the flu or another debilitating illness, you may remember that apart from the sickness itself, you lost interest in your surroundings and just wanted to be left alone. You did not want to answer the phone or deal with anyone. The flu was accompanied by changes in your behavior and outlook. Similarly, research is showing that physical symptoms of illness can accompany shutdown.

Studies involving alpha-interferon to treat some patients with viral illness and cancers have shown a link with depression.[3] Approximately 30 percent of patients who undergo this kind of chemotherapy also develop psychiatric disorders, most notably depression. The explanation may have its origins in how chemotherapy works. Numerous scientists have looked at the psychiatric side effects associated with chemotherapy as possibly linked to interferon. Interferon is a cytokine that affects cell communication and is used to treat infections. Like hormones, cytokines help regulate the immune system. They do this by promoting inflammation.

The links run from interferon to immune system activity to inflammation and finally to depression. Sicknesses induced by excess cytokines have been so closely associated with depression that the link has been called "striking."[4] The conditions produced by cytokines and depression have numerous similar symptoms, such as a withdrawal from daily life, pain, and inflammation.

Furthermore, the inflammatory cytokines may well be fueling depression symptoms. This was shown by Naomi Eisenberger and colleagues at the University of California, Los Angeles, who gave study participants a tiny piece of a bacteria cell wall called endotoxin, which increases pro-inflammation cytokines.[5] Two hours later, the researchers asked the participants, who were in an fMRI scanner, to complete a task involving anticipating financial rewards. The scanner focused on the brain's reward center, the ventral striatum, where activity indicates a person's desire for reward.

Those who received endotoxin had decreased activity in the ventral striatum when they reacted to reward cues. In addition, those who received endotoxin reported feeling more depressed. Those who received a placebo did not.

It makes sense that shutdown helps healing after an injury or infection. At the same time, the apparent connection between depression and physical symptoms associated with healing needs a caveat. Although the pain of inflammation can be associated with sadness and can encourage a period of healing, it can sometimes feed depression. It can be difficult to know which is the chicken and which the egg.

Occasionally, I see patients whose shutdown and physical complaints have a kind of symbiotic relationship. This was the case with Yuki. At the beginning, Yuki's depression appeared to arise from her relationship with her husband. She said that chronic hip pain had restricted her mobility so they were spending less time together. They had been married almost twenty years, and he struck me as a nice, and somewhat passive, man. During our sessions, she did most of the talking, largely complaining about how he treated her. It took a few months for me to understand what she meant. Over that time, he eventually opened up and would liberally criticize her in an understated tone using words like *clueless* and *incompetent*. More than once he joked about whether he should have married her.

She did not push back but internalized his barbs. She began to believe he was right and that she was worthless. Her depression was not full-blown at first but instead fell into the dysthymia category. Less severe than major depression, dysthymia is also chronic and marked by lack of appetite, no energy, disrupted sleep, and low self-esteem. It is also common for someone diagnosed as dysthymic to have a chronic physical illness.

Yuki's husband stopped coming to sessions, but she continued. In many of our sessions, I just listened to her talk about her feelings and activities. She felt surrounded by gloom and misery. Her feelings of bleakness shifted into major depression after she had hip replacement surgery and her hip pain, instead of improving, became markedly worse and she grew housebound. As you will read later, this is not the end of her story.

Genetic Underpinnings

There is plainly a genetic factor to depression, and a number of recent studies explore how genes may interact with people's environment to the point of promoting depression. Given that depression carries a 40 percent likelihood of being inherited, the genetic component is hard to dispute.[6]

Scientists have discovered a short allele in the promoter region of the serotonin transporter gene in the brain of people diagnosed with major depression.[7] Normally this gene works in the brain to help modulate the effects of stressful events on people. The gene with the distinctive mutation has been dubbed the "depression gene" by the popular press because people with the mutation exhibit more signs of depression. Their brain scans show their amygdala reacts more strongly to fearful expressions than it does in people without the allele. Science has much more to learn about this mutation, but clearly genes can have a powerful influence on people who go into shutdown.

Feeling pain from social rejection is more than a matter of being sensitive. On a fundamental level, it can make meeting basic needs extra difficult. People need human connections to survive. I believe that people's need to bond and form communities is one of our survival drives. Its benefits, such as mating, protection, and finding food, make social acceptance good for people's well-being.

A study that probed the effects of social rejection used a game of cyberball, in which a participant tosses around a ball with two other participants and then is excluded from the game.[8] Researchers scanned the participants' brain while they played in order to see which regions were active before and during the social rejection. They discovered that participants who had a certain opioid receptor gene reacted stronger to being rejected than those who did not have the gene. In the rejection-sensitive group, the area of the brain that reacted was the same area that processes physical pain. Social rejection to them was physically painful. When people say they've been hurt by another, that pain is real. (Recognizing this, people who struggle with frequent feelings of rejection need ways to react to and handle it.)

Bleakness in the Brain

Biology provides helpful insights into the world of the depressed person. For one thing, there is an apparent disconnect between the reality of the world and that of the individual. Diane, who became depressed for no apparent reason, is a perfect example. Her bleak view of life and the state of the family business was completely at odds with the facts.

Anyone who's known or lived with someone with depression has probably tried to reason with the individual, pointing out all the good things in their life, all the pleasures to look forward to, all the people who love and value them. Inevitably, even the most persuasive argument falls on deaf ears. Someone in shutdown is essentially incapable of understanding logic or thoughtfully crafted arguments.

Shutdown affects how people process ideas. Much of the blame for this can be pinned on functional and structural abnormalities in the brain. As with so much of what happens in the brain, how sensory information can produce shutdown is enormously complicated. An fMRI scan is an invaluable tool for understanding what happens in the brain of people like Diane. The studies on shutdown appear to point toward three basic conclusions.[9]

First, there are changes in the blood flow to various parts of the cortex in depressed patients. Second, amygdala activity is greater in most patients with depression. Finally, there is little functional connectivity between cortical areas and the amygdala. This suggests that the amygdala acts on its own or in concert with neuropathways that lead directly from the cortex to the PAG, resulting in depression and shutdown.

Studies suggest that the amygdala appears to be more active in someone like Diane with major depressive disorder, especially when she tries to control her sadness.[10] Researchers have found a strong connection between a constantly active amygdala and powerful emotions. An fMRI study of neural circuitry in people with depression showed they had trouble handling feelings of sadness. With an overactive amygdala, someone may be unable to control their emotions and prone to dwelling on negative feelings, a hallmark of depression.

A depressed person may feel emotionally swamped. Researchers asked people with major depression to do emotionally loaded tasks, like matching angry or happy faces, while their brain was scanned.[11] An equal number of people without depression were scanned doing the same task. The difference between the two groups was notable. As expected, the depressed patients showed more activity in the amygdala compared with nondepressed patients when performing a task involving the processing of emotions. The scientists especially noted that depressed patients have decreased connections in one particular area and increased connections in another. The area of the brain with the increased connections, scientists believe, is more involved in people's processing of negative information related to themselves. This impaired connection may explain why a depressed individual is unable to think rationally when coping with strong emotions.

Negative emotions may smother a person's thinking. In the face of strong emotion, someone with major depression is truly crippled. The brain gets hijacked by a super active amygdala, the reasonable cortex is less active, and signals run to the shutdown neurons in the PAG to launch an avalanche of oppressive symptoms.

A Gray World

One of the more universal symptoms of depression is the negative way people see the world. Researchers believe there is a physiological connection between depression and perception of the world.[12] Depressed people do not see sharp, well-defined images but instead faces, scenery, and objects with a gray-on-gray cast. It's like the opposite of rose-tinted glasses—for someone who's depressed, they are dull gray.

This may sound like a metaphor for depression, but a German study has shown that it is literally true.[13] Depression alters people's visual perception and changes the appearance of their surroundings. Depressed people are less sensitive to visual contrast, seeing more darkness and gray, and more dark colors. Researchers in Freiburg presented depressed and nondepressed people with a series of visual patterns ranging from a vivid, high-contrast checkerboard pattern to a checkerboard with little contrast. The researchers monitored the electrical signals of individual retinas as each participant viewed the checkerboards.

The results were dramatic. These two checkerboards show the difference in the brain-wave patterns recorded in the eyes of normal

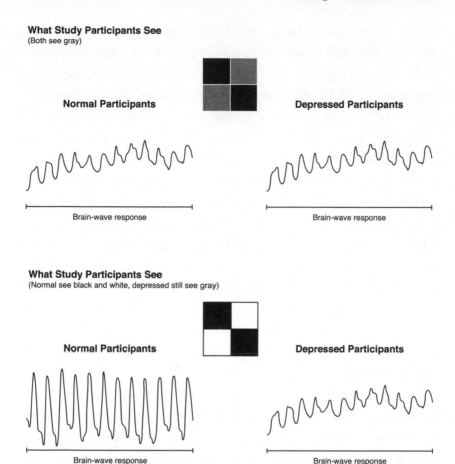

What Study Participants See
(Both see gray)

Normal Participants

Depressed Participants

Brain-wave response

Brain-wave response

What Study Participants See
(Normal see black and white, depressed still see gray)

Normal Participants

Depressed Participants

Brain-wave response

Brain-wave response

participants and depressed participants. The brain-wave response to the first checkerboard reveals that both groups saw the gray boxes. However, the brain-wave patterns in response to the second checkerboard, with the vivid black and white checkers, show that thirty-seven of the forty healthy participants recognized the contrast but that thirty-nine of the forty depressed participants still saw gray. The Germans' study, "Seeing Gray When Feeling Blue? Depression Can Be Measured in the Eye of the Diseased," confirmed that depressed people see the world differently.

Flawed perception also affects how people read facial expressions.[14] Depressed individuals, when viewing happy, sad, or neutral facial expressions, respond more to the sad faces. Looking at sad faces, their brain's emotional processing areas are more active and they pay more attention. When seeing a neutral face, brain activity slows. Researchers suggest that this may explain why depressed individuals have a hard time with personal relationships. They may be reading faces wrong.

Regardless of the cause, a few individuals are so impaired by depression and shutdown that their life is in jeopardy. This happened with Diane. Her shutdown was so consuming that I wondered how she was able to get dressed and drive to my office. Before she got sick, she had been an energetic triathlete who juggled work with training. She linked her downward spiral to a big race she had trained months for and placed second in her age group. Although disappointed, she said that her group had over forty contestants. We agreed that coming in second was no slight accomplishment, yet it was the only noteworthy event around the same time she slipped into bleakness.

She remembered waking up one morning soon afterward and thinking she had no reason to get out of bed and wanting only to sleep. She tried to get back to normal, especially for Dave, but she had neither the will nor the energy. Most days she was on the couch in her sweat clothes. She didn't go out, putter around the house, read, or engage with anyone. She was in a stupor.

The first inkling I had that she might be suicidal was when she declared, "Life is too hard." I asked what she meant, and she rambled on about shin splints and energy fields. When I asked about how she and Dave were getting along, she mentioned how needy and demanding he was and that she was afraid of getting old because she would not be able to do things with him.

Diane's shutdown was plain in her unkempt appearance and listlessness. Yet her voice had an upbeat, almost manic, note.

"I can't go on. It's too hard, but I've solved the problem. It's going to be over soon—I'm going away. I feel good about this decision."

Going where? I wondered.

"To the water, in the car," she said with finality. "It's the best thing, really. Be happy for me, doctor."

I pressed her on her plans, and she said Dave would be better off without her. I had no doubt that she intended to kill herself. By the end of the day, I had admitted her into the hospital. Diane's fractured thought processing was immune to logic or gentle persuasion. Even her marriage bond had become twisted. She could not help herself because the abnormal wiring and chemicals in her brain were driving her destructive behavior.

Scientists believe some people who are suicidal possess a subtle difference in their depression circuitry.[15] While diagrams of brain circuitry look like a New York subway map, they have zeroed in on certain areas. Depressed patients with a history of suicide attempts, compared with those who haven't attempted it, had less gray matter volume and a larger amygdala. Scientists believe that the diminished region of the cortex in suicidal people can have a profound impact on making decisions and could spark more impulsive behavior.

Treatment

Depression causes people to shut down long after any survival benefit and beyond what a body and brain need to recover. Depression pushes the PAG button for shutdown and doesn't let up. The rheostat is locked on high, and the dutiful servant has disappeared. Treating depression requires resetting the rheostat, and to do that, neurosignals have to be recalibrated. One way to relieve this problem is by being honest with yourself. Ask yourself whether you're the kind of person who automatically goes passive when someone criticizes you. You may become quiet, not react, or neither accept nor argue with what you are hearing. If this kind of reaction is a pattern with you, realize it is automatic and, like the rheostat, it needs resetting.

You reset by constantly reminding yourself that your reactions, your rheostat, can malfunction and need regular attention. You do this by instructing your "servant" that the rheostat has to go back to normal. The servant, of course, is your thoughtful, cognizant brain.

If it is difficult to reset the rheostat by yourself, you may need help. Talk therapy can be the solution even though many people do not like talk therapy and offer countless reasons. One of the most common ones is resistance to asking for help. They feel it is a sign of weakness or inadequacy, or they may be embarrassed or think it pigeonholes them as a certain kind of person. I understand, yet I also believe that life is too short to feel miserable. I strongly recommend giving talk therapy a chance. The goal is to feel better, and depressed people need to do whatever they can to reach it.

When I first started as a psychiatrist, I often wondered how talking about something you could not actually change, like a child's disability or the death of a parent, could help alleviate shutdown. A study I mentioned in chapter 2 showed that labeling an emotion on a face activated a person's cortex and slowed amygdala activity.[16] The process of labeling—talking about things that bother you—could shift brain activity to structures where reason, not emotions, are in charge. I have seen firsthand numerous patients for whom talking about troubled events dramatically improved their mood.

Admittedly, talk therapy does not always work, probably because the connections between the cortex and amygdala are not strong enough to calm the amygdala, so the amygdala remains in charge. For such patients, antidepressants are effective. Antidepressants like Prozac (fluoxetine) do this by altering neurochemicals in the cortex, limbic system, and PAG. Fluoxetine reduces signals from the amygdala and increases metabolism in the cortex so that more reasoned behavior is possible.[17]

With patients for whom neither talk therapy nor antidepressants help, I often recommend a trial of electroconvulsive therapy (ECT). Also known as shock therapy, ECT entails placing electrodes on a person's head, giving them a quick-acting sedative and then deliver-

Software for the Immune System: Cytokines

Cytokines are small proteins that affect communication between cells. They have been called "the software that runs the immune system" because they can both stimulate inflammation and/or curb it.[18] When an immune cell encounters a destructive invader, a pathogen, it releases cytokines. The body may produce cytokines not only when there is an infection but also when a person has gone through a physical trauma. Cytokines are released locally or throughout the body. Those produced in the brain can change brain cell function and are associated with loss of appetite, fever, sleep, and dementia.

The first cytokine discovered was interferon. You may have heard of it because it's used in chemotherapy to attack cancer tumors. This cytokine was named for its interference with the production of viruses, bacteria, and tumors by stopping cells from multiplying.

Cytokines affect various biological responses, but their immune system action is the best known. Some types of cytokines create inflammation, and others reduce it. The pro-inflammatory cytokines have been linked with many ailments, including Alzheimer's, cancer, heart disease, and depression. Anti-inflammatory cytokines have been connected with chronic pain.

---

ing bursts of electricity to the brain. I know that ECT has critics, and certainly they have valid concerns. For some patients, memory disturbance can be troubling, especially when receiving ECT. However, almost every form of medical treatment has side effects. Others are leery of ECT because its neurological impact is not fully understood. It is not clear why an electric shock to the brain that causes a brief seizure relieves depression. Yet there are many other effective treatments that medicine does not understand. The best way to explain why the debate surrounding ECT does not stop me from recommending it is to tell the rest of Yuki's story.

Yuki, you might remember, came to me because of depression

and an unhappy relationship with her husband, both of which were aggravated by severe hip pain. Despite hip replacement surgery, her pain grew worse and her depression spiraled into shutdown. She became housebound except for our sessions and her visits to other doctors.

Over the months, it was clear that Yuki's outlook was not improving with talk therapy and medication and that she needed more aggressive treatment. I recommended ECT and explained how it worked. It involved a series of treatments done at a local hospital. For each, she would be sedated and given an electrical stimulus to the head to induce a seizure. She would be unconscious during the procedure and would wake up about five minutes later.

Yuki shook her head through most of my description. She had made up her mind as soon as I mentioned another kind of treatment. Telling her that I had many patients who had gotten much better after a course of ECT did not persuade her. Instead of pushing her, I later contacted her husband to enlist his help. Although he had stopped coming to sessions with Yuki, I knew from the earlier ones that he cared for her. His barbs at her were partly prompted by his feelings of helplessness over his inability to help her feel better. I explained ECT, emphasizing that the odds were very good that it could succeed where other treatments had not. I also told him that I knew ECT was controversial but that I believed strongly that patients should pursue any kind of treatment that helps.

"ECT works," I said. "Among the hundreds of patients I have administered it to, a large proportion of them have improved."

Prodded by her husband, and the friends he enlisted in the cause, Yuki finally agreed to ECT. The first two treatments made a small improvement. After the second, I noticed that Yuki was more engaged in our sessions and seemed to move with more energy. Her lifelessness and feelings of hopelessness appeared to be evaporating. The sixth treatment brought dramatic results. When both she and her husband came to a therapy session, they were holding hands and Yuki was so bubbly, I almost didn't recognize her.

Summing Up

- Depression has a purpose and can be healthy in its purpose to give a person time to heal and recover from a trauma.

- Depression is a feeling of sadness, and shutdown is the behavior that sometimes follows. Both can strike a person for no reason or as a response to a trauma or crisis.

- There is evidence for genetic contributors to depression and shutdown.

- Neurological activity in people who are depressed is markedly different than in healthy people. This distorts their view of reality, makes their world look gray, and causes them to misread people and events around them.

Stone-Cold Predators

Making Headlines

Psychopaths are a popular subject these days. The TV series *Dexter* is a huge hit and in its fifth season. The show's "hero" is a young man who has a day job as a forensic analyst and spends his evenings obsessed with stalking and dismembering people he feels deserve to die. The book *The Psychopath Test*, about a writer's investigation into the world of psychopaths, hit the *New York Times* bestseller list when it came out. And all the popular media outlets in late October 2012, including ABC News, Discovery Channel, and Yahoo!, were carrying stories about a study showing that psychopaths have distinctive ways of speaking.

Anger	○	○	Fight
Fear	○	○	Flight
Depression	○	○	Shutdown
Absence of Emotion	●	●	**Predatory**

From my perspective, this attention is good news–bad news. The unfortunate element is that there appears to be a tendency to glamorize the accounts, with the men's fearlessness made to look like a positive character trait. Some of the stories contain a suggestion that these people are victims of their violent urges and bear little responsibility. To the contrary, psychopaths are truly sick yet have the capacity to make right and moral decisions. The good part about these stories is that they have turned the spotlight on the science of psychopathy. Neuroscience is beginning to understand this illness and is deciphering a whole spectrum of emotions and behaviors that never made much sense until now. Nevertheless, there is still a long way to go.

When I began developing my neurological model, it clearly included predatory, psychopathic behavior. In Allan Siegel's studies mentioned in chapter 4, a cat stalked the rat in its cage. This behavior raised the question, what emotion set off this predatory behavior? My model was not telling the whole story. There appeared to be a blank space, but as I delved into it, the predatory button began to make sense. The area of the PAG tied to predatory actions did not correspond to an identifiable emotion but instead to the absence of emotion. This lack of affect generated a unique kind of aggression. Instead of defensive rage, hitting this PAG button produced another version of aggression: predatory stalking.

Remember the Halloween cat? In experiments stimulating its PAG, the cat could be prompted to react with defensive rage—the typical posture of bared teeth, fur standing up, body and lungs inflated, all to make it look larger—as if it were threatened. But when this same cat was provoked in another way, when a separate area of its PAG was stimulated, the animal did not react with fear or rage but instead as a predator. By stimulating neurons only millimeters from other PAG neurons, unique emotions and behaviors emerged. The cat did not show rage, flight, or shutdown, only determination. And it did not start a fight, run away, or curl into a ball but instead

Hare Psychopathy Checklist (Revised)

Traits are scored 0 (not present), 1 (may be present), or 2 (definitely present). Most normal people score around 5, and anyone with a score of over 30 is considered a psychopath. The traits are organized into three groups.[1]

Personality

- Glibness / superficial charm
- Grandiose sense of self-worth
- Pathological lying
- Cunning / manipulative
- Lack of remorse or guilt
- Shallow affect
- Callousness / lack of empathy
- Failure to accept responsibility for own actions

Lifestyle

- Need for stimulation / prone to boredom
- Parasitic lifestyle
- Poor behavioral control
- Lack of realistic long-term goals
- Impulsivity
- Irresponsibility
- Juvenile delinquency
- Early behavior problems
- Revocation of conditional release

Other Traits

- Sexually promiscuous
- Many short-term marital relationships
- Committing many varieties of crime

slowed its breathing, minimized motion, and quietly watched its target before slowly creeping up on it.

This cat and its unlucky prey came to mind when I met Jacob.

Jacob's Story

Jacob grunted as he sat in the leg press machine at the gym pumping hundreds of pounds. As he strained, he watched a pretty woman in the Pilates studio, hoping she'd notice all the weight he was working. He'd seen her before and knew her every-other-day schedule. They'd even spoken—light banter about boring workouts. She sort of reminded him of his second wife, the one who put a restraining order on him, but was much better looking.

He finished and moved to the quad machine closer to the studio so he could keep an eye on her. But as he searched around for weights to add to the machine, another man slid into the machine's chair. The interloper, a middle-aged man in baggy shorts and a gut-hugging T-shirt, began flexing his legs, his eyes straight forward.

"What the hell?" Jacob snarled, walking around to confront the man. "That's my machine. I was just getting weights."

The man closed his eyes and continued to pump.

"I'm talking to you," Jacob demanded, not raising his voice but trying to sound authoritative.

The man opened his eyes and nodded without looking at Jacob. "Yeah, yeah. But it was empty and I'm here, so chill. I'm almost done."

Jacob's face hardened like cold metal. The man wouldn't even make eye contact, as if Jacob were a nobody. He glanced about, noting if anyone was watching while he gauged his options. The man briefly halted, took a swig from a water bottle beside him, and began another set of repetitions.

"You and your fat ass are going to be sorry," Jacob stated as he walked away. For the rest of his workout, he kept track of the man, following him with his eyes through the gym and toward the locker room. Twenty minutes later, Jacob observed him leaving and walking toward the stairwell that led to the gym's underground garage.

Jacob stopped his routine, grabbed his towel, and sauntered past the front desk toward the stairs. No one was staffing the front desk. *A good thing,* he thought. As soon as he hit the stairwell, he quick-stepped down, hearing only his own breathing and the footfalls in front of him. The stairs were empty, a sign that this was meant to be.

He caught up with his prey on a sub-basement landing and grabbed the man by his arm, wheeling him around. "Think you can get away from me?" Jacob said.

"What the hell are you doing?" The man, now in a suit, yanked his arm away as he recognized Jacob's sweaty face.

Jacob lunged for the man and slammed him against the concrete wall. One hand was on the man's neck in a wrenching grip, and the other was about to collide with his face.

"This is what you get for dissing me. For not respecting me. For not having simple decency," Jacob announced as he pummeled the man, delivering blows to the fleshy gut in between punches to his ears and sagging jaw. Blood flowed from the man's mouth and nose.

At one point, Jacob stopped so he could observe the man's expression.

"Please stop," the man begged, his mouth half open in terror and anticipation of what was to come. His face bloody, he crumbled into a ball.

"You brought this on yourself," Jacob announced as he continued to beat and kick the scum who had defied him.

God, this feels good, he thought. Like the rush he got from a snort of coke. This was worth it, to feel almighty power.

Faulty Fear Processing

I have a limited number of patients like Jacob, men who are predators possessing no social conscience and unable to empathize with or

The Female Predator

Research involving women in prison has found that, like their male counterparts, they are callous, antisocial, and aggressive.[2] Although they score high on tests that measure psychopathy, they differ from male predators. Female psychopaths are not as violent and don't have as high rates of criminal behavior. And they process emotions differently, reacting more to threats, showing more emotion, and better controlling their behavior. A possible explanation is that research comparing brain volume of male and female psychopaths finds that men have larger volume deficits in their frontal gray matter. This may underlie their more violent, cold behavior.

even understand someone else's feelings. In contrast to the domestic abuser or the patient in shutdown, a predator's behavior appears to be triggered by a fault in his fear-processing system.

Their brain does not process fear normally.[3] Laboratory tests have shown that they don't startle like normal people when surprised by a painful shock, a fearful sound, or gruesome pictures. But they can feel threatened, as did Jacob when the other man challenged his supremacy on the weight machine. The threat was especially acute because Jacob was trying to impress the woman in the Pilates studio, so the man's slight became a challenge to his manhood.

Jacob's episode of beating the man can be interpreted as revenge, but his description of the attack indicated that he was more propelled by wanting to feel the satisfaction of dominating and hurting the man than wanting to exact revenge. His behavior had components of raw aggression as well as elements of being driven by reward of the pleasant feeling he got from inflicting pain.

In examining Jacob's behavior, I wondered at the possibility that the same pathway that drives the stalking cat could also drive the human predator. Predatory behavior is offensive and rooted in survival. This primitive drive makes a stalker indifferent to its victim's survival and culminates in the pleasure and satisfaction of a successful hunt. Aggression is rewarded.

What Makes a Psychopath?

Jacob's aggressive predatory actions, coupled with a collection of traits stemming from the lack of empathy, fearlessness, and callousness, make him a psychopath. Psychopathology is a singular psychiatric disorder, even though the psychiatrists' *Diagnostic and Statistical Manual of Mental Disorders* assigns its distinctive traits to "antisocial personality disorder." The term *sociopath* is sometimes used interchangeably with *psychopath,* but they are not the same. What distinguishes a sociopath is anti-social behavior, which isn't necessarily violent. Psychopaths, however, offend when they are younger, are more violent, and are much more likely to commit new crimes when released from prison.[4]

The most distinctive quality of psychopaths is the lack of empathy. They have no regard for the feelings or physical pain of their victims. This lack of empathy is an emotional hollowness. Their often cold, emotionless expressions reveal that they possess no deep emotions whatsoever, although they can be very clever at faking feelings. Two leading researchers into psychopathology, Kent Kiehl and Joshua Buckholtz, describe it best: "They don't feel particularly deeply about anything at all."[5]

This absence of empathy takes many forms. In a broad sense, it is antisocial behavior. Psychopaths have little interest in people around them or in the good of the community. It is difficult, if not impossible, for them to form friendships or strong attachments.

Because of their inherent lack of emotion, they have no visceral feelings about others. This also makes them incapable of understanding other people's perspectives. Because they don't share their basic emotions, they cannot understand how others think or feel.

Callousness is another facet of the lack of empathy. It is more cold-blooded, however. The callous psychopath is immune to the distress or pain of others. A study involving monkeys begins to explain this inability to feel empathy.[6] When one monkey performed a simple function, like moving an arm, the same neurons were active as those in a second monkey that merely watched the first one's arm moving. There was identical neuron activity. This implied that the second monkey could learn by watching and imitating. What made this possible is a network in monkey and human brains called the mirror neuron system.

Although this system first offered an explanation for learning motor functions, science now has evidence that it may apply to some emotional learning. For example, a mother smiles at her baby and the baby smiles back. Similarly, pain activates the network—when people imagine or see others in pain, their mirror neurons react the same way as the injured person. Have you ever winced when you saw someone else in the dentist's chair getting a tooth drilled? That reaction is based on your mirror neurons. The parts of the brain especially involved with emotional mirroring are the insula and anterior cingulate. Here's the kicker: early studies using emotional scenarios suggest that psychopaths do not activate these areas as much as healthy people do. And without active mirror neurons, they don't share others' pain.[7]

Tests with psychopaths in prison (15–35 percent of the prison population are psychopaths) have found that they are often oblivious to emotional cues from others.[8] Emotional signs that crop up in people's facial expression or tone of voice are usually lost on psychopaths. They don't see or hear them. Another blank spot in psychopaths' sensory perceptions is emotional subtleties in language. Again, studies with select inmates have found that they don't react to emotional words. Studies examining the electrical activity of their brain while they are exposed to a string of emotional and neutral words reveal that words like *scar* and *blood* elicit the same brain activity as *house* and *milk*.[9] Psychopaths appear to have other language idiosyncrasies too. They often do not understand metaphors and have difficulty recognizing the underlying meaning in abstract nouns like *love* and *deceit*. Kiehl and Buckholtz offer an example, explaining that a psychopath is likely to judge the metaphor "Love is an antidote for the world's ills" as a negative statement. The researchers conclude about a psychopath's understanding of language: "They know the words but not the music."

A separate study about how psychopaths use language reveals that their word choices and verb tenses create language patterns that provide additional information about their thought processes.[10] Led by Jeff Hancock, a computer science professor at Cornell University, the study, "Hungry Like the Wolf: A Word-Pattern Analysis of the Language of Psychopaths," compared the speech patterns of fourteen psychopaths with the speech of thirty-eight convicted murderers not diagnosed as psychopathic.

The psychopaths and murderers were asked to talk about their crimes. Hancock and his colleagues found that psychopaths use more conjunctions like *because* and *since,* implying that their actions had justifiable, compelling reasons. While the psychopaths used reasons to suggest they had little choice in their actions, their words showed that they were motivated by personal rewards. Compared with the murderers, they used many more words related to food, drink, and money. The murderers, on the other hand, spoke more of social needs, like family and religion, as reasons for their crimes. When it came to verb tenses, the psychopaths much preferred the past tense. Hancock and his colleagues believe that past tense gave the psychopaths a psychological detachment from their crimes.

While fear is a great motivator for other extreme emotional reactions, psychopaths possess a dysfunctional fear-processing network. They do not sense danger like normal people do. They seem truly fearless. Their malfunctioning neural system makes them oblivious to the consequences of their actions. When planning an assault, they are not concerned about harm to themselves or others, or about the legality of their action. For most people, a fearful face has a halting effect. But psychopaths feed on fear. Researchers have found that, starting in childhood, they don't pick up on expressions of fear or disgust.[11] This may explain why their absence of caution in potentially violent or dangerous situations may imply a lack of a conscience. They plunge ahead, except when fear of getting caught checks them.

Personal reward, whether it is the exhilarating sensation of dominance, control, or making people suffer because they have disrespected a psychopath, seems to compel the psychopath to act. Stalking is classic predatory behavior. It is aggressive but quietly so, without any show of emotion or nervous system agitation and with a slow-beating heart. It's very goal oriented and often triggered by the presence of someone who's vulnerable. Stalking itself, involving a game of plotting and planning, may give psychopaths a feeling of exhilaration along with a heightened sense of self-esteem, self-confidence, and even sadistic pleasure.[12]

Research has shown that psychopaths with high degrees of impulsivity, aggression, and substance abuse have more dopamine release in the brain's reward center after being given a stimulating drug than non-psychopaths do. Similarly, when the psychopaths instead expected a financial reward, their brain scans showed higher blood flow again to their reward center. These results strongly suggest that some behavior is rewarding for them.[13]

The Everyday Psychopath

Many ruthless, ambitious people have mild versions of some psychopathic traits. They are not violent, although they may have a temper or psychiatric difficulties. As with the other behaviors in the PAG model, there are degrees of appropriate and inappropriate predatory traits. In people with socially accepted psychopathic traits, the PAG button for lacking emotion and predatory behavior is pushed intermittently and mildly. Perhaps they feel a business situation demands

Who Are the Stalkers?

Forensic psychiatrists in Australia interviewed 145 stalkers, whom they identified through treatment programs.[14] They found that 79 percent were men and over half had never had an intimate relationship. The reasons for their stalking were broken into five categories: rejected, intimacy seeking, incompetent, resentful, and predatory. The mean amount of time they stalked was twelve months (actual time ranged from four weeks to twenty years). Their victims were ex-partners, professional or work contacts, and strangers. The study concluded, "Most stalkers are lonely and socially incompetent, but all have the capacity to frighten and distress their victims."

---

telling grandiose lies and manipulating coworkers. Or maybe people become infatuated with making a sexual conquest and so feign affection and thoughtfulness, along with a constant barrage of glib compliments.

"Not all psychopaths are in prison. Some are in the boardroom"— this is how psychologists Paul Babiak and Robert Hare, experts in the study of psychopaths, sum up the phenomenon of functional psychopaths.[15] They have made an extensive study of such people, and their publications, such as *Snakes in Suits: When Psychopaths Go to Work,* highlight their belief that such people are not uncommon, especially in business.

Hare has studied psychopaths since 1960, when he started working as a psychologist at a prison in British Columbia. He sees psychopaths all around and has developed a twenty-item list for medical professionals and others to use in identifying such individuals (see sidebar, page 149).

To understand how prevalent psychopathic traits are in business, researchers surveyed 203 corporate professionals.[16] Led by Babiak, the researchers sought to discover whether psychopathy could explain the widespread incidence of Ponzi schemes, embezzlements, insider trading, mortgage fraud, and internet schemes. How common, they wondered, is corporate psychopathy? They found a remarkably high correlation between managers who scored high for psychopathy traits and good communication skills, strategic thinking, and creative ability along with low scores for management style and being a team player. Although Babiak could not answer the question of whether the crooks and moral sleazeballs in the news are psychopaths, he did conclude that psychopath qualities do not necessarily limit someone's success in a company.

Other fertile grounds for finding functioning psychopaths include the military, law enforcement, politics, and medicine.[17] Scientists say that people with psychopathic traits who are not in jail or murdering people could be Machiavellian mothers-in-law, bullying bosses, or conniving coworkers.

While researchers who study psychopaths point to their charm as a prop to enhance their deceit and achieve their goal, I see it as predatory behavior with the psychopath angling to gain control, to ensure domination, or to disarm someone. Of course, lots of normal people know how to turn on the charm, and this does not necessarily make them psychopaths. Charm in a normal person is generally ingratiating with an aim of bringing people together. The only real way to know the difference between the two is to let time pass and to evaluate whether a charmer is evil or just trying to get a date.

The Psychopath as a Stalker

A patient recounted to me her experience with a psychopath. The man was a neighbor who had a small bike repair shop in his garage, and he often fixed flat tires or made small adjustments on neighborhood kids' bikes for free. She admits she had a crush on him, largely because he reminded her of James Dean, and she would fabricate reasons to take her bike to him. Gradually, he reciprocated the attention, inviting her on long rides. Twice she went with him but made sure they stayed on public paths. He was much older than she was, so she thought of him as an eccentric uncle.

The friendship continued for months, and during that time, he grew increasingly demanding, showing mock anger when she didn't bring her bike to him for a weekly tune-up and leaving notes on her door about future rides. Rather than distance herself since he lived so close, she often acquiesced to his demands that they go riding together. Many Saturdays, he appeared at her door ready for the day's outing.

Then his demands acquired another dimension: he began suggesting the clothes she wear and offered to buy her tight spandex shorts and cropped biking shirts. On two or three occasions, she went to his house to watch a movie about a biking event like the Tour de France. Each time she briefly felt uneasy, especially when he got physically close, but then he would defuse the situation with a funny story, flattery, or promises to help her get into competitive biking.

One afternoon she went to his house to pick up a biking DVD, and he invited her in and offered her a beer. She just wanted the DVD but was afraid to seem rude, and so she lingered. As he handed her the beer, he wrapped his arm around her shoulders, and at first she thought it was a friendly hug. But he held on to her so long, she became very afraid. She fought to break free, but he didn't let go until she went limp almost in a paralyzed state of shutdown. This woman's attacker was obsessed with her, which goes along with the single-minded focus of a psychopath.[18] When in predator mode, they see little other than their prey. They do not notice and are unable to process any peripheral information surrounding their target. This laser-like attention is devoted exclusively to their prey. As a result, during an attack, psychopaths do not hear or heed the pleas of their victims. They also are blind to anything in their surroundings that might make a normal person move more slowly, proceed more cautiously, or abort an attack. From the outside, psychopaths look fearless because they acknowledge no threat to their single-minded drive. From their perspective, they have eyes and ears only for their prey.

Dealing with a Psychopath

Short of a formal diagnosis by a medical expert, there is no way to know for certain whether you are involved with a psychopath. However, if you suspect someone in your life is one or shows many of the symptoms, psychologist Robert Hare, who developed the Psychopathy Checklist, suggests taking these steps:

• Be wary of what might be fake behavior and exaggerated claims, such as constant over-the-top compliments, glibness that doesn't stand up to reason, eye contact that goes beyond romantic and becomes staring, and insistence on too much control over the relationship.

• Be alert to someone exploiting your weaknesses or insecurities. Hare tells the story of a woman encountering a psychopath who repeatedly told her she had beautiful eyes and complimented her appearance. When she stopped talking to him, she felt totally disarmed.

• Don't wear blinders, and try to be realistic about the other person. Psychopaths are con artists and often prey on people's wishful thinking. Try not to be blinded by the attention or declarations of love.

• Be careful in vulnerable situations, like a singles bar, a blind date, cruises, foreign travel, and internet romances.

• Don't blame yourself if you've been duped or hurt by a psychopath. These people are skilled manipulators and do not play by normal rules, only their twisted rule book.

• Psychopaths may blame you for their misery. Don't buy into it.

• Watch out for power struggles. Psychopaths like to control and dominate, and standing up for yourself may put you in harm's way. Better to get away.[19]

As I explain later in this chapter, there are neurological reasons for psychopaths' relentless drive. There is a malfunction in the mechanisms for control and processing sensory information, rendering psychopaths deaf and blind to stimuli outside their predatory drive.

The Psychopath's Brain

The cluster of neurons in the PAG that indicate the absence of emotion and produce predatory behavior are within millimeters of the other PAG buttons. Predators are distinguished from other patients by an instinct that is ignited by a strong reward drive more than fear or an overt threat. While psychopaths may detect a threat in someone's attitude, tone of voice, or expression, they are launched by an aggressive reflex. Neuroscientists know this from hundreds of brain scans that show an abnormal fear-processing network, and this may be what pushes their PAG button.[20]

Predatory behavior in response to a survival drive is an appropriate, effective reaction in some circumstances.[21] The police officer who is tracking a dangerous criminal needs predatory skills to protect the public and himself. The hunter who pursues animals for food needs to know how to stalk. The soldier looking for insurgents needs predatory skills. In healthy, normal individuals, the signal to their PAG is not damaged but comes or goes as circumstances require. In psychopaths, the signal is flawed because of faulty control mechanisms that process sensory information.

Defects appear to be in the amygdala. As mentioned in earlier chapters, the amygdala is vital to putting together pieces of information that enable you to acquire fear conditioning. For instance, when you were little and you beat up your younger sibling, your parents probably punished you. In this way, you learned that your behavior brought punishment and so you feared it and presumably didn't do it again. Your amygdala enabled you to learn to couple fear and punishment. Psychopaths don't seem to have learned this. A study of twenty-seven psychopaths revealed that their amygdala was on average 18 percent smaller than that of normal people.[22] And those with the smallest amygdalae were the extreme psychopaths.

Other brain structures, such as the anterior cingulate, insula, and prefrontal cortex, are involved in fear conditioning too. Researchers have shown that people with psychopathic symptoms have less gray matter around these areas.[23] This reduction may be one reason for psychopaths' frayed communication system and what's referred to as "impaired executive functioning," meaning thinking unclearly, making bad decisions, or engaging in antisocial behavior. Aggression may be unchecked. The significance of this area is clear from what happens to people who have suffered brain damage in it. A thirty-five-year-old security guard who was attacked by a gang and clubbed repeatedly on the head showed no physical damage, but his personality changed.[24] Weeks after, he became irritable and argumentative, began drinking, and got into fights.

Compounding the problem for psychopaths is poor connection between this cortical region and the amygdala.[25] The practical implications of these abnormal brain structures came to light in a study of fear conditioning in psychopaths and healthy participants. Brain scans were done on each group as they viewed faces with neutral expressions and then received an unpleasant shock. Brain scans on the psychopaths showed different activation, and this showed in their reactions. They did not make the emotional connection of face and pain. The researchers concluded that this could lead to a lack of emotional involvement with the consequences of their behavior.

Abnormalities All Around

Other psychopathic symptoms can be traced to flaws and misfiring elsewhere in the brain.[26] The insula plays a seismic role in people's emotional life. It manages negative emotions like disgust, pain, and hunger as well as moral feelings like guilt and empathy. And part of its machinery is devoted to reward-driven behavior that can produce addictions. It also integrates sensations from the body into positive or negative emotions, making it a functioning mind-body structure. As a participant in the paralimbic-limbic network, the insula suffers along with the amygdala from sluggish activation and flawed processing of emotions. Similarly, the anterior cingulate cortex does not work properly in the psychopath. This part of the cortex operates as a neural alarm system that goes off when something is wrong—for instance, when there is physical pain or the emotional pain of social rejection. So psychopaths do not experience normal pain, or thus react like most people do.

The brain abnormalities of psychopaths became news during a court hearing on the fate of a convicted murderer, Brian Dugan, serving two life sentences.[27] Kent Kiehl, a neuroscientist who has done fMRI scans on more than one thousand psychopaths, mainly from the New Mexico prison system, testified about abnormalities in Dugan's brain. Dugan had already been given life sentences for two horrendous murders and rapes and was being sentenced for a third. Before the hearing, Kiehl put Dugan through ninety minutes in an fMRI scanner and an in-depth psychiatric interview. Kiehl's testimony made headlines, in part because of the immensity of Dugan's crimes. It was also memorable because he linked abnormalities in Dugan's brain—deficiencies in the paralimbic system and decreased activity around the amygdala—to Dugan's near-perfect score on the twenty-item Hare Psychopathy Checklist.

Dugan's lawyer argued that the murderer knew the difference between right and wrong but was unable to make a moral decision. The court disagreed, finding it did not diminish Dugan's culpability. He was sentenced to death. A psychiatry professor for the prosecution made a persuasive argument when he declared, "Brains don't kill people. People kill people."

Tackling Treatment

Many brain experts—neuroscientists as well as psychiatrists—believe that psychopaths are so neurologically abnormal that no treatment can touch the disorder. Predators pose some of the most challenging and problematic cases. Little helps in treating a predator. Medication is unable to target the systems in their brain that malfunction, and talk therapy requires a patient who admits to a sickness and wants to be helped. Part of the psychopathic disorder is an ability to deceive not only others but also themselves. Perhaps the biggest obstacle is that psychopaths do not seek out treatment. They don't think they are sick. Many of them deny they have a problem and point to others or society in general as being at fault.

A study of thirty-five psychopaths conducted in the Netherlands entailed giving subjects a series of moral dilemmas and comparing their judgments about what to do in decisions of right and wrong with the judgments of normal people.[28] Surprisingly, the psychopaths' conclusions matched those of the non-psychopathic individuals. Maaike Cima, the lead investigator, summed up the study findings in its title: "Psychopaths Know Right from Wrong but Don't Care."

Perhaps the road into psychopaths' psyche lies in making them care. Armed with knowledge about how survival-driven they are, treatment professionals could focus on appealing to their self-interest. During treatment sessions, psychopaths have at times expressed an openness to thinking about how their behavior is counterproductive to what they truly want. It puts them in prison and hospitals, robs them of freedom, and imposes unpleasant limits. Helping them draw a connection between their behavior and confinement or unpleasant consequences might make an impact.

This may sound like applying a Band-Aid to treat a compound fracture, yet it is a promising start—promising because it goes to the heart of the disorder, the underlying neurological deficits that feed it.

As science gathers more data about the neurological functions of the psychopathic brain, physicians will be able to develop protocols that control the disorder.

Summing Up

- Psychopaths do not feel fear the same as normal people do.

- Psychopaths are noted for a lack of empathy and callousness toward the suffering and pain of others.

- Psychopaths are motivated more by personal goals, like the exhilaration of dominating someone, than by fear or threats.

- In some situations, like business, the military, and criminal justice, psychopathic traits can be appropriate and useful.

- Brain scans of psychopaths reveal numerous brain abnormalities.

Held Hostage by Trauma

Everyone Is Dodging Bullets

Trauma is a fact of life for everyone. Domestic violence, fatal car accidents, hurricanes, fires, terrorist attacks, wars, violent crime, and painful deaths are all too common. Everyone has been there one time or another. Trauma experts say that three-quarters of the population goes through at least one trauma in a lifetime.[1] After the 9/11 attacks in New York, health care professionals estimated that 58 percent of the city's residents suffered at least one symptom of PTSD, and at least 10,000 police, firefighters, and civilians were diagnosed with PTSD.[2] Most of us have had experiences that hurt us to the core, like

Anger	●	●	Fight
Fear	●	●	Flight
Depression	●	●	Shutdown
Absence of Emotion	●	●	Predatory

losing a job, suffering from a major illness or disease, or being hit by a natural disaster. We are all just dodging bullets. Unfortunately, some of us do not recover from the wounds.

I often use the Slinky example as a visual image to help patients understand the symptoms that grow out of their trauma. The Slinky is a metal coiled spring that bounces, moves across the floor, and even slides down stairs. It is flexible and tough, and you can stretch it to the limit and then watch it spring back into its original shape. Occasionally, though, one of its coils gets bent and when this happens, it stays bent. Trauma patients are like Slinkys because they are twisted or besieged by a trauma, and their lives are never the same. These traumas are not the death of your favorite grandmother or a burned turkey at Thanksgiving dinner. Instead, they are events that typically involve actual or threatened death, serious injury, or threatened well-being. The trauma is a threat to personal security or survival. And that's not all—the event also triggers profound, intense feelings of fear, helplessness, and even horror.

PTSD is a collision of forces arising from a trauma that results in specific symptoms. The forces that make someone vulnerable to such a trauma include early-life stressors such as domestic violence, child abuse, parents' messy divorce, and sexual assault.

People's neurological makeup can interact with the environment to alter their wiring. Their nervous system may be changed. Distortions in neurotransmitter activity plus the inability of neuropathways to turn off the threat reaction can make everyday experiences traumatic. It's as if the nervous system changes from a peaceful day at the beach to a turbulent thunderstorm, which may last for a short period or for a lifetime.

A trauma pushes every button of the PAG rheostat, as the diagram above shows. With PTSD, the pathways and wiring to the PAG repeatedly malfunction, so at least three buttons—anger-fight, fear-flight, depression-shutdown, and perhaps flat emotion–predatory—are activated at one time or another.

There is no set period of time that is considered normal for someone to rebound from a traumatic experience. Some patients bounce back within weeks, and others take many months. By and large, most people possess enough resilience to spring back to their original emotional state within months of the trauma. Researchers continue to explore why this is so but have yet to fully answer the question of why some people can go through a horrible trauma and not develop chronic PTSD while others do. They strongly suspect it is exposure to a trauma plus a combination of predisposing genetics and environmental influences.[3]

I had been a psychiatrist for years before I began to comprehend the far-reaching and profound effect that certain traumas have on people's lives. Patients who frequently seek treatment for panic attacks or depression often reveal a major trauma buried in their past. They grew up in a violent or abusive home, were sexually abused, or went through a life-threatening experience. It's only with probing questions that their earlier traumas come to the surface. For most people, these memories are very painful, and it can be especially painful to confront the trauma again. The question for me becomes, are the present symptoms just the tip of the iceberg? As the stories here reveal, PTSD symptoms fall into three clusters of behavior that can come alive in a traumatized individual.

Domestic Violence: Damage for Generations

So far I have talked about domestic violence from the perspective of the perpetrator. I now want to focus on the victims. There is often more than one victim in domestic violence. Children who witness domestic violence can be traumatized. It's like a tsunami that destroys not only the lives in its path but also entire families. And it is not unusual for children who grew up in a household with domestic violence to later become direct victims themselves.

I believe that domestic violence is one of the biggest causes of PTSD in society. It pervades lives and homes. The figures on domestic violence are staggering: One in every four women will experience domestic violence sometime in her life, and an estimated 1.3 million women are victims every year.[4] Men are also victims of domestic violence but have much fewer injuries because women are usually smaller and not as strong.[5]

Karen painted a common picture. The violence with her husband, Roy, began gradually with shoves, slaps, and painful arm twisting. Occasionally the violence happened because of a particular situation, like an argument over Karen's spending or Roy's anger over something their seven-year-old child, Whitney, did. More often it was a kind of intimate terrorism. Spurred on by anger and feelings of powerlessness in his job, resentment over Karen's modest success as a pottery maker, and annoyance with Whitney, Roy belittled and berated Karen constantly. He called her useless and a pathetic mother, then punctuated his anger with physical attacks. This gradually escalated into physical attempts to control Karen and assert himself. It became a pattern, and Karen became a battered wife.

Judging from her account, I gathered that Karen showed signs of PTSD after enduring months of Roy's violence. Most obvious were her nervousness and wariness. She was always alert for signs that Roy was in a bad mood. The cracking sound of his metal heel savers on the kitchen floor signaled that he was angry. When Karen heard them, she would go into the bathroom and lock the door. When she and Roy arrived for treatment sessions, she kept an eye on him and would not precede him through the door but trailed behind, always watchful. A couple of times, she flinched when Roy tried to give her a gentle pat. She didn't sleep well, either, and was startled awake by the slightest noise or movement in the bed. She believed that she would not live long enough to see her daughter grow up.

Karen was not the only victim. Whitney was harmed too. Her behavior at school changed dramatically, Karen said. Her cheerfulness was replaced by sullenness. She cried frequently, especially when anyone raised their voice. Her reaction to her parents' fighting was understandable. She had probably spent many nights lying awake in bed, listening to them yell and scream at each other, along with the sounds of her mother experiencing pain. Karen recounted that after a particularly vicious argument with Roy, she found Whitney huddled in the cabinet beneath the bathroom sink. Despite Whitney's pleas for them to stop, the violence continued, only heightening her fears. For a child, such an experience may produce profound damage not only psychologically but also neurologically.

Children growing up where they do not feel safe and where parents can instantly become a source of fear instead of comfort may be forever scarred. Whether physical or verbal, the violence makes children fearful about the future. Is Mommy or Daddy leaving? What's going to happen to me?

Parents may be so buried in their own painful interactions that they don't realize that they are permanently scarring their children just by exposing them to their domestic violence. The abuse can be as damaging as if the children were physically hurt. A couple's violence puts their child at a significantly higher risk for alcoholism, depression, becoming an adult abuse victim, and developing PTSD in adulthood.[6]

The abuse may produce genetic changes. A team of neuroscientists led by Avshalom Caspi examined a number of studies into the link between childhood abuse and trauma and the later development of depression and other mental disorders.[7] This was a groundbreaking study because it showed that people's past can interact with their genetics and result in changing their behavior as adults. They found that for some people, there is an interaction between the presence of a short allele of the serotonin transporter gene and childhood abuse, which increases the risk for depression as an adult.

Childhood abuse can also produce structural changes in the brain.[8] In a study of thirty-one women diagnosed with PTSD and histories of childhood sexual abuse, scientists in the Netherlands looked at gray matter volume in parts of the brain associated with trauma. Compared with a group of non-traumatized women, the PTSD subjects' brain was strikingly different. The gray matter concentrations

Are You Suffering from Trauma?

You can develop PTSD at any age, after a personal trauma or after a friend or family member has gone through a trauma. These are its symptoms, according to the psychiatric manual:

- Exposure to a traumatic event, either by experiencing, witnessing, or confronting, that involved actual or threatened death or serious injury, and a response involving fear, helplessness, or horror

- Distressing recollections of the trauma in any of the following ways: intrusive thoughts or images, dreams, hallucinations, flashbacks, exposure to things that remind the patient of the trauma or a physical reaction to reminders of the trauma

- Generally feeling numb and avoiding associations with the trauma, including activities, places, or people

- An inability to remember important aspects of the trauma

- Feeling detached or estranged from others

- Numbed emotions or a small range of emotions, an inability to love

- A feeling of a foreshortened future, like not expecting to have a career, get married, or having a normal lifespan

- Persistent feelings of increased arousal, for example, difficulty sleeping, irritability, difficulty concentrating, hypervigilance, or an exaggerated startle response[9]

---

had atrophied, especially in the hippocampus as well as the anterior cingulate cortex and amygdala. And the number of the differences corresponded to the severity of the childhood abuse. A smaller hippocampus has been linked to certain people's impulsive behavior. And less gray matter in the anterior cingulate cortex has been connected with the PTSD symptom of hyperarousal, like being easily startled by a slight sound.

A study traced a history of psychiatric illness and perhaps suicide to a history of childhood abuse and genes in the hippocampus that affect cortisol metabolism.[10] The abuse, such as severe physical abuse or neglect, appeared to alter the children's cortisol receptor genes involving the regulation of the stress response. This suggests that the childhood abuse brought about changes in gene expression. Another landmark study of the inheritability of trauma symptoms involved the offspring of Holocaust survivors and also looked at cortisol.[11] The offspring were divided into two groups, children of a mother who survived the Holocaust and healthy volunteers whose mothers were not caught in the Holocaust. Low levels of cortisol are considered a biomarker for PTSD, so researchers focused on that in the mothers and the offspring. Led by Rachel Yehuda at Mount Sinai School of Medicine, researchers discovered that the children of a Holocaust mother had markedly lower levels of cortisol than the non-Holocaust children. They had a higher incidence of developing PTSD sometime during their lifetime. It is unclear whether low cortisol levels are the result of a trauma or contribute to a trauma disorder. Nevertheless, the unusually low cortisol in traumatized mothers and children suggests a genetic effect.

Layers of Trauma: Rape and Sexual Abuse

It's hard to overestimate the profoundly devastating impact of rape and childhood abuse on people. RJ described what happened to her after being raped by her stepfather. Her mother had just gotten remarried, although she and RJ had lived with the man for a couple of years before the ceremony. Only after the official marriage did the man begin raping her. It usually happened when RJ and her stepfather were in the car alone. After picking her up from a sporting event or before driving her to the mall, he would drive to a deserted area and make her perform oral sex while he penetrated her with his fingers.

The first time RJ saw Eric's penis, she began to hyperventilate while her heart pounded, she shook, and she felt dizzy and nauseous. "I felt out of control, like I couldn't control my body, like it wasn't mine," she said. "I couldn't push away. I couldn't talk."

During an attack, RJ would go into a kind of robotic coma, and it took hours for her to lose the spacey sensation and feel somewhat normal again. As the attacks continued, RJ began to compulsively pull out strands of her hair and acquired bulimia.

The first few times, she tried to reason with Eric and talked about how much her mother loved him. When that didn't work, she tried curtailing her activities, avoiding anything that Eric might drive her to, but her mother insisted—and since her mother did not drive, RJ felt trapped. Adding to her feelings of despair was a suspicion that her mother knew what was happening and was not going to stop it. The attacks finally stopped when RJ reached age sixteen and was no longer dependent on Eric's driving. She got a driver's license, started dating boys with cars, and acquired a reputation for being promiscuous. Within two years, she had become infected with several STDs and had had an abortion.

It's important to stress that childhood sexual abuse, including incest, is not as uncommon as readers might think. According to a Dr. Richard Kluft writing in *Psychiatric Times*, incest between a daughter and a birth father occurs in one in twenty instances, and between daughter and stepfather, one in seven.[12] Rape, sexual abuse, and incest are like a plague on society, yet there is a great silence surrounding them. The case involving a coach at one of America's premier universities, Penn State, highlighted the iniquitousness of childhood sexual abuse. As commonly happens after one victim goes public about being attacked, numerous other victims have come forward. In a newspaper commentary about the case and his own abuse experience, one victim wrote, "The worst thing we can do is pretend that the negligent behavior at Penn State is the exception and not the norm. The reality is that people everywhere are hiding the same kind of secrets." This silence deepens a victim's trauma.[13]

The extent of the damage of sexual abuse on children depends on the assault itself. How long the abuse went on, how frequent it was, the amount of force or violence involved, whether there was penetration or not, the relationship of the perpetrator to the children, and the amount of support for the abused children all come into play. In helping children heal from such trauma, it's vital to give children a sense that they are not bad and to help them shift their feeling of being wrong from themselves to the abuser. It's also essential that the abuse stop.

While there is much overlap in research findings about childhood abuse and childhood sexual abuse, sexual crimes seem to be especially traumatic because they create in a victim a disturbing collision of survival instincts. Victims often feel so physically vulnerable that during an attack, they go into shutdown and tacitly acquiesce. They protect themselves from possibly fatal attacks by not resisting or provoking their attacker. At the same time, the assault may stir sexual feelings driven by the reproductive and reward system. Stimulating the genitals activates the brain's insula, which sets off not only feelings of disgust but also the body's reproductive drive.[14] This kind of touching can have such a neurological impact that it alters the brain. This happens with men and women.

As a result of these conflicting, disturbing sensations, abuse, incest, and rape victims often feel disgusted with themselves, even years after an attack. Self-loathing and disgust were predominant emotions for RJ. "Why didn't I fight? Why didn't I scream?" were common refrains. Although her body went into shutdown during the attacks, she was left feeling dirty and worthless. She also felt guilty, as if she had caused the attacks. The fact that her mother seemed complicit in the assaults reinforced RJ's feeling that she deserved the abuse. There was no one in RJ's life to tell her otherwise, so her feelings of disgust and worthlessness became permanent beliefs.

Disgust is considered a core emotion, meaning it promotes survival. It's biologically vital to feel disgust because it engages the senses and prompts the body to reject poison, contamination, filth, or unhealthy substances. The moral disgust people feel about incest activates brain pathways that overlap those connected with physical disgust. With child abuse, I believe that a feeling of disgust signals that the behavior is wrong. Pregnancy from incest can result in the expression of recessive genes that can impair the survival of future generations. Moral disgust is wired into people and can color their personality by undermining self-image, self-esteem, relationships, and everyday functioning.[15] Turned inward, this survival emotion can become destructive.

Internalized disgust is probably behind the reasons women who have been abused or raped as children often become promiscuous. People who are disgusted with themselves cannot believe that anyone would want them, so sex becomes a way for rape or abuse victims to get others to act as if they care. Alternately, disgust may make victims seek out self-defeating relationships because that's what they feel they deserve.

Promiscuity may also be driven by the victims' need to gain control of their body. Right before an attack and afterward, sometimes for years, their nervous system reacts to the overwhelming fear that the attack activated. In many respects, PTSD is a fear disorder. The psychological and physical symptoms of the trauma are the result of the brain's fear-processing network being out of control. At the center of this uncontrollable fear is a hyperactive amygdala. It is broadcasting alarm signals to trigger survival behavior. Victims have little control over this fear processing. But being promiscuous—deciding with whom and when to have sex—is behavior they can control.

The harm done by complicit family members is that not only are victims not protected, but also their primary source of support is not there. Victims need to be reassured that they did not cause an attack or allow it to happen. Without care and comfort from the people closest to victims, self-loathing and disgust are much more likely. Damage to children can be diminished if parents, once they learn of the assault and assuming they are not involved, take action to protect the children. Making children feel safe again could make the difference between a healthy adulthood and a lifetime of psychiatry appointments.

The damage from a sexual attack can be as long lasting for adults as it is for children. Women abused when they were children are more likely to develop psychiatric disorders including PTSD and major depression, abuse alcohol or drugs, engage in prostitution, attempt suicide, and be the victim of rape or sexual assault.[16] A study of male Vietnam veterans found that those who had been victims of childhood abuse had much higher rates of PTSD than vets who had not been abused. The difference was 26 percent versus 7 percent.[17]

Adding to victims' pain is that often the memory of a sexual assault stays with them for years with the memories truly burned into their mind. Assault victims remember a sexual attack different from other traumas. A group of women who were victims of sexual violence were asked to recall the trauma as well as a pleasant experience.[18] Their answers revealed that their memory of the sexual attack was more vivid and more detailed than their memory of an experience they enjoyed. The researcher who conducted the interviews concluded that contrary to popular belief, victims over time do not forget what happened to them. Sexual trauma is "remembered all too well," she concluded.

Fear, Helplessness, and Horror

After domestic abuse, rape, and sexual abuse, one of the more common traumas in modern life comes from car accidents. This happens especially when young people who are inexperienced drivers drink or use cell phones. One such patient, Carole, had been in a horrible car accident as a teenager. She was eighteen at the time and, along with four friends, driving home in the early morning from a New Year's Eve party. Everyone had been drinking, including Carole. The party had been in the suburbs, so to get home, she had to negotiate long, winding roads that were unfamiliar to her. As her car

What Makes a Person Resilient?

Researchers believe that a person's ability to control emotional responses may form a kind of protection against developing PTSD.[19] A study examined women who had been sexually assaulted, with half of them having developed PTSD and half not. Researchers used fMRI to look at the women's neural activity while the subjects viewed negative pictures.

While viewing the pictures, the women were asked to elicit different emotional reactions. They were to diminish, enhance, or maintain their emotions during the viewing, and they were instructed how to do this. To diminish their feelings, researchers told them to imagine a less negative outcome for the scenes in the pictures. To enhance, they had to imagine a worse result. The third instruction was to maintain their emotional response.

The researchers discovered that the women who had not developed PTSD were better at diminishing their emotional responses. The resilient, non-PTSD women also showed more activity in their prefrontal cortex, meaning they engaged more thought and fewer instinctive survival reflexes.

---

rounded a bend, it began to skid, either because of speed or black ice. Either way, it flew off the road and slammed into a tree.

Because Carole was wearing a seat belt, she was flung toward the windshield but not thrown out. Her two friends in the passenger seats did not have seat belts on and were ejected from the car. Carole was briefly unconscious and then woke to the sounds of screams from the back seat. To this day, she doesn't remember if there were three or four people in the car, and she tries not to talk or think about it. Her friends' cries were so terrifying that she avoided looking at them. She wrestled herself free from the seat belt, climbed through the broken windshield, and staggered about. She did not see the two bodies that had been thrown from the car and were in a heap in the darkness. For a few moments, she stumbled about and then started walking toward the road. A passing motorist picked her up fifteen minutes later.

That was more than ten years ago, but when Carole came to me, it was as vivid as if it were yesterday. She had become a recluse, rarely leaving the home she still shared with her parents. She avoided any reminders, like driving or riding in a car at night. Her mother drove her to her appointments with me. We talked about her depression, her problems sleeping, and her fear of the outside world. She said she hated going out because everyone stared at her and the noises of the street easily startled her. At home, she got into shouting matches with her parents and generally stayed in her room behind pulled curtains watching television. She did little else and had become obese, creating an assortment of health complications.

Carole was haunted by the screams of her friends, and I watched her closely for signs of suicide thinking. Her trauma was rooted deep in her memories of helplessness, horror, and fear. The feeling of helplessness was acute and stemmed from both the accident itself and her life after it. Her failure to help her dying friends created a memory that she will probably never forget. She believed she did not help them because she had no medical training or knowledge of what to do. Regardless of why she did this, running away sealed the memory of her inability to rescue them along with lasting feelings of guilt. Her feelings of helplessness continued as her life spiraled out of control afterward. She could not control her emotions or reclaim any sense of normalcy. During the trauma, she could not save her friends, and afterward she could not save herself.

Carole's case, like those of most patients who develop PTSD, raises the question of why she developed the trauma disorder. Not all people who are in fatal car accidents develop the disorder, so why did she? A number of factors probably made her vulnerable.[20] Alcohol surely contributed to the accident, making her more likely to be in a traumatic situation. Poor coping strategies put her at risk too. These were plain from her troubled school years, which consisted of numerous visits with school authorities and truancy officers. After the accident she did not have much support. She did not get along with her parents, and after she left school, they grew weary of fighting with her and left her alone. While this worked for her because they made no demands, it also meant that they weren't there to offer care and support when she got into trouble. Afterward, her depression helped solidify the trauma disorder. Carole's symptoms were typical for PTSD: re-experiencing the trauma, avoiding any reminders of it, and hyperarousal. These persisted beyond the one-month marker of the trauma, indicating that her temporary PTSD had become chronic.

The Hallmarks of PTSD

One cluster of Carole's symptoms revolved around re-experiencing the event. Intrusive thoughts about the accident and her role in it flooded her thinking almost daily and often stirred up nightmares. The natural survival value of reliving a traumatic experience is understandable in temporary situations. A tornado survivor must remember not to be in the wrong place again, and the assault victim must remember how it happened, at least in the short term, in order to recognize other dangerous situations. On some level, the body and mind believe that if they forget, the person could die. Being seized by the memory of a trauma for years afterward, though, pushes victims into pathology.

A second cluster involves hyperarousal symptoms. Carole's sleep difficulties also made sense as a temporary survival mechanism. You are most vulnerable when you are asleep, so the body struggles to stay awake and vigilant. Another facet of hyperarousal is irritability and anger that can boil over into rage. These, too, are protective in the aftermath of a trauma but destructive as long-term personality characteristics. Constantly scanning your environment, looking for danger or threats, is also part of this cluster. Although Carole did not go out often, she said that whenever she went to a restaurant, she sat with her back to the wall and obsessively watched the door.

When people are always on edge, looking for where the next assault is coming from, concentration is difficult. Their attention is pulled in multiple directions, too stimulated to settle down to a single focus. Everything sets them off, like the combat vet who trembles at the sound of a traffic helicopter because it instantly reminds him of attacking choppers.

A third cluster of symptoms has to do with avoidance. People with PTSD go out of their way to avoid reminders of the trauma. Not only do they avoid places and activities that might remind them of the trauma but also anyone connected with the event. Researchers at a veterans facility in Georgia describe a combat veteran who quit his job after he came home because the smell of the workplace reminded him of the combat zone.[21] Carole's isolation as well as her choice not to drive ensured that she could, more or less, keep a lid on her disturbing memories. Her avoidance added unhealthy complications, namely obesity. Among men with PTSD, alcohol and drug problems are common accompaniments to their inability to cope. Addictions help them sleep and go numb, becoming an essential, albeit a counterproductive, coping tool. Ultimately, their symptoms will get worse.

Beyond the normal three clusters of PTSD symptoms, I have found that sufferers experience a sense of a foreshortened future. Traumatized individuals get a feeling that they will die young or not live a full life. It is as if the trauma has stamped a canceled sign on their future. As a result, they have low expectations for their present life and make plans only day by day, nothing farther out. This feeling of not having a future can show up in various types of behavior. Abused teens may drop out of school, avoid friends, and stay in their bedroom. Drug and alcohol abuse can arise from this feeling, too, because it can make them feel numb and indifferent to tomorrow. Again, this is a version of survival thinking—for them, life demands only immediate reactions, and thinking ahead distracts them from the job of surviving. There is a lid on feelings of joy and happiness, and the ability to love or trust is diminished. Such feelings can jeopardize survival in a threatening environment. They shift the mind away from survival to thoughts of nesting and mating, giving power to other people.

Pushing All the PAG Buttons

The emotions of PTSD are part of your survival system. Each reaction, whether fear, anger, or depression, helps people survive traumas that threaten their life. Regardless of whether the threat is physical or psychological, it still demands a survival reaction. A life-threatening trauma mobilizes brain structures—like the hippocampus, prefrontal cortex, and amygdala—that affect the PAG. When this happens, each of the four PAG buttons may be activated. Imagine a broken pinball machine with the ball bouncing off the bumpers and sides, back and forth, bells ringing, lights flashing, always in motion. That's what happens in the PAG with PTSD. The bouncing ball never stops; alarms are always going off.

The source of this uncontrollable survival reflex is a faulty connection between the cortex and the amygdala. A major trauma stimulates the amygdala to launch survival reactions. In a normal situation, after a threat passes, the amygdala slows and the cortex quiets the fear. This does not happen with PTSD patients. The survival reflex does not slow.

A distinctive feature of trauma is its effect on the immune system. Trauma sets in motion fight-or-flight reactions, and the body straps on its armor and prepares to defend itself. This armor includes the immune system. Immune reactions release clotting factors and inflammation-causing cytokines (inflammation heals wounds by delivering repair chemicals and removing toxins). But with PTSD, the system soon malfunctions and doesn't shut off. Scientists believe that the unchecked immune reaction may explain why PTSD patients have a high incidence of inflammatory and autoimmune disorders like psoriasis, eczema, atopic dermatitis, and other skin problems.[22]

The hippocampus suffers in trauma.[23] Numerous brain scans have shown that PTSD patients have less gray matter in their hippocampus, a key structure for storing and retrieving memories. While noting that chronic PTSD patients often have small hippocampi, researchers are not certain whether this smaller brain region is the result of trauma or a preexisting condition that contributed to it. Some scientists say that this is the most profound consequence of trauma, a smaller hippocampus altering memory retrieval and learning.

Patients with PTSD typically have a distorted memory-processing system.[24] Their memory for negative information or details of a trauma is much sharper than for neutral, non-traumatic events. This bias toward disturbing information applies to experiences and personal memories of moods and feelings. Vietnam combat vets with PTSD have been studied extensively, and research has consistently demonstrated that their memory for words related to combat is stronger than that for neutral words, and their memory of the emotions they feel while looking at combat photographs leans strongly toward unpleasant feelings. More noteworthy is that they show difficulty remembering or focusing on positive experiences or feelings.[25] This memory bias toward disturbing, upsetting events and feelings may well fuel people's trauma disorder.

Living with a Trauma Experience

PTSD can cut a wide swath of damage. Spouses and partners say that it can be enormously painful living with someone with PTSD and that the relationship is often riddled with frustration, bewilderment, and feelings of helplessness. In couples, one person may not be aware that his or her partner was abused as a child, raped as a teen, or the victim of some other type of trauma until they are well into the relationship. It takes time and closeness to know someone's history, especially if it was traumatic. There may be signs that someone has been traumatized—an emotional distancing, an avoidance of closeness or intimacy, a lack of trust. Of course this can create problems in relationships, especially if one person doesn't know about the other's earlier trauma.

The difficulties are not resolved even after a couple has talked about the trauma. Although most spouses, as well as friends and family, want to be supportive and sympathetic toward people who have suffered trauma, there is often the unspoken thought, *It happened. Get over it. Let's move on.*

The underlying calamity is that people with PTSD may find it very difficult to "get over it," no matter how badly they want to. In many PTSD victims, the trauma they suffered may have altered their brain. They may be neurologically changed, and this in part could be driving their behavior. They may well have no control over their symptoms, making it difficult to manage their reactions to other people.

If you think about a life-threatening trauma, be it child abuse, rape, domestic violence, or a war experience, the behavior that comes with PTSD has survival value. PTSD symptoms, such as hypervigilance, hyperarousal, and insomnia are good things because they can keep you safe when you are vulnerable to some kind of assault. Just like the other PAG emotions and behaviors, there are times when PTSD behaviors are appropriate and useful as well as times when they are inappropriate and destructive.

The problem with PTSD is that once the trauma situation is over, the symptoms can remain. To understand why some people develop PTSD, researchers have been exploring the effects of environment and genes and how they might interact to cause lasting changes in behavior. It's the age-old nature-versus-nurture debate, with an aim to discover whether these two forces function together in some people. Already, studies have shown that people with certain genes who have also been abused as children are more likely to develop PTSD as adults.[26]

It makes sense that our brain and body would change and adapt when survival is threatened. The logic is elegantly simple: PTSD emerges when people have encountered a life-threatening event (even internalized disgust can be life threatening if people regularly expose themselves to dangerous situations). We, meaning our internal biological survival mechanisms, would rather overreact and survive than underreact and die. Repeated overreaction causes dramatic changes to the nervous system that last for a long time and can potentially be passed to the next generation.[27]

It's part of our survival mission to want to equip our young with the behaviors needed to protect themselves in a hostile environment. Here's where we encounter the intersection of nature and nurture. In order to survive in the face of overwhelming danger, a body alters its nervous system by a process called epigenetics. In epigenetics, genes themselves (which are the basic parts of DNA) are not changed but instead their function is changed. Researchers have focused on genes involved with the stress response that helps regulate cortisol metabolism.[28]

A group of pregnant women who were exposed to the 9/11 attacks at the World Trade Center and developed PTSD had babies with lower cortisol levels than babies born to mothers who did not develop PTSD.[29] One interpretation of this finding is that lower cortisol predisposes children to developing PTSD in the future if they are exposed to trauma.[30] It is possible that when cortisol levels are down, adrenaline levels go up, and adrenaline solidifies traumatic memories.

Even though scientists are beginning to understand how a trauma like childhood abuse can alter brain processes, they do not know how to influence this activity. It's reasonable to think that genetic alterations that change the brain can also change it back. At present, there is no cure for the neurological impairments that may come with PTSD. This leaves us with a modest arsenal of treatments.

Extinguishing a Traumatic Memory

An alert, active fear system is essential for survival, as you know. For PTSD patients, this mechanism is broken. The brain and body are in constant survival mode long after the danger has passed.

A symptom of this dysfunctional system is the repeated intrusion of memories of a trauma. They are so strong that people feel like they are reliving the event. The details and sensations can be so vivid that they can cripple people. This is what happens when a rape victim cannot walk across an empty park because such a place was where her attack happened years earlier.

A goal of treatment is to extinguish these traumatic memories by dampening the conditioned fear responses that often develop in reaction to sights, sounds, or situations associated with the trauma. It's an automatic response that no longer has a connection to danger. Treatment aims to uncouple the link between stimuli associated with a trauma and the brain's fear response. This is done mainly through prolonged exposure therapy.

As its name suggests, the therapy repeatedly confronts patients with memories and descriptions of their trauma. It works similarly to the way physical exposure conditioning works, like getting accustomed to very cold water by sitting in a bathtub of ice water (competitive open-water swimmers really do this). For trauma victims, it entails recalling the experience in detail, dredging up memories and associations connected with it, and when possible, revisiting the place or circumstances in which the original trauma occurred. Computers able to create a virtual reality and closely duplicate the trauma are a powerful tool in exposure therapy. They are especially helpful with veterans and disaster victims traumatized by events long past.

A *New York Times* story about people coping with PTSD years after 9/11 profiled Margaret Dessau.[31] From her apartment window, Dessau witnessed the burning and plummeting bodies from the twin towers and later developed PTSD. To this day, she regularly listens to a tape she has made recounting what she saw. She says listening to the tape is like taking cod liver oil. While she still avoids looking at the skyline where the towers once were, the exposure therapy has helped quiet her fears.

Another facet of overcoming the automatic fear reaction is learning a different way of reacting when trauma stimuli and memories flood your mind. Slowing the response of an overactive amygdala requires imposing new thoughts and new ways of behaving.

Extinction and exposure therapy are not foolproof remedies, and many experts believe it is impossible to truly extinguish a traumatic memory. At best, therapy helps generate new memories that write over the trauma memory but does not erase it. People with trauma disorders have found themselves in the throes of reliving a distant experience because a new encounter has brought it all to the surface. A panic attack, a random act of aggression, or a personal tragedy and thoughts of suicide can rekindle the memories. Margaret Dessau was again plunged into fear and anxiousness when her husband died years after the twin tower attacks. The *New York Times* noted about her husband's death, "His quick death revived the sense of helplessness she had felt watching people jump from the towers."

Drugs can be an effective treatment for trauma sufferers. I have seen the best results with Prazosin, an alpha-blocker that relaxes blood vessels so that blood flows more easily through the body. Normally prescribed for high blood pressure and migraines, it eases a number of PTSD symptoms, especially sleep disturbances, nightmares, and anxiety.

Other classes of drugs also reduce trauma symptoms, each with degrees of efficacy depending on the individual. One truism for all people and drugs is that nothing will work if a patient drinks during the treatment. You cannot get well when you are drinking. Alcohol actually changes a brain. A study in *Nature Neuroscience* showed that alcohol alters the structure of the neurons in the prefrontal cortex important for extinguishing fear.[32] As a result, the cortex could not tamp fear down. It was as if the subjects' fear-reduction machinery had been disabled.

It is nearly impossible for people to recover from PTSD if they keep drinking. It's like throwing gasoline on a fire. As you will find in the next chapter, alcohol inflames not only PTSD but also all sorts of extreme emotions.

Summing Up

- Domestic violence, rape, and fatal car accidents are among the most common traumas.

- PTSD is the result of a range of survival behaviors stimulated in the PAG that persist after danger has passed.

- Symptoms can be grouped into three clusters of related reactions: re-experiencing the trauma, avoidance behavior, and hyperarousal.

- Treatment for PTSD focuses on extinguishing traumatic memories by dampening the conditioned fear response to certain things and by exposure therapy that repeatedly recalls the event.

10

Another Route
to Survival
or Sickness:
The Reward
Pathway

The Iron Fist of Addiction

You may have noticed in my patient stories that alcohol frequently played a part in their troubles and was a huge contributor to their irrational emotions and out-of-control behavior. A man may have been in danger of losing his job because his boss has smelled alcohol on his breath, in danger of breaking up his marriage because his wife is tired of failed rehab attempts, or in danger of going to jail because of repeated DWI charges. Yet he continued to drink. Alcohol sets things in motion by acting as a neurological accelerant for patients' inappropriate emotions. Of course, countless people drink, even heavily, but do not lose control or become alcoholics. Some people, however, appear to have a neurological flaw that makes them vulnerable to the troubles that alcohol can cause.

I have often told alcoholic patients that they have a problem and need to stop drinking. Thinking back on these conversations, I wonder what the patient must have thought. For those in denial, it might have been a wake-up call, but for many more, my telling them to open their eyes and smell the coffee must have sounded simplistic to the point of ridiculous. I imagine them thinking, *Gee, doc, that was brilliant. Thanks for sharing.*

Many of these people had a detailed understanding of their addiction. They had been living with its consequences for years and had long ago become stuck in an endless quest to capture the original high or ward off the physical and emotional pain that arose whenever they tried to stop. They did not need or want one more person telling them they messed up their lives. Rather, they needed help in solving their problem.

I recall Clay, a middle-aged man I had been treating for depression who brought his wife, Anne, to one of our sessions. She was a big-time real estate agent, dealing in million-dollar homes, and an alcoholic. Clay had been nagging Anne to quit or at least cut back, and he wanted me to be part of the discussion. He said her drinking was a major irritant in their relationship and that much of the time he felt helpless and frustrated because she resisted his pleas to stop. An arrest for DUI and complaints from other family members, along with a bad job performance evaluation that mentioned "frequent absences" and "erratic behavior," finally persuaded her to come along with him.

We began talking about how they related to each other and her take on what was wrong. When I brought up the subject of alcohol, Anne vehemently denied that she drank too much. She only drank after work and only enough to smooth her out, she declared. Clay offered his take on her drinking.

"You know why I don't like your drinking? It's because you're a mean drunk. I can always tell when you've hit three glasses of wine because then you start arguing with me, a waiter, other guests at a dinner party, anybody around. You start cutting people down, getting sarcastic, and making snide asides."

Anne was taken aback. The portrait he painted reminded Anne of her mother, and she was appalled. Many alcoholics believe that they can control their drinking and that every time they raise a glass, they are making a conscious choice. As I explained to the couple, this is only partially true. More is going on inside their head than deliberate thought. Another part of their brain, the primitive reward system, frequently has a louder say in people's behavior. Over the course of my research, I've learned just how influential the reward system can be.

A bingo moment in my approach to alcoholic patients came when I read a paper about cravings and addictions.[1] Written by scientists at Brighton and Sussex Medical School in the United Kingdom, it introduced the idea that addiction hijacks a person's reward system. Their use of the word *hijacking* implied that a system in the brain that usually functioned normally had been sent in an unintended, wrong direction. It meant that the reward system could not only spark normal survival behavior but also inappropriate, destructive behavior. Like drinking too much.

Framing alcoholism as a problem arising from the reward system explained a lot. Addiction is not simply a lack of willpower or a hedonistic drive. It is more powerful than personal psychology. It is a relentless neurological phenomenon that grips you with an iron fist. Its power comes from tapping in to one of the brain's essential survival networks, the reward system. Just as a threat can cause you to employ extreme emotions and behaviors to survive, so too can your reward drive.

Many people fight some type of addiction. Alcoholism, overeating, and smoking are the obvious ones, but addictions to certain foods, shopping, gambling, marijuana, prescription drugs, pornography, caffeine, video games, internet surfing, and even exercise dominate countless lives. The power of addictions arises from the brain's

Are You Dependent on Alcohol?

These questions are based on the list of symptoms for alcohol dependence according to the *Diagnostic and Statistical Manual of Mental Disorders, Fourth Edition.* Three affirmative answers relating to a twelve-month period indicates dependence.

1. Do you require increasing amounts of alcohol in order to feel good?

2. Have you found that the amount of alcohol that once made you feel good does not anymore?

3. Do you feel physical or emotional withdrawal symptoms (shaking, sweating, nausea, obsessing about alcohol) when you do not drink? Do these symptoms disappear when you drink?

4. Are you drinking more and more than you intend?

5. Do you frequently think about cutting back or try to cut back?

6. Do you spend a lot of time planning, doing, hiding, or recovering from your drinking?

7. Have you quit or limited social, work, or leisure activities because they get in the way of drinking?[2]

reward system, and food addictions offer a vivid illustration of how it works.

Food Addictions: A Window into Your Reward System

You already know how a threat triggers survival behavior. A threat sparks emotions and behaviors that you need to protect yourself. It may be surprising to learn that your brain has another way of ensuring your survival. This is the reward system, a neurological highway dedicated to seeking pleasing, rewarding sensations that also have essential survival value, like eating and sex.

Eating provides a window into how the reward system functions. If you don't eat, you don't survive. Imagine that it has been twelve hours since you have eaten and you are starved. Physically, you feel weak and have hunger pangs and a vague headache. But you have learned that when you eat, these negative feelings go away. This is the reward. It's plausible that without the discomforts, you might forget to eat and die.

But we are fickle. We do not like to eat tasteless slop, no matter how nutritious. Food has to taste good—otherwise we are less inclined to eat. Taste is only one of the rewards of eating. The brain offers other enticements. Sensory signals about food's pleasant smell, sight, and texture travel to the reward system. External cues make you want to eat—the appealing ambiance of a restaurant, the sight of something sweet or salty, the presentation of a plate, the smell of tantalizing spices, the friendly clatter of dishware.

Some foods are considered addictive. In a study of self-described chocoholics, participants gradually ate individual chocolate squares, with some participants consuming seventy-four.[3] After each piece, the chocolate lovers rated the chocolate's pleasantness or unpleasantness. During all this, researchers watched what happened in their brain. As the chocoholics eagerly consumed the chocolate, blood flow to the reward center increased and heightened the pleasant, rewarding sensations. This area of the brain is the same place that becomes active when someone goes through other kinds of addictions, like to alcohol or cocaine.

The researchers also noted that when people ate chocolate, after eating enough to make them feel full, a different region of their brain became active, not the reward system. The chocolate was pleasant to them only when they weren't full. The research team, led by Dana Small, concluded that people have two motivation systems: the reward system that pushes us to eat when it is pleasant and an avoidance system that prompts us to stop when it is unpleasant.

Dieters often talk about how stress stimulates their appetite for fattening foods like high-carbohydrate treats, even when they are not hungry and they don't feel much pleasure from eating. Researchers have found that the reward system plays an active role in stress-related eating.[4] Both a steady dose of stress-induced cortisol and a steady stream of highly palatable food stimulate the release of opioids and reward system activity. Scientists believe that this can lead to the reward system malfunctioning, with the result being compulsive overeating.

The reward system has redundancies—multiple pathways and processes to ensure that we do the things necessary for survival. The fact that redundant systems are activated by eating is in part what has foiled the development of an effective diet pill. Because eating activates numerous pathways, a pill that suppresses appetite does not shut down the entire reward system or drive to eat. And any drug aimed at the entire reward network could create disastrous side effects. If one system breaks down, it has a backup. This is good for survival, but it also presents opportunities for malfunctioning, which is what happens with addictions.

The reward system, just like the systems that stimulate the PAG model, can help us or hurt us. The system can become impaired and actually threaten our survival. This is what happens with addictions—they piggyback on your basic need for food and sex, using the reward system to deliver a steady stream of pleasant sensations. Over time this drive for the good feelings delivered by the reward system becomes so strong that it cannot be controlled. Basic neurological functions become corrupted and tangled up with extreme emotions and out-of-control behavior. This is the essence of addiction—a hijacked reward system. The best way to understand how this hijacking happens and how it can affect your emotions and behaviors is to look at the design of the reward system.

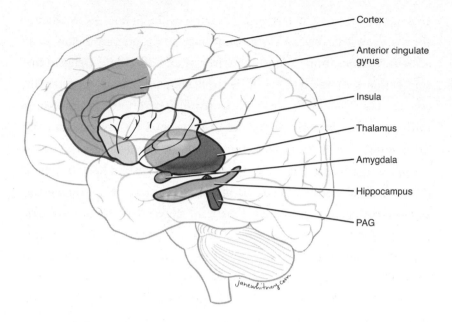

Anatomy of a Hijacker

Reward system pathways spread throughout your brain like a fine web, linking numerous structures. The more influential ones are the amygdala, insula, striatum, and cortex. These work in concert to generate numerous kinds of rewards that push you to engage in pleasurable survival behavior. However, they are also corruptible, as you will see. Each offers possible weak spots for where things can go wrong and addiction can happen. In short, there are many ways for you to become addicted.

The Amygdala: An Unseen Force

The amygdala is vital not only for detecting threats but also for directing your attention to things that are rewarding. It does this so fast that you are not aware of its actions. All you know is that something has sparked a thought or feeling, but you aren't sure what it is.

A study at the University of Pennsylvania School of Medicine showed how the reward system and amygdala operate below conscious awareness and can be taken over by an addiction.[5] Drug addiction patients viewed a series of pictures showing a person preparing cocaine and a couple in an erotic position. The photos appeared for milliseconds, below the threshold of conscious awareness, and the drug addicts didn't know what they would be viewing.

As the pictures flashed, the subjects' reward system became active for both the cocaine and sexual pictures. This was remarkable because cocaine has no survival benefit. Nevertheless, the addicts' reward system recognized the drug and generated cravings and desire without them knowing why. The brain's unconscious reaction to reward cues may also explain why people's efforts to change are difficult. Their reward system is unknowingly betraying them. The system can be hijacked when you feel anxious, stressed, or keyed up from sleeplessness. It can compel you to eat or drink things that diminish fear and unpleasantness but don't aid survival. Alcohol uses the reward system to relieve anxiety. When people are under the influence of alcohol, they don't react to threatening sights or sounds that normally make them alert and anxious. The alarm in the amygdala is not sounded.[6]

Alcohol can change normal reward system functioning by counteracting its impact.[7] It can generate an effect that scientists have dubbed the anti-reward system. At first, alcohol stimulates the reward system and makes you feel good. Then you grow used to the pleasant alcohol-fueled reward system and gradually need more to achieve the same high. Now the anti-reward system begins to rear its ugly head. It changes your reward set point and puts in motion a downhill spiral in which you are driven to drink to avoid unpleasant symptoms, not to find the old high. Your body reacts and produces the unpleasant sensation of withdrawal in the absence of reward stimulation. From here it is a small step to craving. Even though this kind of craving has no survival value, it pushes you to eat, drink, or smoke what made you feel better before. At this point, your reward system has been hijacked—physical cravings, not survival or necessity, are driving you.

This physical reaction can happen with all kinds of excessive behavior, including gambling, overeating, viewing pornography, surfing the internet, and even shopping. These compulsive actions probably travel the reward system. Like alcohol abuse, people use these things to relieve stress, take away anxiety, feel good, or get a familiar high, or because they have developed the habit.

How the Senses Come Into Play

Another player in the reward system is the insula, which takes sensory signals from the body about hunger or other physical sensations and translates them into emotions that drive behavior.[8] It's especially busy when you eat because your taste cortex is situated in it. Taste serves a function beyond pleasing your palate. It is important for survival because it enables you to identify nutrients and poisons. Just thinking about food, even if you're full, can activate your insula.

A study from the Netherlands compared the taste reactions of satiated healthy-weight people versus satiated overweight people and found a notable difference.[9] Both groups looked at pictures of high-calorie, tasty foods and were asked to imagine the taste. The overweight people showed greater activation in the reward region when they were asked just to imagine the taste of high-calorie foods. But when both groups looked at similar pictures of fattening, tasty foods and were not given any instructions, the overweight group's brain showed less activity. It appears that the overweight people felt ambivalent about wanting the taste of a fattening food while knowing they should avoid it, so they deliberately restrained themselves when looking at the pictures of high-calorie treats.

The insula, with its command of sensory sensations, is instrumental in producing cravings.[10] Normally smell, color, texture, and food ambiance stimulate the reward system to make you want to eat. But other sensations, those not associated with survival, can also tap in to the reward system. The burning taste of alcohol, an acid taste of wine, the rush of a snort of cocaine, the pain of a needle full of heroin—these can become paired with the reward to enhance the drive to consume more.

A smoking habit offers a window into what goes on in the insula when you crave something. Smoking shows how cravings tap in to the reward system's redundant nature to add to its grip on a person. A few years back, a now-famous study focused on cigarette addiction by looking at nineteen smokers who had a damaged insula and fifty smokers who had brain damage that did not include the insula.[11] Up to the time of their brain damage, all the patients had smoked at least five cigarettes a day for more than two years. The study discovered that those people with insula damage were able to quit smoking more easily and sooner than those without insula damage. And they stayed off cig-arettes, too, because they no longer felt a physical craving. A patient who stopped immediately after the brain trauma said he quit because "his body forgot the urge to smoke." The smokers' reward system was still functioning, however, as shown by their continued enjoyment in eating. This demonstrated that the reward system indeed has redun-dant pathways for essential functions like eating, and disrupting one route does not shut it down.

Dopamine Can Fuel a Habit

Yet another busy brain structure in the reward system is the ventral striatum, which uses dopamine as its messenger.[12] It sends you signals about experiences that are pleasant, surprising, novel, important, or should be avoided.[13] These messages can benefit survival, so they use the reward system. They do not elicit a big shot of dopamine but just enough to make the experience worth repeating. Steady drink-ing increases dopamine concentrations in the limbic system, as do food and sex, but alcohol produces more and spikes its levels faster.

Dopamine is more than rewarding. It influences people's interest and attention, prompting reward-seeking behavior. It's a motivator.

With repeated drug use, dopamine appears to travel to another area of the striatum.[14] As a result, new pathways become active, and these give rise to a new set of behaviors, namely habits. Brain imaging reveals that for a regular drug user, even the sight of a drug or something drug related excites dopamine release, and study participants reported a craving. The area of the striatum that handles cravings is also involved in acquiring habits.

Habits are often good. Imagine living every day as if it were the first, having to make a decision for everything you do. With habits, you do not have to think about eating meals, taking daily medication, or doing the countless other things you have to do to live a healthy life. But habits, too, can be hijacked and result in misuse of the reward system.

A habit can corrupt the reward system and lead to addiction. Some habits stimulate the reward system more than others. Brushing your teeth every day does not do much for the reward system, but lighting a smoke every time you have a cup of coffee can regularly activate it. In the same way, the habit of drinking when you feel stressed or overeating when you are bored can become addictive.[15]

The automatic feature of a habit—not thinking about what you are doing—can add force to its destructiveness. If you are not thinking about all that you are eating or drinking or smoking, you lose awareness of a problem. For example, you come home from work stressed and frustrated, and you relieve this by getting a beer from the fridge. Now alcohol has become a relief from an unpleasant feeling. The habit of your after-work drink is tied to the reward system, and it wants constant stimulation. The addiction cycle begins with your reward system giving you a pleasant feeling from such pairings, prompting you to go back for more.[16] Over time and repeated use, other reward system pathways become active (remember, it uses multiple pathways), and this creates an addiction.

A Tug of War That Willpower Loses

When you are confronted by a plate of chocolate chip cookies and are not starving, you can chow down now, postpone the pleasure, or not eat them at all. It is your cortex that helps you assert willpower and decide whether to eat them. The cortex is central to handling information related to making decisions about the future, like what eating cookies will do to your waistline. Being the thinking part of the brain rather than the instinctive area, it notes sensory signals about pleasure or pain in the future.

The cortex imposes willpower, which is an antidote to habit. But as everyone knows, breaking a habit and resisting those cookies is easier said than done. This is not because people lack discipline or mental strength. It's because the sight, smell, or even thought of something you crave can prompt your body to trump your willpower.[17] The best way around this is to avoid temptation or use distraction when your mind gets near a temptation or enticing food.

The reason people have trouble asserting willpower, according to renowned neuroscientist António Damásio, is that decisions are influenced by signals from their body that motivate them toward immediate gratification and instant rewards.[18] These signals are sensations and images from viscera and other body parts. Imagine you quit smoking years ago and are now thinking about lighting up again. If that thought makes your stomach go queasy, that's what Damásio calls a "somatic marker." That sensation may prompt you to think again and not return to smoking. Or the thought of smoking may produce an image in your mind of being relaxed and looking cool. This, too, is a somatic marker.

Somatic markers help you make decisions about the future and can act as a warning system signaling unpleasantness or threats, or future benefits. They also can signal that doing something right now will be exceedingly pleasant. The signal may announce, "Danger, danger!" or "Go for it!"

An alcoholic may receive a signal about unpleasant experiences with alcohol and also get messages like, "There's a bottle of my favorite beer." In the alcoholic's mind, the reward messages are louder and more persuasive. Images of immediate, pleasant sensations trump thoughts about long-term consequences. Willpower requires thinking about the future, and it loses out to instant pleasure.

There's also a neurological reason why it's hard for addicts to impose willpower and make good decisions.[19] Their brain has developed what neurobiologist Antoine Bechara calls a "myopia for future consequences." Addiction has created an imbalance between the impulsive amygdala system and the thoughtful cortex system. The amygdala system focuses on immediate pain or pleasure, and the cortex system handles future pain or pleasure. An addiction, such as alcoholism, makes the amygdala system hyperactive. Repeated stimulation of the reward system has reinforced the amygdala's instinctive reactions. As a result, the automatic, impulsive brain overrides thoughts and decisions from the cortex system. Willpower and thoughts about the future are drowned out.

Alcoholism in particular damages other brain structures.[20] Not only does the cortex lose both gray and white matter, but there is also shrinkage in the hippocampus, producing memory and learning problems. These brain changes created by alcohol can last a lifetime. Evidence for this comes from alcoholics who have quit drinking for years, even decades, and then resumed drinking. Despite years of abstinence, within a week of drinking again, they were craving alcohol and soon became dependent. An obvious conclusion is that even twenty years of not drinking is insufficient for a brain to repair itself after years of drinking.

The Hijacker's Helper: Genetics and the Hangover Gene

Genes can make people's reward system more susceptible to hijacking. Alcoholics' genes can add to their vulnerability, accounting for

40 to 60 percent of the risk for addiction.[21] Studies of family histories and twin studies confirm the influence of genes on developing alcoholism. The children of alcoholics are four times more likely to become alcoholics as children without an alcoholic parent. This is true even if the children are not raised by the alcoholic parent. Genetic markers, which are gene variations in a DNA sequence, have also been connected with people at risk for alcohol dependence.

An especially intriguing gene is what scientists call the "hangover gene."[22] A team led by Henrike Scholz at the University of Würzburg, Germany, found the hangover gene affected fruit flies' response to ethanol vapor. Like drunk humans, the flies lost coordination and fell asleep. Twenty minutes later, the fruit flies recovered to a non-drunken state. The researchers then waited four hours and administered the same amount of ethanol vapor. This time some of the fruit flies needed more time to develop the same state of drunkenness. They had acquired a tolerance. The hangover gene had a second remarkable property. It made the fruit flies more susceptible to stress delivered by raising the temperature in their environment. I realize that fruit flies are not people. However, when studying genetic makeup, humans have much in common with them, with about 61 percent of our genes being present in the fruit flies' genetic code.[23] And fruit flies respond to ethanol the same way people do to alcohol. The hangover gene is not proof of a genetic foundation for alcoholism, but it does add to the evidence that it may be involved in human alcoholism.[24]

The genetic impact of alcoholism may cross generations.[25] An alcoholic's abnormal emotional traits, like apathy, emotional flatness, or outbursts, may be passed to the next generation. For instance, a genetic change affecting an alcoholic's tolerance to drink may be passed along so that her children also have a higher tolerance for alcohol. Although scientists have yet to identify specific genes, they believe that alcohol may produce an epigenetic effect and alter genes passed between generations.[26]

The possibilities of a genetic predisposition, a hijacked reward system, and an altered brain structure each present a formidable obstacle for someone who wants to quit any addiction. They also present numerous challenges to treatment. My approach with alcoholics illustrates the strategies and approaches I believe are helpful regardless of the addiction.

Foiling the Hijacker: Treatment Possibilities

Aaron's story has much in common with those of other alcoholics. As often happens, he did not believe that alcohol was the true source of his troubles. He believed it was his anger—and he was right, to a degree. He first sought help after a fight with his wife, Ann, that ended with the police in his home. What he didn't understand was that his anger and other altercations had been intensified by alcohol.

Married almost thirty years, Aaron and Ann had no children, and at times I got the sense that Aaron was more wrapped up in his work than his home life. He was an editor at a large newspaper and faced constant stress from deadlines and demands for news coverage. On the night of the fight, he had gotten home from work late, quickly consumed a couple of strong drinks, and then went out to dinner with his wife. At the restaurant, he had a cocktail and most of a bottle of wine. An argument had started over dinner about whether or not he'd be able to make a trip they had been planning. They got home, and Aaron continued to drink while he and Ann carried on arguing.

The disagreement heated up in the bedroom. Ann was packing her suitcase, presumably for the trip, and Aaron was berating her for not being understanding enough about all the stress he was under. At some point, he became infuriated, grabbed Ann's arms, and threw her against a door. She recovered and then ran from the house to a neighbor's to call the police.

Ann did not press charges after Aaron promised to get professional help. No one specified the nature of this help, and Aaron felt he needed just a dose of anger management.

Hearing his story, I recognized numerous red flags indicating that anger was just the tip of the iceberg. The larger, more dangerous issue was his drinking.

For instance, one of the first things he mentioned when describing the night of the fight was coming home and needing a drink. "It was a really bad day at the office. I wanted to forget about it," he explained.

I asked why he continued to drink at dinner. He mentioned the restaurant's extensive wine list. That environmental cue undoubtedly kept his attention on alcohol. Then he added another reason.

"It was to forget about this vacation Ann had planned. I never said anything, but I really felt that we couldn't afford it. She was booking us into all these four-star places. And I was still trying to pay off a credit card bill I had run up in Atlantic City when I got carried away and lost more than I should have."

Another compulsive behavior, I thought and asked why he continued to drink once they were back at home. By this point, he had no answer other than because drinking was a habit that comforted him. He tried to defend his behavior, declaring that he was rarely drunk and on some days he had only a couple of drinks.

"I'm not an alcoholic," he claimed. "An alcoholic is someone who can't control their drinking. That's not me. It doesn't dictate my life. I decide when I want to drink. You tell me, doc. Do I look like an alcoholic?"

I hear this regularly from alcoholics, and though I suspect they intend it to be rhetorical, I give a truthful answer, which is usually, "I think so."

Nevertheless, the question was a good sign because it signaled his awareness to a possible problem. Even though someone who asks this question is probably not yet committed to stopping drinking, I welcome it for two reasons. It allows us to talk about denial and truthfulness, and to explain about treatment.

Denial: A Common Denominator

Denial like Aaron's is common among patients and makes treatment doubly difficult by sabotaging efforts to change. One estimate claims that 80 percent of substance abusers do not seek treatment.[27] The reason is that dependent individuals are often unaware of how alcohol, or other addictive substances, affects them. They lack insight and self-awareness into how they act, think, and feel when they're under the influence. Heavy alcohol consumption reduces people's self-awareness because it inhibits thinking and instead activates the emotion-based limbic system. Alcohol suppresses people's critical thinking, especially when it relates to themselves.

Research shows that alcohol distorts people's ability to read the emotions of those around them. A study of volunteers, half alcoholics in detox and half healthy, involved showing each person a series of faces expressing mild or intense happiness, anger, or fear.[28] Afterward, the volunteers rated the intensity in each face. The recovering alcoholics dramatically misjudged what they were seeing and overestimated the intensity of both the angry and happy expressions. The alcoholics did correctly interpret the fearful faces. Only angry or happy looks skewed their reactions. The researchers, a team from Brussels, surmised that a history of alcohol abuse may impair people's ability to correctly gauge nonverbal, social cues.

I often begin treatment by asking patients to keep a detailed log of their addictive behavior for a week. If the addiction is alcohol, the log should include how many drinks a day they consume, the size of the drinks, the related cost, and a short note about how they felt about the drinking. I want to know whether they hide their drinking and feel any shame or guilt about the behavior.

I dispense with any thoughts about judging or condemning their behavior, explaining that addictions are powerful, neurological processes that many people struggle with. Backsliding is common, I add, but it isn't the last word. I tell patients that treatment will take time and effort—there is no magic pill that can cure an addiction. Yet each attempt to get better, even those that aren't successful, offers lessons for tailoring and improving the next attempt.

The log is the first productive step, giving me a concrete piece of information to talk about self-honesty. Alcoholics may deny having a problem or on some level know there is a problem. This is apparent in people who try to hide their drinking, mouthwash being the usual cover-up.

Once a problem has been admitted, we examine its dimensions. I talk about practicalities and the cost of alcoholism. This includes not only money paid for drinks but also lost income from missed working days, missed opportunities, and the cost of any alcohol-related damage. This may include car repairs, fines and penalties for drunk driving, repairs around the home for accidents and mishaps, and sometimes costs associated with being a crime victim when drunk.

Next we talk about the cost in terms of the personal dimension—what drinking has done to relationships and family dynamics. The damage can be huge, from broken marriages to children who lose respect and become estranged, to friends and neighbors who sever relationships, to business colleagues who withdraw professional help and support.

Saying Good-Bye

People often hesitate to talk about problem drinking. They may be unconvinced they have a problem or believe quitting will make their life less enjoyable. They may talk about how drinking helps their social life and makes them feel better about themselves (they often forget blurry mornings and social embarrassments because of their behavior). Drinking is a social pastime, and it can make people feel comfortable, like they belong in a group. Some people sense enormous peer pressure to drink. These feelings have to be confronted.

Quitting an addiction is like saying good-bye to a close friend. Once people quit drinking, their life will never be the same. There is going to be sadness and grief over the loss of a way of life and all the comfortable props that go along with the behavior.

Recovering addicts must go through a grieving process, but after they have mourned, they need to rethink their relationship with their so-called friend. If they think about all the destruction their habit created, they realize that alcohol is not their friend and they need to get angry about what has happened to them. Alcohol has stolen normalcy and control from their life. It has been in charge, not them, and they need to get determined about this in order to reclaim it. Determination can give them energy to pursue treatment regardless of how hard it might be.

At the same time, they need to admit the power of what they are resisting. Cravings are strong impulses, and it helps to put these feelings into words. Rather than being ashamed or guilty, alcoholics should acknowledge that they are fighting a powerful urge. The best way to defeat it is with an even more powerful resolve. This requires acknowledging that saying they'll limit themselves to "just one" drink will not work; rather, one drink will send them back to the old ways. It requires articulating all the reasons for quitting and dispensing with the rationalizations for drinking that have enabled them to keep doing it.

Creating New Habits

A few years ago, I took a course on how to interview prospective employees. The instructor told us each to prepare a question that we would ask an applicant. Mine was, where do you see yourself in five years? The instructor seemed displeased with my question. A much better question, he said, and one that I have since used to shape my treatment approach, was, how do you see yourself getting to where you want to be in five years?

This is a better question because it goes to the heart of the problem—finding a process for achieving success. I ask alcoholic patients a form of this question too: How are you going to break your addiction?

I may then explain that I cannot solve their problem, but we can work together. I add an important caveat: this is going to be hard. Using a basketball metaphor, I explain that there are few shots possible from the half-court. The ball has to be patiently worked, passed back and forth, before it goes through the hoop. It will take day-by-day persistence and diligence. For many, treatment is a combination of Alcoholics Anonymous and Weight Watchers. The AA part is the one-day-at-a-time philosophy. Don't look at the mountain, just the boulder in front of you, and count every day sober as an achievement. The AA element is also dedication. It demands patients be constantly vigilant and never forget that they are vulnerable. Another useful element of these programs is praise and symbols of success, whether it's a mark on a calendar, a chip, or a rousing ovation. Some people may regard these as insignificant or patronizing, and dismiss them. I tell them to not only take them to heart but also find ways to reward themselves. I remind them about how bad they felt physically when they were drinking and how much better they feel clearheaded and alert. I may suggest they use the money they have saved from not drinking on something they've coveted.

The Weight Watchers strategy is especially effective because it emphasizes that changing a habit is not going to be a two-week affair but a new lifestyle. A person has to change an array of habits. Whether it is food or alcohol, you cannot cut back or quit for just a few weeks until you feel better or have lost 10 pounds. The success will be so short-lived as to be pointless. Only a permanent change in behavior and a major lifestyle alteration will work.

For patients to make the lifestyle adjustment, they must know the enemy. Where are they vulnerable? What activities, places, and people in their life can hurt them? Do they expose themselves to situations that strain their willpower or are too tempting to resist? A source of trouble may be habits. The part of the brain that handles automatic, impulsive behavior may not be communicating well with the part that makes them stop and think.

Like soldiers who practice for battle, alcoholics have to prepare for situations where they will be challenged. This means talking about how to respond when someone offers a drink at a party, when a friend wants to take you for a beer to celebrate a special occasion, or when someone gives you a bottle of wine as a hostess gift. Verbalizing your struggle helps quiet instinctive reflexes and engages thoughts about consequences.

Alcoholics deciding whether to drink wrestle with clashing thoughts. On the one hand are the cues and signals, like the sight of a bottle of wine or feeling stressed and needing to reduce anxiety, that fuel an impulsive decision to drink. Other thoughts engage not the reward system but the higher cortical areas. These thoughts are slower and weigh a decision to avoid the short-term negative effects of drinking, postpone the immediate reward of alcohol, and opt for the deferred gratification that comes from quitting. The difficulty for alcoholics is that their reward system has gained more influence over their decisions than slower thought processing. Reversing this imbalance will be hard work.

A family history of alcoholism can compound the difficulty. There may be a genetic risk and the hangover gene. However, genes are not destiny. They indicate risk and vulnerability, but they are not absolute predictors of future behavior.

I also talk with patients to identify things that can weaken their resolve or kindle their desire to drink. For instance, fatigue, stress, and lack of sleep can weaken some people's determination. They need to anticipate these and find other ways of coping. Some patients, when stressed, go to the gym instead of staying home during cocktail hour. When they're fatigued, they may find a relaxing activity like watching a movie, listening to music, or getting a massage. People have to know their own stress points—for instance, being late or arguing with their spouse. By being aware of stress points that can push them to resort to habit and drinking, people can avoid them.

Recovering alcoholics have to look around and pinpoint the external cues that trigger thoughts of drinking. These may include situations like after-work gatherings; being around certain people, like a fishing buddy; going certain places, like a wine bar or a popular tavern; or certain rituals, like the after-dinner drink. Each reminder needs to be identified and avoided. Bad habits have to be replaced by neutral or good ones. There cannot be a void because the old habit will slip back in. So we talk about automatic behavior and how to halt it by replacing it with new routines, new activities, and new venues.

An essential part of creating a new lifestyle is rebuilding relationships. Addictions produce collateral damage to marriages, families, friendships, and coworkers. This is particularly true for alcoholics who have repeatedly tried and failed to quit. Friends and family may well feel deceived by previous attempts. It's vital to rebuild these relationships because alcoholics need help and support. They cannot do it alone. The rebuilding will take time and talking. The walls that families build to protect themselves from alcoholics' destructive influences have to be dismantled brick by brick. This is done through constant communication—explaining and reassuring—and reestablishing trust. Sometimes patients chafe at the idea that they must account for their actions and reassure loved ones that they have not been drinking. Yet this is the only way people will again trust alcoholics.

The pleasant, sometimes euphoric high of drinking has to be replaced with another reward. Each successful day of not drinking should be acknowledged, and positive results celebrated. People should reward themselves for resisting the craving and triumphing over that urge. It may be a small, momentary victory but it is significant, and over time, it gets easier to withstand the urge. Even with brain impairment from alcoholism, neuroplasticity may well help heal the damage. The reward can be symbolic, like recognizing that not drinking makes you feel better and look better. The simple act of adding up how much money is being saved by not drinking can be a reward. Enjoying improved relationships is also rewarding.

People with addictions need to tell their physicians, no matter how difficult or embarrassing. Addictions like alcoholism affect your health and can undermine even the healthiest of lifestyles. Also, your physician may be able to help. For instance, there are medications that help with alcoholism. Naltrexone, acamprosate, and topiramate have shown good results with some alcoholics.

Dealing with Setbacks

I warn alcoholics in treatment that they may experience setbacks. Having a drink or getting inebriated during treatment will feel like failure, so I tell them that not only is it common but it can be instructive. Each so-called failure should be examined for the triggers and conditions that weakened their determination. They need to know what set them off so it can be avoided in the future.

I describe the process as a journey on a long country road that has many peaks and low spots. In the dips, the road up may look impossibly steep, but it is the best way out. Every time you get bogged down offers a lesson on where you need to concentrate your efforts and where the greatest obstacles lie. And the peaks may feel like the summit, but there is truly not one final scenic overlook where you can rest. There are steep drop-offs all around. It's a never-ending journey but one that can offer gorgeous views and years of peaceful cruising. There is always more road. There is a reason for hope despite the pain, difficulties, and setbacks. They can reclaim their lives.

Summing Up

- The brain's survival network uses its reward system to ensure that you eat and procreate. Many non-survival-related substances, like alcohol and drugs, tap in to the reward system, producing pleasant sensations.

- The reward system has redundant processing networks to ensure its survival functioning.

- The reward system can become hijacked, which can jeopardize survival by being repeatedly activated. When this happens, habit and instinctive behavior overrule thoughtful decision making.

- Treatment requires a strong personal commitment to replacing the habitual, instinctive behavior that has hijacked the reward system with thoughtful decisions about the benefits of being free of addiction.

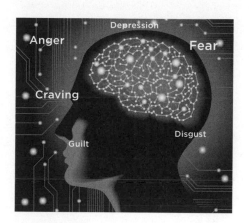

Part III

Seeking Healthy Emotions

Smothering the Fire: Treatment

Using the PAG Model to Understand

The emotions and behaviors that sidetrack people often result from everyday events. I have included a list of these issues in a sidebar on page 220 to illustrate two points. Some of these things are beyond your control—you don't cause them, they happen to you. Then there are problems you do create. Nevertheless, every situation presents you with choices and the opportunities to make good decisions. The biggest danger is ignoring the need to do something.

Treatment begins with honesty about who you are, what you've done, and where you're going. You acknowledge your issues and take steps to control them. Personal dilemmas can often be addressed without professional help. You do not need a psychiatrist for everything that provokes you. Hopefully the PAG model can help.

One of the goals of this book is to provide a framework for you to understand the origins of your emotions and behaviors, and to

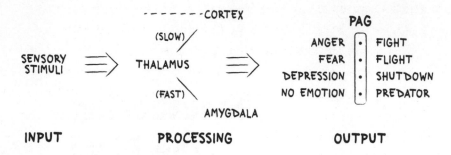

determine whether they are appropriate or inappropriate. The model's four groups of neurons, what I call buttons, each correspond to an instigating emotion and a resulting behavior. The sketch here, which you also saw in chapter 4, illustrates how the senses first detect something threatening and pass a message via the thalamus to the cortex for thoughtful processing or to the amygdala for a survival reaction. Extreme threats go to the amygdala, and it sends the signal to the PAG, which launches behavior.

The model can help you understand your behavior. Each patient story in this chapter shows how a person's life and relationships kindle particular emotions and behaviors. Following the description of how their emotions and behaviors came about, I offer my perspectives based on the PAG model and ideas on how therapy can address their problems.

Vern: Always Angry

Vern had been married for twenty-five years, was the father of two teenagers, and worked for the government. Since he was a kid, he remembered having problems with bad moods, lashing out in temper tantrums, or becoming gloomy and apathetic. The moods came less often as he grew up and married, but they never disappeared completely. When they struck, his go-to remedies included drinking to numb himself and getting away from his family.

It was after a budget cut in his office, when his department was downsized and coworkers let go, that feelings of anger and depression started to come back regularly. If he was around the house, he would not speak for days, sometimes weeks. If he said anything, it was snapping at his wife and kids. He never hit anyone but he would slam doors, throw pans around the kitchen, and explode at anyone who tried to talk to him. He'd call them stupid and idiotic then clam up. There was no normal family life during these times, and the wife and kids would walk on eggshells, watching for signs of Vern's mood lifting. When that happened, he acted as if everything was normal. No one spoke of his moods.

He finally sought treatment because he was afraid he might lose his job. In his first session, we talked about his job and family life. He struck me as a good man who genuinely cared about his family. Yet he was also resentful and confused, and skeptical about whether therapy could help. I asked him to bring his wife, Jody, the next time. The session with them started slowly, with Vern sharing about his fears and inadequacies and the wife sitting stone-faced, her arms crossed, her eyes studying him as if waiting.

As soon as he brought up the subject of his physical health—frequent headaches and fatigue—she pounced. She ripped into him about his drinking and not helping around the house.

Vern didn't react or argue. He sat mute, shaking his head and clenching his hands. Jody finished, and we were silent for a moment.

"What do you think, Vern, about what Jody just said?"

"I dunno," he shrugged. I pressed him.

"I don't know what I'm feeling. I feel like I'm hanging by my fingers on a trapeze, scared to death that I'm going to fall, angry because someone put me there, sad because awful things keep happening to me."

His response was one of the great teaching moments for me as a psychiatrist. The man had just shared his feelings, making himself vulnerable, and his wife reacted with disrespect and venomous words. Yet Vern did not react. I was flabbergasted. I expected, given his history, that he would go ballistic, but instead he made a statement about not understanding his emotions and talking about being on a trapeze. It made no sense to me.

The PAG model gave me some insight, reminding me that emotions and behaviors can arise for a valid reason, for a dubious reason, or for no reason. It seemed to me that Vern would have been justified to become angry at Jody's verbal assault, yet he did not. He had no idea why Jody's anger didn't provoke him. His "I dunno" told me that there were no reasons behind his emotions, whether anger or lack of anger.

It was like the oil light in a car's instrument panel. If the oil light goes on, you pull into a gas station and add more oil so that the light goes off and everything works. This is normal, emotional behavior. But some people, like Vern, have topped off their oil and the light is still on. So they pull into a station again, check the level, and the oil reservoir reads full. Now there's a dilemma—they cannot trust the oil light and don't know how to fix the problem.

Your brain wants to be rational, and when it does not make sense to be angry, it tries to explain it. For a person like Vern, his desire to understand his anger often made him blame others for causing it. He'd blame his wife for messy housekeeping or the children for making too much noise. Outside the home, another driver honking his horn or a pedestrian who walked too slowly would set him off. As you read in the shutdown chapter about how depressed people see the world as gray, this same distorted worldview happens with anger. Angry people see threats and anger all around them. Trivial incidents that would just annoy a normal person made Vern furious. He saw them as personal attacks and responded in kind. As a result, his anger made those around him angry, and emotions escalated.

But the story does not end there. His anger was equally confusing for his family. Vern's wife and children did not understand why he was coming at them. Their reactions to his anger only inflamed the situation more. When they tried to withdraw, walking on eggshells or avoiding him, it made him angrier because he felt ignored and disrespected. At other times, believing they had done something wrong and trying harder to please him, the result was equally ineffective. They thought their behavior could change the situation. In this instance, it didn't help because their behavior did not cause it. Vern was angry regardless of what they did. It wasn't them, it was him. His anger stemmed from a survival-driven amygdala constantly pushing the PAG's anger-fight button.

Vern's anger made Jody lash back with both vocal attacks and subtle barbs and digs. Her reaction at the time was a conditioned fear response. I realized that her angry outbursts were persisting months into treatment. Vern was on antidepressants for controlling his angry episodes and feeling more in control, able to think before he went off. But Jody was still lashing out at him. Why?

Jody had lived with this man's anger and rage for decades. I believe at some level her nervous system had changed. Suppose you are arguing with your neighbor over his dog regularly fouling your lawn and, with no warning, he explodes and hits you. Your relationship has just changed and the next time you see him, you back away. This change is a conditioned fear response. You no longer wait for your neighbor to get close enough to hit you before you respond. Now you respond to him when you see him at a distance. Even the thought of him living next door makes you uneasy. Vern calling home to say he would be late from work or the sound of his car pulling into the driveway triggered a similar defensive reaction from Jody.

Treatment for Vern had to begin with him understanding his anger. The first step for getting it under control was to stop drinking. Alcohol makes a person's survival reactions go faster. For an angry person, it shortens the fuse. Then we addressed the cycle of threat

Everyone Is Vulnerable

To treat emotional and behavioral disorders, people need to recognize the threats and fears that ignite them. Until you stop and think about your life, you may not be aware of all the pressures and demands that can push your buttons. This list of life's trials is by no means complete, but it will give you a place to start:

Marriage: lost commitment, sexual conflict, adultery, poor communication, in-law problems, abuse (physical, emotional, spiritual), rejection or disrespect by spouse (physical, intellectual, vocational), elderly parents, ex-spouse problems

Financial: debt, foreclosure, bankruptcy, mortgage, taxes, budget, savings, giving, spending, spouse irresponsibility, retirement

Children: infertility, pregnancy, death of a child, discipline problems, academic problems, learning disability, self-image problems, two or more children under age six, stepchildren, leaving home, health/handicapped, lack of spouse support, teens/puberty

General: death in the family, death of a friend, alcoholism, drug abuse, retirement, education, legal problems, vacations, holidays

Personal: friends, work, schedule, priorities

Health: illness, injury, diet, weight, exercise, back, heart, cancer, ulcer, sexual dysfunction, sleep problems, depression

Work: change in management, firing, budget difficulties, conflicts, relocation, added responsibilities[1]

and defensive rage. The Halloween cat offers a good example. When a cat is angry at being provoked and is defending itself, you do not box it into a corner. You give it space.

In therapy, I try to give patients space by always being on their side and expressing concern. I explain that inappropriate behavior is not in their best interest. I avoid any statement that could be interpreted as a threat and fuel defensive behavior. Instead I ask about their anger and what they think is setting it off. I try to help them see that the angry outbursts are out of proportion to the circumstances.

When Vern said he was reacting to feeling disrespected and challenged, I explained that he was not going to get respect and feel safe with people who were targets of his anger. His anger pushes people away and forces them to defend themselves.

Vern had a neurological malfunction. His cortex was unable to control his amygdala, and as a result, he reacted to tones of voice and other provocations before he had time to think. His periods of silence, a form of shutdown, were his brain's attempt to limit sensory stimulation.

As I explained this to Vern and Jody, she directed her anger at me. Why was it that Vern could be congenial and friendly outside the home and only go into a rage with his family? Because, I said, people react differently to different sources of provocation, depending on the environment. Vern was more sensitive to the people and events in his home than at work. He felt more threatened by family members than by outsiders. Her eye rolling would make him furious while he would ignore a coworker doing the same thing. Friends, coworkers, and bosses did not push his buttons as severely as Jody and the kids did.

Vern had to reestablish trust and a feeling of safety at home. This would take time because he would have to overcome their weariness from his countless apologies and promises to change that never happened. He had to realize that they did not believe that he was truly going to change and that only time and repeated demonstrations of his new behavior would convince them. His wife and kids had probably heard "I'm sorry" numerous times, but it needed to be said over and over, and with sincerity. Putting some meat into "I'm sorry" included taking steps to avoid the triggers that set off his anger, be they stress at work, his wife's tone of voice, or money worries. "I'm sorry" had to be the beginning of a continuing conversation about anger and what everyone in the family needed to feel safe and supported.

Vern was used to being in control, making demands, and intimidating people, and he had to give up that behavior. His family was not the enemy, and he could not treat them like they were. With this new perspective, coupled with meds to decrease his anger and stopping drinking to give him time to think, Vern could begin to create new, anger-free memories for his family.

John and Margie: We Don't Communicate

John and Margie's marriage was wracked by argument and hurt feelings, and neither knew how to break the pattern. They both worked, he writing history books in a home office and she commuting to a company where she was chief counsel. John also functioned as the stay-at-home dad taking care of their elementary school–aged son. He enjoyed the role tremendously yet resented Margie's long work hours. Most evenings, she came home late, and each would slip into familiar roles.

Margie usually called when she could not be home by seven, but then some nights she would not get home until after ten. While John appreciated the heads-up, he suspected that she used the calls as a way of avoiding coming home and having to do the trivial chores a family requires. When she arrived at home, John at first was relieved. He worried about accidents, breakdowns, and crime so was glad when he heard her come in.

Soon after the relief came accusations. John berated her for treating him like a babysitter and not spending enough time with their son. This infuriated Margie because she felt like he didn't appreciate all the time and effort she was putting into her job. As the primary breadwinner, she provided them with a comfortable life with lots of perks. But John didn't seem to appreciate it, or to understand the pressure and expectations she had to deal with. He treated her, she said, like an ATM. Each time, one of them finally stomped off and they quietly seethed until bedtime. By morning, they were civil again but their flash points were right below the surface.

Their arguments always covered the same ground and never settled anything. On weekends, they argued about different things but with common themes. John got annoyed because Margie didn't help around the house and instead went shopping, and she was perturbed with him for acting like a martyr and making no effort to do things with her.

With the PAG model in hand, I could predict that their arguments always had three outcomes. They'd exchange nasty, hurtful words along with broad, sweeping statements usually beginning with, "You never . . ." Fear then crept into their arguments and was expressed by one of them trying to escape. One of Margie's preferred ways was to suddenly stop arguing, announce she was tired of his belittling her efforts, and then retreat to the den to call her sister for sympathy. John's usual retort was leaving the house with "I'm out of here." Right before they came to me for therapy, he dropped the marriage bomb: "I want a divorce." The third response was each of them going into a form of shutdown. Margie would declare, "I just want peace" and say no more. John would hole up in the TV room for a marathon viewing of crime shows.

John and Margie believed they had a communication problem and that the other person was so self-absorbed that he or she would not listen. Each regarded the other as unreasonable and deliberately mean. In truth, there was heaps of communication, but neither liked what the other was communicating. Both felt threatened and afraid, but they did not know of what. They lived in a state of fear, braced for the next confrontation, and ready to defend themselves. It was as if they lived in a house with bars on the windows and an elaborate alarm system while they were being robbed by a live-in nanny.

Therapy for John and Margie had to begin with identifying what they felt threatened by and why they were afraid. They had to truly communicate—not merely swap accusations but listen and understand what each was saying. John was afraid of losing Margie's love and their marriage. He was afraid that her job was more important than he was. His self-esteem was in jeopardy, too, from Margie's ignoring his contributions to their son's upbringing and making a home for all of them. Margie's fears were similar. John rarely acknowledged all that she was sacrificing for the high-paying job that was benefiting all of them. She did not feel loved or respected.

Couples like John and Margie, who don't talk but only argue, represent a huge segment of the population. They are well-intentioned people who believe they love each other and want peace, not conflict. Yet they repeatedly slip into confrontations, believing the other person is unreasonable and saying hurtful things they later realize they shouldn't have. There is no great pathology here, just ordinary people grappling with life's ups and downs.

Another physician, a good friend of mine, once faced a similar situation with his wife. He was working long hours, rarely home before eleven P.M., and his wife was stuck at home with the kids. Weekends were just as bad, as he frequently had to make rounds in the early morning. He loved his job and felt he was building something for both of them, but she was discontented. My friend asked me to talk to her and explain why he worked so hard and really didn't have control over his schedule.

I gave Ralph an incredulous look: "You must be crazy," I declared. At first he didn't get it, but then he realized that I understood the problem all too well. It wasn't that his wife was being clingy or unreasonable. Just the opposite—maybe he was wrong and had been blindsided by his single-minded drive.

John and Margie had to open their eyes to the other's perspective and understand the fears as well as their differences. Each wanted the other to buy in to their point of view, but sometimes people will never agree. This does not have to be a source of conflict. While the amygdala may sense something threatening in a different point of view and stimulate an emotional response from the PAG, you can learn not to give in to this reaction. Different ways of thinking can, on the surface, appear threatening but be healthy for a marriage. More important than agreeing are understanding and recognizing that we are different, accepting this, and being willing to keep engaging the other person instead of constantly arguing or giving up on the relationship. Therapy for a couple like John and Margie entails creating goals and strategies for achieving them. One such goal was finding a balance between earning a living and spending time together. Another was finding more time for John to pursue his book writing projects.

The threats that cripple a marriage are often complicated and messy, possessing layers of experiences and memories. Sometimes people give up trying to understand what's driving them, feeling overwhelmed by the complexity of their emotions. It is not uncommon for people to throw up their hands in helplessness.

The PAG model can help, beginning with defining the threat. Often couples believe that their arguments about ordinary events, like getting home late from work, is the problem. They need to dig deeper into fundamental threats, like feeling they don't matter and believing that a spouse values a job or the kids more than a mate. Couples argue about the wrong problem, so it's no wonder nothing is ever solved.

Once the true threat is identified, the emotions and behaviors need clarifying. Activation of the anger button can result in seeing a spouse as the enemy. Activation of the fear button can result in loss of self-confidence, or in the ultimate flight behavior, threatening divorce. Shutdown may result in seeing marriage and family life as dull and pointless, like the depressed study participants who saw the world as gray.

At this point I talk about the power of words and how describing threats and fears enables them to gain control. I might also mention the research of neuroscientist Ahmad Hariri and his finding that people can control their emotional responses through the use of words. He showed that using language and thinking of words calmed down an emotional reaction.

With a couple like John and Margie, the road to recovery began with just talking and addressing the fundamental questions: Do I matter? Am I important? Talking bonds a couple, knitting them into a team so that when one feels threatened, they respond together. It enables them to accept differences in each other, to not feel threatened, and to say, "I'm sorry" and "I see your point" and mean it. This is the beginning of communication.

Jill: Traumatized for Life

Jill's parents divorced when she was five, so she was raised by her mother with her father visiting sporadically. The time she did spend with her father was strained and punctuated by long periods of silence. Jill felt that he was more interested in the children from his second marriage and noticed that he never said he loved her. Jill's mother did not have much time for her either. She worked two jobs and frequently had male friends stay overnight.

School offered little support. Jill had a hard time focusing on her studies and was easily distracted by anyone who paid attention to her. She began dating at age thirteen and soon acquired her first boyfriend. He was a senior, and she was flattered by his eager pursuit. On their second date, he drove her to a well-known make-out place, which she interpreted as meaning he loved her. Eager to please him, she got into the back seat. But the groping went too far and she tried to stop it, but he wouldn't stop. He said he would teach her what love was all about, and then he forced her to have sex. When he was done, he dropped her off at the end of her block. The only time she saw him after that was at school when he would turn away whenever she approached.

Gossip about her night with the senior boy got around school, and soon she had many dates. She accepted them all, hoping to erase feelings of loneliness and disgust. Her schoolwork fell off and she ditched as many classes as she could get away with. Her mother tried to intervene but was not around enough to impose much discipline. As a last resort, her mother took her to therapy. Therapy didn't last long. Jill refused to go after the therapist made her feel like a loser when he described her behavior as "acting out."

When Jill came to therapy with me, she was forty and in her third marriage. She was depressed, had trouble sleeping, and was having frequent panic attacks. Alcohol numbed her pain, so she drank steadily. Emotionally she was all over the map. She and her husband fought often, usually about money, and rarely had sex. This contentious relationship made her even angrier, and her temper had cost her repeated jobs.

Being raped as a teenager was a central trauma of her life, and that night was stuck in her mind as if she had swallowed something filthy. It is noteworthy that during this time her mother, instead of protecting her, had largely ignored her. This lack of support and reassurance about Jill's goodness and value scarred her for life. Forever after, she thought of herself as a slut.

Jill had a biological reaction to the rape. When she was raped, her insula generated feelings of disgust, which she turned inward. The rape and feelings of disgust sparked other emotions that fueled her PTSD. Feeling abandoned by her father and mother, her dysfunctional home life growing up, and being exposed to her mother's promiscuous behavior were meshed together in her traumatized life. She had never felt truly safe.

Individuals with PTSD have a neurological malfunction that alters the connections between the cortex and the amygdala. As a result, the amygdala stimulates the buttons in Jill's PAG, which goes into steady survival mode. Her nervous system also goes on high alert.

Jill's "acting out" was probably the result of an out-of-control feeling produced by faulty neural connections.

I cannot get into someone else's mind and know firsthand what they are feeling, but I have firsthand experience with feeling out of control and know how disturbing it can be. When I was traveling in Uganda, I remember a bus ride through a bustling city. The streets were busy and vibrant with shoppers and children, and as we bounced along, I noticed that the driver had one of his feet on the dashboard and was occasionally turning around to chat with passengers behind him.

The instant I realized he was not paying attention, my pulse began to race. I anxiously scanned the road ahead, praying that no one dashed in front of us and that the bus stayed on the road. Then a dog ambled into the road, and I ducked my head, ready for a collision. None came, and as I looked up, still on the edge of panic, my eyes slipped to the passenger seat at the front of the bus. On the "wrong" side, I saw a man with both hands on the wheel, expertly steering us down the street. This country had been British—it was right-side driving. I felt safe, my blood pressure plummeted, and my PAG went quiet.

If broken into separate actions, Jill's behavior revealed that almost every button in the PAG model was active. Anger, fear, and numbness—a form of shutdown—were all there. Usually just one behavior predominates, but it is logical that the brain can initiate a battery of survival behaviors. When she was a teenager, these behaviors probably resembled those of other teens. Even non-abused teenagers engage in extreme, survival behaviors probably because their immature brain and young nervous system have not developed proper control mechanisms. As they age, controls in the form of discipline, new habits and automatic behavior, and family support act as a brake on immature survival behavior. Jill never acquired these brakes and was still going through the rapid mood changes and the out-of-control or acting-out behavior of her youth.

Also, her family history, especially her mother's behavior, may well have created a genetic or epigenetic effect on Jill. As mentioned in the trauma chapter, an individual's environment, which includes parental influences, can alter genes within a single generation. This alteration could well have added extra stimulus to her survival behavior and made her hypersensitive to threats.

The effects of a trauma changed her nervous system, and her sleep was broken by nightmares. Her body was geared for survival, and anything in her environment that could be interpreted as threatening, like an unfamiliar noise in the middle of the night, alerted her brain and launched a defense reaction. Whereas another person might roll over, Jill woke up.

Her relationship with her husband was also steeped in survival behavior. Her irritated tirades and her lack of interest in sex were behaviors intended to protect her. These behaviors had been hardwired into her. Part of the fallout from her trauma was an acute sense of vulnerability. Emotionally, she counteracted this by avoiding intimacy and holding herself in check. She felt unable to love or to be close to her husband. I suspect that on some level her husband sensed this distance between them, and this affected how they related to each other. Her sense of vulnerability may also be why, as is typical with many PTSD sufferers, she had a bleak view of her place in the world and felt that she had no future.

Therapy with Jill involved addressing these issues while ensuring that her survival reflexes were not regularly inflamed by alcohol. She had to understand how alcohol accentuated the extreme feelings she had and she would never find normalcy unless she reset her system without drinking. In therapy, she received the support and reassurance she did not get growing up. This meant convincing her that she was not a bad person, that her difficulty in relationships was not because of some flaw in her character but had a neurological explanation. She needed to feel worthy and valuable for who she was.

A combined treatment involving exposure therapy and extinction especially helped. In exposure therapy, patients repeatedly recall or relive a trauma that has instilled crippling fear while they are in a safe environment. It may entail imagining an experience or recounting the actual one or writing an account of it that someone else reads. By airing her fearful reactions, Jill created new images and associations to connect with the trauma. Exposure therapy enabled Jill to review the circumstances surrounding the rape and see that she was not at fault. And she learned new ways of reacting in situations and to slow her automatic survival reflexes. This gave her new memories that would become the foundation for normal behavior.

The Power of Talk Therapy

My goal in therapy is to change people's dysfunctional thinking habits and assumptions by offering alternative ways of reacting. My primary tool is words, and my main goal is getting people to abandon maladaptive, instinctive emotional responses and find ways to manage their actions. Changing behavior can be difficult and painful because it demands that people examine their lives and relationships in new ways and with an honesty that they may not have done before.

There are many misconceptions about talk therapy, one of them being that it delves into people's childhood to discover causes for particular emotions or ways of behaving. While patients and I sometimes delve into history if it's relevant to the present situation, I am much more focused on current symptoms and relationships they may have. When it's successful, therapy dials down people's emotions, lowers the volume, so to speak, so insight and reasoning can have more influence on their behavior. With emotions quieted, they have a better chance of learning new, healthier ways of feeling and behaving. As a result, I have found talk therapy to be effective in treating anger, rage, domestic violence, anxiety, and PTSD.

If you were to ask me what is the most prevalent, most destructive emotion I encounter, I would answer: fear. This is why talking is so important—airing strong emotions can reduce a person's fears. Of course there is good fear, and there is pathological fear. The good fear is what keeps you safe and healthy—it makes you protect yourself, avoid danger, and follow rules. Pathological fear can damage you in two ways: you can be a victim of your fears, and you can be a source of fears in others, thus sabotaging relationships.

Most fear can be controlled, no matter how forceful it is. While you may not be able to control events outside yourself, your fear is your creation. In therapy sessions, we frequently explore people's fears. As if they were buried land mines, we dig them up and examine them in detail and go to work on disarming them. On occasion, we cannot disarm them. We don't know whether to cut the red wire or the green wire, so we leave it alone. In these cases, people learn to live with uncertainty and make mental preparations just in case the fear unexpectedly leads to a troubling situation. Nevertheless, fear that has been examined and picked apart is much less harmful than fear that is ignored or denied.

With experiences that happened long ago, people have a better chance of controlling fear if old memories are modified by new information. This is where I hope to help people gain insight by using the PAG model as an explanation for inappropriate emotional reactions and toxic behavior. This does not erase the memory but changes and enhances it. Extinction is more about new learning than forgetting.

Not everyone gets better with talk therapy. People who don't do well are those who, probably because of an overactive amygdala, are especially sensitive to threats. Years of feeling threatened and having their brain on constant alert, ready to launch into fight or flight, has so frayed their neural connections that signals are amplified. In short, they are always fearful. For patients in this state, medication and support may help.

How to Use the PAG Model

When patients come to me, they are often upset and confused. They cannot control their emotions, whether anger or fear or depression or some combination of these. And they often do not understand why they feel the way they do. Their emotions frequently make no sense to them. Another common feeling is shame or guilt over things they have done, relationships they have damaged, and lives that have been damaged.

For this reason, early in our treatment I explain how their brain processes emotions and the role of the PAG in sparking behaviors. I show them my sketch of the PAG and its buttons, pointing out that what they have been experiencing has an underlying neurological explanation. In the next breath, however, I add that their active involvement in treatment and commitment to making changes is essential. I explain that the model presents a number of critical junctures—moments in their emotional life when they face a decision or action that will determine the course of their treatment. What follows here is a distillation of the PAG model into a series of steps or decision points that I hope will be helpful to anyone who sometimes struggles with emotions.

- Recognize the importance of sensory stimuli, and identify which of your senses you are most sensitive to and are most likely to set you off.

- Decide whether you need to remove yourself or get away from certain situations or sensory stimuli.

- Talk to a spouse, friend, or colleague about what sets you off. Verbalizing your reaction and feelings is enormously helpful in defusing explosive emotions.

- Consider how well you are handling stress and whether it may be intensifying your reaction to sensory stimuli.

- Assess whether you are reacting to a genuine threat to your physical or psychological well-being or to a fictitious threat. Remember that threats come in all shapes and sizes—not just from a mugger but also from internal emotional or physical reactions and from your environment.

- If your emotions include fear, examine it closely. Make a list of each of the fears besetting you. Think about how to tackle each one: Confrontation? Avoidance? Repeated exposure for a feeling of familiarity? Realize that you may not be able to defuse all your fears—you may need to learn to live with them.

- If your reward system is stimulated and you feel a craving for a particular pleasure, explore ways to get your mind off it. Even a distraction for a few minutes can quiet the reward drive.

- If you are feeling threatened, either physically or psychologically, remind yourself that this feeling will trigger your survival machinery. Certain parts of your brain will react automatically, sparking emotions or behavior so fast that you are unaware of what's just happened. Remember that it is natural at this point to act to protect yourself or get away from the threat.

- Ask yourself whether your reaction is appropriate to how threatened you feel. Is your behavior out of proportion to your fear or are you on your PAG button for a legitimate reason?

- If you feel that you are overreacting, remember you can slow the process down by pausing to think. Different ways of pausing are making lists, plans, and getting support or professional help. Taking a deep breath helps reset your nervous system. These steps impose cortical control over your survival machinery. You are disengaging your autopilot by applying methodical thinking and deliberate behavior.

- If you feel out of control most of the time, consider whether you were traumatized as a child. A buried trauma may be at the core of your wild emotions.

- Watch your alcohol intake. Ditto for caffeine or any other stimulants. These make it harder to control your emotions.

- Look for ways to reset your emotional ignition point so you are not set off so easily. Possible ways are through exercise, taking time off away from stress, forging more realistic expectations or learning to say no, developing a support network, and trying out ways of verbalizing or writing about your feelings.

Summing Up

- An essential first step of treatment is overcoming denial and acknowledging the extent of the problem and how it's affecting your life.

- The PAG model offers an explanation for spinning out of control as well as possible treatment approaches.

- Therapy entails understanding the hypersensitive fear and threat-driven survival instincts that set off inappropriate emotions and behaviors.

- Talk therapy works because it offers alternative ways of reacting to situations.

The Blame Game and Taking Personal Responsibility

Being Honest with Yourself

I always remember this patient. Barney was an eighty-year-old man coping with depression who came for therapy every Wednesday evening. Although he was married and had issues with his wife, I did not meet her until months after therapy began. Then one evening he showed up with her in tow. I greeted him at the door and, with barely a word, he motioned to his wife and marched to my office. Barney was scowling.

I had never seen him like this. Normally, he was soft-spoken and always attentive to respectful niceties. We settled in for a session, and I introduced myself to his wife.

"Enough. I can't take her anymore. This is the final straw. She's driving me crazy," he declared, shooting his wife a blistering look.

"We certainly should talk about this. Something obviously has happened. Can you tell me about it?" I asked, glancing back and forth between them.

"That's right, something did happen, and my life has been a mess ever since," Barney said.

"When did it happen? What was it?" I asked.

"Forty years ago. We got married. My life has been hell ever since," he declared.

It had been forty years since Barney decided to marry a woman who made him unhappy and frustrated. The consequences of his choice tormented him, but instead of rectifying it, he brought his wife to me. He intended her to be Exhibit A: The Reason I Am Miserable.

Miserable, eighty-year-old Barney never paused to consider that his wife's nastiness toward him was a response to his attitudes. He did not realize that his lifetime behavior of treating her like a mistake made her feel threatened. He made her feel as if their marriage was a sham, so she struck back to defend all that she valued. The result was a never-ending spiral of misery for each of them.

It is no accident that I am ending with this story. The majority of the couples I see come in with Exhibit A, Exhibit B, and Exhibit C in hand. They all have multiple reasons for why they have been behaving the way they have. Their reasons are all around them. Common refrains are "He made me do it" or "She gave me no choice" and the universal "It's not my fault."

My goal in writing this book has been to help you to better understand your behaviors and the people around you. The question now becomes, where do you go from here? When it comes to actions driven by strong emotions, people often feel that the outcome is beyond their control and they are an innocent victim. However, in all their explanations and litanies of complaints, I rarely if ever hear them admit personal responsibility. That's where the journey starts.

Who Do You Blame?

When I see patients for the first time, I take their history to get an assessment of where they have been, both emotionally and behaviorally, and where they are today. Without an accurate assessment, it is difficult to identify problems and find solutions. This can be painful and not for the fainthearted, but honesty is critical to the process.

Some will blame themselves for everything. This is a way of obscuring truths and avoiding thinking about what's really going on. Others will overlook key information, like the man who says his wife has left him but leaves out the fact that it was his affair that drove her away. Or it's the alcoholic who said she hadn't had a drink in ten years but didn't mention a recent urine test positive for drugs. Or it is the mother who is estranged from her children but doesn't mention that she's rarely home for a family meal.

A simplistic line of thought reduces the dilemma to the either-or question, am I to blame, or did you make me do it? This obscures a third and most probable answer, which is along the lines that it takes two. Wild emotions and extreme behavior do not come about in a vacuum. It is not as if they are launched into space never to return. They always ricochet back to you. Your emotions affect people around you, and they react, especially in a marriage. Even if your anger arises for no legitimate reason, when you express it, others react accordingly. Both individuals are at fault, and both have a chance and a responsibility to stop the damaging cycle.

The question of personal responsibility in a book about how brain networks govern emotions and behaviors may seem incongruous. There is a mountain of scientific research showing that the brain's survival mechanisms dictate how people react in difficult situations. It is understandable to believe that the brain is the prime mover behind your emotions and actions. A natural corollary to this is that you have little power over your feelings and actions, and you are compelled by basic drives. Given that your brain is directing your actions, the next logical step is thinking you bear little responsibility for your actions. The reasoning goes, "It isn't my fault that I can't control my temper or that I am depressed. It's my brain's." People blame the brain. This is a familiar argument, but it is flawed.

It is flawed because most people do not understand their behavior.

As this book has pointed out, people constantly process and react to the world around them to promote survival. But in some people, this system has been altered and their emotions and behaviors arise totally out of proportion to a situation. So they find themselves between a rock and a hard place. They don't want to blame others, yet their efforts to pull themselves up by the bootstraps and overcome deep emotional problems is often met with disappointing results. So blame, Barney's Exhibit A, becomes the default response.

Take Charge of Your Behavior

Denial can be a comforting way of thinking. Yet ultimately it is destructive because it prevents you from making positive changes. One way to tackle the denial issue is to assess your life and behavior. Ask hard questions and look for answers not only from yourself but also from those around you. These questions are the type that you should be asking yourself and your spouse, friends, and perhaps coworkers.

- Are my kids terrified of me?

- Is my drinking a problem?

- Is my anger hurting my relationships?

- Am I often defensive with suggestions about my behavior?

- Do I run away, either physically or emotionally, from problems?

- Am I capable of intimacy, love, and trust?

- Does fear keep me from reaching my potential? Fear can be expressed as lack of confidence, feelings of incompetence, inadequacy, or passivity.

- Have I taken on too much and don't know how to say no?

- Am I a bully? Do I enjoy controlling people, being bossy, or always being in charge?

- Do I have relationship problems?

- Do I avoid forming close relationships? Why?

- Is my language or tone of voice destructive?

Suppose you go to your doctor and he finds multiple polyps in your colon. Or you have a mammogram that shows suspicious calcifications. You might be inclined to blame your genetic heritage and ignore these conditions, but as everyone knows, blaming doesn't fix these conditions. In truth, you have to pay attention to potential problems or be faced with worse ones down the road. It is the same with emotional and behavioral problems. They need addressing early and maybe even often. There are no easy solutions here, but it is undeniably true that if you do not address your fears, they will persist or get worse. They will torment you and hold you hostage—you'll be miserable.

Responsibility is acknowledging that your emotions and behaviors are imperfect and can have a profound impact on your life and those around you. You are defined by your choices and actions. Regardless of what is going on in the brain, regardless of the wiring, neurochemicals, and genetic influences, life becomes meaningless without responsibility.

Acquire Insight

Acquiring insight into personal behavior is like genetic testing. Everyone has predispositions, whether they're a propensity for breast cancer because of family history; heart attacks because of cardiovascular disease; or inappropriate displays of fight, flight, shutdown, or alcoholic behavior because of defective neurological control mechanisms. It is the same for external factors. Patients frequently say that they hate their job, that it's boring and pointless, and gives them no satisfaction. Regardless of whether your life is constrained by a biological flaw or dissatisfaction with a lifestyle, you have a choice: you can feel defeated and accept that your life is going to be messed up, or you can recognize the problem and make changes to manage your issues.

In the same way, insight tells you about psychological weak spots, like addictive behavior, depression, or mood disorders. Similarly, knowing you have the hangover gene or depression gene, or that Aunt Sally spent years in a psychiatric hospital is useful but not a prediction. It is material for monitoring and motivation for change. The same is true for psychological proclivities. They indicate only where you are susceptible.

Making the effort to develop personal insight into emotions and behaviors is a practical, immediate way of discovering where you need to pay attention. With insight, you learn if you do not handle stress well, are extra sensitive to facial expressions or what people say, tend to be overly anxious, or have a temper. Insight begins with understanding your fears. With insight, you learn what needs special attention.

Most of the time, you know what's bugging you, whether it's an attitude from a store clerk, a driver flipping you off, or a spouse ignoring what you say. Other times, you feel angry or depressed but can't pinpoint why. You feel like saying, "I want to tear someone's head off," or "Everything makes me sad." Knowing that sensory input influences your emotions can alert you to something in your environment that is setting you off. If a threat is nebulous, withdrawing from your surroundings can help. Putting distance between yourself and people who might be a source of irritation, tasks that cause frustration, or places that disturb you can silence the alarm.

An essential insight is realizing that you do not think well and your memory cannot be trusted when your emotions are stirred up. When you are emotional, you remember how you felt at the end of an experience, not how you felt at first or during the experience.

Acknowledging that your emotions may not be reliable is vital. It forces you to look elsewhere for insights, namely at your actions.

Acquiring insight into how your brain reacts to threats is a way of taking control. With this information, you are better able to grapple with changes for tomorrow. Instead of being bogged down in toxic emotions, you figure out how to override your brain's imperfect wiring.

Face the Elephant in the Room

One of the reasons taking responsibility is difficult is that it can come with a feeling of guilt, loss, or shame. It can mean admitting and talking about what you never want to talk about.

It's the man whose father abandoned him when he was six and now struggles with depression. It was difficult for him to talk about the abandonment, and at first when he did, he vowed never to be that way himself. But it wasn't until he admitted that he now rarely sees his own child that he began to make progress.

It's the woman first admitting her alcoholism and then ultimately talking about the friends and husbands she has lost because of it.

It's the young man who talks about loyalty and family duty then finally admits that he has been crippled with guilt because he abused his sister.

It's the woman being treated for depression who talks about a childhood memory of crying herself to sleep at night because her father abused her and her mother never intervened.

It's the man who admits that he lost the best job he ever had because he could not control his temper and blew up at his boss.

It's the woman who hasn't talked to her sister in years because of a fight over a birthday cake.

Like everyone else with emotional struggles, these people must begin with honesty, no matter how painful. This is because honesty is ultimately freeing. Just a simple, heartfelt "I'm sorry" is a monumental first step. It is no small task, I know, but it must start somewhere.

Don't Let Fear Rule

No one can live a life cloistered from stress or fear. If you live in a bubble with no fear or threats, you will never learn to handle them. Avoiding them entirely is not a good strategy because you are unprepared for the inevitable encounter. You need to know how to react when your survival system sounds the alarm. Even more, you need to know how to modulate survival behavior.

The model shows that feeling threatened can arise from someone or something happening around you or for no reason at all. Keep that in mind—no reason at all. The threat may be genuine or just as easily be fictitious, such as an unintended slight, or it may be out of the blue. A lesson of the model is that it is useful to consider whether the threat is truly a survival situation or a false alarm. Remind yourself that your neurological wiring can malfunction. Your brain can misread fear. The brain's survival system can go haywire, sounding alarms when no threat is imminent.

Listen to Your Inner GPS

Changing behavior is immensely painful. It is much easier to continue with the status quo or to abdicate responsibility and go passive. I know that patients frequently hit a wall at some point during therapy, thinking, *This is too hard, I can't do it.* I wish I had easy or simple answers for them, and I can only remind them that not changing, not taking responsibility, is not in their best interest. Their irrational emotions and destructive behaviors are sabotaging everything good about them and their lives.

It helps sometimes if I describe what they are going through as a kind of road trip with the guidance of an inner GPS system. At some point in their journey, the GPS voice announces, "You missed your exit. Redirecting." This can throw people into turmoil. They don't know how they missed the exit, they feel lost, and they worry about never reaching their destination.

When they hear this voice, they have three choices. They can ignore it and continue ahead, not really knowing where they are going. They can unplug the device and try to find the correct road by wandering about on their own. Or they can listen to the GPS and follow the directions for getting back on the right road. I encourage them to listen.

Their new road will be unfamiliar and perhaps even circuitous. Their journey will never be as they first imagined. Much will be new territory, and at times they will wonder, *Is this really the right way?* However, I reassure them that this is the only way. They must redirect, they must change their route to reach their destination.

My hope is that people will have the courage to listen to their GPS—acknowledge where they have gone wrong, face their behavior and change, or get help. This is a tall order, but it starts with small, incremental changes that will ultimately produce a sea change. It is possible to overcome emotional and behavioral flaws. Doing so requires taking responsibility. This means making a choice. On the one hand, you can be a victim and blame your brain function, genetics, or the environment; persist in denial; and avoid any insight. Or you can take action. Along the way, cut yourself some slack and give yourself credit for tackling the problem.

It's my dream that people realize that how they behave matters and to take their behavior seriously. I want engaged parents, thoughtful spouses, and a caring community. I want children to feel safe, I want adults to face their fears, and I want couples to communicate. It begins with acting responsibly, reclaiming self-respect, and realizing that everything you do matters—to you, your family, your community. This is perhaps the ultimate lesson I've learned from my patients. It is possible to take control. I have seen it happen, and I know it can happen.

Redemption.

Acknowledgments

This book has been a labor of love for both of us. For Ted, it represents a lifetime of psychiatry, research, and, hopefully, helping patients. For Lisa, it represents the culmination of years of writing about mental health, psychiatry, and the brain. Yet this book would never have happened without the help of others. Our agent and tireless champion, Gail Ross, brought us together and we can't thank her enough for that. She then found us a wonderful editor, Nancy Hancock, whose cogent insights and deft editing elevated our manuscript immeasurably. Thanks also to her assistant, Elsa Dixon, who has kept us organized, and Ali McCart, a meticulous copyeditor. Our illustrator, Jane Whitney, did a great job producing skilled drawings.

Last and surely not least, we must thank our families. Tim George provided the original concept and inspiration for the book, and Ted's daughter Becky had a great idea for the cover design. His daughter, Heather, and daughter-in-law, Lauren, were always there with suggestions and encouragement. Ted's wife, Angie, was an astute and thoughtful editor. She frequently saved us from embarrassing ourselves. And Lisa's husband, Ted Culp, not only provided support and understanding but put up with our countless working weekends and late-night meetings with barely a grumble.

Notes

Chapter 1: Patient Zero

1. P. Bard, "A Diencephalic Mechanism for the Expression of Rage with Special Reference to the Sympathetic Nervous System," *American Journal of Physiology* 84 (1928): 490–515.

2. D. T. George et al., "Lactate-Induced Rage and Panic in a Select Group of Subjects Who Perpetuate Acts of Domestic Violence," *Biological Psychiatry* 47, no. 9 (2000): 804–812.

3. P. L. Johnson et al., "Neural Pathways Underlying Lactate-Induced Panic," *Neuropsychopharmacology* 33, no. 9 (2008): 2093–2107; Stephen M. Roth, "Why Does Lactic Acid Build Up in Muscles? And Why Does It Cause Soreness?," *Scientific American,* January 23, 2006.

4. A. Siegel and C. B. Pott, "Neural Substrates of Aggression and Flight in the Cat," *Progress in Neurobiology* 31, no. 4 (1988): 261–283.

Chapter 2: It's All About Survival

1. G. F. Loewenstein et al., "Risk as Feelings," *Psychological Bulletin* 127, no. 2 (2001): 267–286.

2. J. S. Morris et al., "A Neuromodulatory Role for the Human Amygdala in Processing Emotional Facial Expressions," *Brain* 121, no. 1 (1998): 47–57.

3. J. S. Morris, A. Öhman, and R. J. Dolan, "Conscious and Unconscious Emotional Learning in the Human Amygdala," *Nature* 393, no. 6684 (1998): 467–470.

4. R. Garcia et al., "The Amygdala Modulates Prefrontal Cortex Activity Relative to Conditioned Fear," *Nature* 402, no. 6759 (1999): 294–296.

5. Keith Oatley, *Emotions, A Brief History* (Maldon, MA: Blackwell Publishing, 2004).

6. A. R. Hariri, S. Y. Bookheimer, and J. C. Mazziotta, "Modulating Emotional Responses: Effects of a Neocortical Network on the Limbic System," *NeuroReport* 11, no. 1 (2000): 43–48.

Chapter 3: What Ignites Your Emotions

1. P. Ekman, "Darwin's Contributions to Our Understanding of Emotional Expressions," *Philosophical Transactions of the Royal Society of London* 364, no. 1535 (2009): 3449–3451.

2. J. C. Westman and J. R. Walters, "Noise and Stress: A Comprehensive Approach," *Environmental Health Perspectives* 41 (1981): 291–309.

3. Paul Ekman, *Emotions Revealed: Recognizing Faces and Feelings to Improve Communication and Emotional Life* (New York: Henry Holt: 2007); "Facial Expression and Emotion," *American Psychologist* 48, no. 4 (1993): 384–392.

4. Paul Ekman, *Emotions Revealed*, 54.

5. A. R. Hariri et al., "The Amygdala Response to Emotional Stimuli: A Comparison of Faces and Scenes," *NeuroImage* 17, no. 1 (2002): 317–323.

6. J. C. Britton et al., "Facial Expressions and Complex IAPS Pictures: Common and Differential Networks," *NeuroImage* 31, no. 2 (2006): 906–919.

7. A. D. Lawrence et al., "Selective Disruption of the Recognition of Facial Expressions of Anger," *NeuroReport* 13, no. 6 (2002): 881–884.

8. P. J. Whalen et al., "Masked Presentations of Emotional Facial Expressions Modulate Amygdala Activity Without Explicit Knowledge," *Journal of Neuroscience* 18, no. 1 (1998): 411–418.

9. R. Adolphs, "A Mechanism for Impaired Fear Recognition After Amygdala Damage," *Nature* 433, no. 7021 (2005): 68–72; R. Adolphs et al., "Impaired Recognition of Emotion in Facial Expressions Following Bilateral Damage to the Human Amygdala," *Nature* 372, no. 6507 (1994): 669–672.

10. S. Baron-Cohen, S. Wheelwright, and T. Jolliffe, "Is There a 'Language of the Eyes'?," *Visual Cognition* 4, no. 3 (1997): 311–331.

11. E. Fox and L. Damjanovic, "The Eyes Are Sufficient to Produce a Threat Superiority Effect," *Emotion* 6, no. 3 (2006): 534–539; L. J. Burklund, N. I. Eisenberger, and M. D. Lieberman, "The Face of Rejection: Rejection Sensitivity Moderates Dorsal Anterior Cingulate Activity to Disapproving Facial Expressions," *Social Neuroscience* 2, nos. 3–4 (2007): 238–253.

12. S. K. Scott et al., "Impaired Auditory Recognition of Fear and Anger Following Bilateral Amygdala Lesions," *Nature* 385, no. 6613 (1997): 254–257.

13. Westman and Walters, "Noise and Stress."

14. Westman and Walters, "Noise and Stress."

15. A. E. Ziemann et al., "The Amygdala Is a Chemosensor That Detects Carbon Dioxide and Acidosis to Elicit Fear Behavior," *Cell* 139, no. 5 (2009): 1012–1021.

16. L. R. Mujica-Parodi et al., "Chemosensory Cues to Conspecific Emotional Stress Activate Amygdala in Humans," *PloS One* 4, no. 7 (2009): e6415.

17. S. Gelstein et al., "Human Tears Contain a Chemosignal," *Science* 331, no. 6014 (2011): 226–230.

18. L. Conty et al., "Searching for Asymmetries in the Detection of Gaze Contact Versus Averted Gaze Under Different Head Views: A Behavioral Study," *Spatial Vision* 19, no. 6 (2006): 529–545; S. R. H. Langton, R. J.

Watt, and I. V. Bruce, "Do the Eyes Have It? Cues to the Direction of Social Attention," *Trends in Cognitive Science* 4, no. 2 (2000): 50–59.

19. William James, "What Is an Emotion?," *Classics in the History of Psychology,* http://psychclassics.yorku.ca/James/emotion.htm.

20. M. R. Rosenzweig, S. M. Breedlove, and A. L. Leiman, *Biological Psychology,* 3rd ed. (Sunderland, MA: Sinauer Associates, 2002).

21. J. A. Herd, "Sixteenth Bowditch Lecture: The Physiology of Strong Emotions—Cannon's Scientific Legacy Re-Examined," *The Physiologist* 15, no. 1 (1972): 5–16.

22. D. S. Charney, "Psychobiological Mechanisms of Resilience and Vulnerability: Implications for Successful Adaptation to Extreme Stress," *American Journal of Psychiatry* 161, no. 2 (2004): 195–216.

23. F. Lederbogen et al., "City Living and Urban Upbringing Affect Neural Social Stress Processing in Humans," *Nature* 474, no. 7352 (2011): 498–501; D. P. Kennedy and R. Adolphs, "Social Neuroscience: Stress and the City," *Nature* 474, no. 7352 (2011): 452–453.

Chapter 4: An Answer in the PAG

1. George et al., "Lactate-Induced Rage and Panic in a Select Group of Subjects Who Perpetrate Domestic Violence."

2. Siegel and Pott, "Neural Substrates of Aggression and Flight in the Cat"; N. J. Weinshenker and A. Siegel, "Bimodal Classification of Aggression: Affective Defense and Predatory Attack," *Aggression and Violent Behavior* 7, no. 3 (2002): 237–250; A. Siegel and J. Victoroff, "Understanding Human Aggression: New Insights from Neuroscience," *International Journal of Law and Psychiatry* 32, no. 4 (2009): 209–215.

3. R. Bandler et al., "Central Circuits Mediating Patterned Autonomic Activity During Active vs. Passive Emotional Coping," *Brain Research Bulletin* 53, no. 1 (2000): 95–104; R. Bandler and K. A. Keay, "Columnar Organization in the Midbrain Periaqueductal Gray and the Integration of Emotional Expression," *Progress in Brain Research* 107 (1996): 285–300.

4. Herd, "Sixteenth Bowditch Lecture," 5–16.

5. J. LeDoux, *Synaptic Self: How Our Brains Become Who We Are* (New York: Penguin, 2003), 211; J. E. LeDoux, "Emotion Circuits in the Brain," *Annual Review of Neuroscience* 23 (2000): 155–184.

6. D. Dougherty et al., "Anger in Healthy Men: A PET Study Using Script-Driven Imagery," *Biological Psychiatry* 46, no. 4 (1999): 466–472.

7. X. An et al., "Prefrontal Cortical Projections to Longitudinal Columns in the Midbrain Periaqueductal Gray in Macaque Monkeys," *Journal of Comparative Neurology* 401, no. 4 (1998): 455–479.

8. A. Siegel and J. Chabora, "Effects of Electrical Stimulation of the Cingulate Gyrus upon Attack Behavior Elicited from the Hypothalamus in the Cat," *Brain Research* 32, no. 1 (1971): 169–177.

9. B. S. Nashold et al., "The Midbrain and Pain," in *Advances in Neurology,* ed. J. J. Bonica, vol. 4 (New York: Raven, 1974): 191–196.

10. D. Mobbs et al., "Where Fear Is Near: Threat Imminence Elicits Prefrontal-Periaqueductal Gray Shifts in Humans," *Science* 317, no. 5841 (2007): 1079–1083.

11. Hariri, Bookheimer, and Mazziotta, "Modulating Emotional Responses: Effects of a Neocortical Network on the Limbic System."

12. S. Izawa et al., "Cynical Hostility, Anger Expression Style, and Acute Myocardial Infarction in Middle-Aged Japanese Men," *Behavioral Medicine* 37, no. 3 (2011): 81–86; L. D. Kubzansky et al., "Healthy Psychological Functioning and Incident Coronary Heart Disease: The Importance of Self-Regulation," *Archives of General Psychiatry* 68, no. 4 (2011): 400–408; S. Shivpuri et al., "Trait Anger, Cynical Hostility and Inflammation in Latinas: Variations by Anger Type?," *Brain, Behavior, and Immunity* 25, no. 6 (2011): 1256–1263.

Chapter 5: Hair-Trigger Tempers and Anger Unleashed

1. E. F. Coccaro et al., "Intermittent Explosive Disorder—Revised: Development, Reliability, and Validity of Research Criteria," *Comprehensive Psychiatry* 39, no. 6 (1998): 368–376.

2. D. T. George et al., "Serotonin, Testosterone and Alcohol in the Etiology of Domestic Violence," *Psychiatry Research* 104, no. 1 (2001): 27–37.

3. B. Schiffer et al., "Disentangling Structural Brain Alterations Associated with Violent Behavior from Those Associated with Substance Use Disorders," *Archives of General Psychiatry* 68, no. 10 (2011): 1039–1049; D. T. George et al., "A Select Group of Perpetrators of Domestic Violence: Evidence of Decreased Metabolism in the Right Hypothalamus and Reduced Relationships Between Cortical/Subcortical Brain Structures in Positron Emission Tomography," *Psychiatry Research* 130, no. 1 (2004): 11–25.

4. "Intermittent Explosive Disorder," in *Diagnostic and Statistical Manual of Mental Disorders,* 4th ed., ed. American Psychiatric Association (Arlington, VA: American Psychiatric Association, 2000), http://psycho. silverchair.com/content.aspx?aID=15671&searchStr=intermittent+explosive +disorder.

5. V. L. Holt et al., "Civil Protection Orders and Risk of Subsequent Police-Reported Violence," *Journal of the American Medical Association* 288, no. 5 (2002): 589–594.

6. K. Schubert, et al., "Differential Effects of Ethanol on Feline Rage and Predatory Attack Behavior: An Underlying Neural Mechanism," *Alcoholism: Clinical and Experimental Research* 20, no. 5 (1996): 882–889.

7. T. M. Lee, S. C. Chan, and A. Raine, "Hyperresponsivity to Threat Stimuli in Domestic Violence Offenders: A Functional Magnetic Resonance Imaging Study," *Journal of Clinical Psychiatry* 70, no. 1 (2009): 36–45.

8. George et al., "A Select Group of Perpetrators of Domestic Violence,"

Psychiatric Research 130, no. 1 (2004) D. T. George et al., "A Model Linking Biology, Behavior and Psychiatric Diagnoses in Perpetrators of Domestic Violence," *Medical Hypotheses* 67, no. 2 (2006): 345–353.

9. *National Intimate Partner and Sexual Violence Survey, 2010 Summary.* Centers for Disease Control.

10. R. J. Davidson, K. M. Putnam, and C. L. Larson, "Dysfunction in the Neural Circuitry of Emotion Regulation—A Possible Prelude to Violence," *Science* 289, no. 5479 (2000): 591–594.

11. J. L. Stewart et al., "Anger Style, Psychopathology, and Regional Brain Activity," *Emotion* 8, no. 5 (2008): 701–713; B. A. Bettencourt et al., "Personality and Aggressive Behavior Under Provoking and Neutral Conditions: A Meta-Analytic Review," *Psychological Bulletin* 132, no. 5 (2006): 751–777.

12. Coccaro et al., "Intermittent Explosive Disorder—Revised."

13. Lawrence et al., "Selective Disruption of the Recognition of Facial Expressions of Anger."

14. E. F. Coccaro et al., "Amygdala and Orbitofrontal Reactivity to Social Threat in Individuals with Impulsive Aggression," *Biological Psychiatry* 62, no. 2 (2007): 168–178.

15. Caccaro et al., "Amygdala and Orbitofrontal Reactivity to Social Threat in Individuals with Impulsive Aggression," 168–178.

16. D. T. George et al., "Fluoxetine Treatment of Alcoholic Perpetrators of Domestic Violence: A 12-Week, Double-Blind, Randomized, Placebo-Controlled Intervention Study," *Journal of Clinical Psychiatry* 72, no. 1 (2011): 60–65.

Chapter 6: Desperate to Escape: Panic

1. J. LeDoux, *The Emotional Brain* (New York: Simon and Schuster, 1998), 161.

2. LeDoux, *Synaptic Self,* 207.

3. A. Öhman, A. Flykt, and F. Esteves, "Emotion Drives Attention: Detecting the Snake in the Grass," *Journal of Experimental Psychology* 130, no. 3 (2001): 466–478; A. Öhman, "The Role of the Amygdala in Human Fear: Automatic Detection of Threat," *Psychoneuroendocrinology* 30, no. 10 (2005): 953–958.

4. Rosenzweig, Breedlove, and Leiman, *Biological Psychology.*

5. Rosenzweig, Breedlove, and Leiman, *Biological Psychology.*

6. "Anxiety Disorders," in *Diagnostic and Statistical Manual of Mental Disorders,* 4th ed., http://psycho.silverchair.com/content.aspx?aID=3037&searchStr=panic+attacks#3037.

7. LeDoux, *The Emotional Brain,* 230.

8. LeDoux, *The Emotional Brain,* 180.

9. K. Mogg, M. Garner, and B. P. Bradley, "Anxiety and Orienting of Gaze to Angry and Fearful Faces," *Biological Psychology* 76, no. 3 (2007): 163–169; G. A. Georgiou et al., "Focusing on Fear: Attentional Disengage-

ment from Emotional Faces," *Visual Cognition* 12, no. 1 (2005): 145–158; J. M. Cisler and E. H. Koster, "Mechanisms of Attentional Biases Toward Threat in the Anxiety Disorders: An Integrative Review," *Clinical Psychology Review* 30, no. 2 (2010): 203–216.

10. E. Becker, M. Rinck, and J. Margraf, "Memory Bias in Panic Disorder," *Journal of Abnormal Psychology* 103, no. 2 (1994): 396–399.

11. I. Indovina et al., "Fear-Conditioning Mechanisms Associated with Trait Vulnerability to Anxiety in Humans," *Neuron* 69, no. 3 (2011): 563–571.

12. J. Becker et al., eds., *Sex Differences in the Brain: From Genes to Behavior* (New York: Oxford University Press, 2007).

13. A. E. Meuret et al., "Do Unexpected Panic Attacks Occur Spontaneously?," *Biological Psychiatry* 70, no. 10 (2011): 985–991.

14. A. E. Meuret and T. Ritz, "Hyperventilation in Panic Disorder and Asthma: Empirical Evidence and Clinical Strategies," *International Journal of Psychophysiology* 78, no. 1 (2010): 68–79.

15. B. A. Teachman, S. B. Smith-Janik, and J. Saporito, "Information Processing Biases and Panic Disorder: Relationships Among Cognitive and Symptom Measures," *Behavioral Research and Therapy* 45, no. 8 (2007): 1791–1811.

Chapter 7: Going into Shutdown

1. Bandler et al., "Central Circuits Mediating Patterned Autonomic Activity During Active vs. Passive Emotional Coping."

2. J. Wacker, D. G. Dillon, and D. A. Pizzagalli, "The Role of the Nucleus Accumbens and Rostral Anterior Cingulate Cortex in Anhedonia: Integration of Resting EEG, fMRI, and Volumetric Techniques," *NeuroImage* 46, no. 1 (2009): 327–337.

3. C. Debien et al., "Alpha-Interferon and Mental Disorders," *Encephale* 27, no. 4 (2001): 308–317.

4. R. Dantzer et al., "From Inflammation to Sickness and Depression: When the Immune System Subjugates the Brain," *Nature Reviews: Neuroscience* 9, no. 1 (2008): 46–56; C. L. Raison, L. Capuron, and A. H. Miller, "Cytokines Sing the Blues: Inflammation and the Pathogenesis of Depression," *Trends in Immunology* 27, no. 1 (2006): 24–31.

5. N. I. Eisenberger et al., "Inflammation-Induced Anhedonia: Endotoxin Reduces Ventral Striatum Responses to Reward," *Biological Psychiatry* 68, no. 8 (2010): 748–754.

6. P. F. Sullivan, M. C. Neale, and K. S. Kendler, "Genetic Epidemiology of Major Depression: Review and Meta-Analysis," *American Journal of Psychiatry* 157, no. 10 (2000): 1552–1562.

7. A. Caspi et al., "Influence of Life Stress on Depression: Moderation by a Polymorphism in the 5-HTT Gene," *Science* 301, no. 5631 (2003): 386–389.

8. B. M. Way, S. E. Taylor, N. I. Eisenberger, "Variation in the Mu-Opioid Receptor Gene (OPRM1) Is Associated with Dispositional and Neural Sensi-

tivity to Social Rejection," *Proceedings of the National Academy of Sciences of the United States of America* 106, no. 35 (2009): 15079–15084.

9. J. L. Price and W. C. Drevets, "Neurocircuitry of Mood Disorders," *Neuropsychopharmacology* 35, no. 1 (2010): 192–216; T. Johnstone et al., "Failure to Regulate: Counterproductive Recruitment of Top-Down Prefrontal-Subcortical Circuitry in Major Depression," *Journal of Neuroscience* 27, no. 33 (2007): 8877–8884.

10. M. Beauregard, V. Paquette, and J. Lévesque, "Dysfunction in the Neural Circuitry of Emotional Self-Regulation in Major Depressive Disorder," *NeuroReport* 17, no. 8 (2006): 843–846.

11. S. C. Matthews et al., "Decreased Functional Coupling of the Amygdala and Supragenual Cingulate Is Related to Increased Depression in Unmedicated Individuals with Current Major Depressive Disorder," *Journal of Affective Disorders* 111, no. 1 (2008): 13–20.

12. E. Bubl et al., "Seeing Gray When Feeling Blue? Depression Can Be Measured in the Eye of the Diseased," *Biological Psychiatry* 68, no. 2 (2010): 205–208.

13. Bubl et al., "Seeing Gray When Feeling Blue? Depression Can Be Measured in the Eye of the Diseased."

14. S. Surguladze et al., "A Differential Pattern of Neural Response Toward Sad Versus Happy Facial Expressions in Major Depressive Disorder," *Biological Psychiatry* 57, no. 3 (2005): 201–209.

15. E. S. Monkul et al., "Fronto-Limbic Brain Structures in Suicidal and Non-Suicidal Female Patients with Major Depressive Disorder," *Molecular Psychiatry* 12, no. 4 (2007): 360–366.

16. Hariri et al., "The Amygdala Response to Emotional Stimuli."

17. A. S. New et al., "Fluoxetine Increases Relative Metabolic Rate in Prefrontal Cortex in Impulsive Aggression," *Psychopharmacology* 176, nos. 3–4 (2004): 451–458.

18. Mary Ann Liebert, Inc., Publishers, "What Role Do Cytokines Play in Autoimmune Diseases?," *ScienceDaily*, October 27, 2011.

Chapter 8: Stone-Cold Predators

1. R. D. Hare, *Manual for the Revised Psychopathy Checklist* (2nd ed.), 2003. Toronto, ON, Canada: Multi-Health Systems.

2. A. Raine et al., "Sex Differences in Orbitofrontal Gray as a Partial Explanation for Sex Differences in Antisocial Personality," *Molecular Psychiatry* 16, no. 2 (2011): 227–236.

3. N. Birbaumer et al., "Deficient Fear Conditioning in Psychopathy: A Functional Magnetic Resonance Imaging Study," *Archives of General Psychiatry* 62, no. 7 (2005): 799–805; R. J. Blair, "The Amygdala and Ventromedial Prefrontal Cortex: Functional Contributions and Dysfunction in Psychopathy," *Philosophical Transactions of the Royal Society of London* 363, no. 1503 (2008): 2557–2565.

4. K. A. Kiehl and J. W. Buckholtz, "Inside the Mind of a Psychopath," *Scientific American*, August 19, 2010.

5. Kiehl and Buckholtz, "Inside the Mind of a Psychopath."

6. E. A. Shirtcliff et al., "Neurobiology of Empathy and Callousness: Implications for the Development of Antisocial Behavior," *Behavioral Sciences and the Law* 27, no. 2 (2009): 137–171; G. di Pellegrino et al., "Understanding Motor Events: A Neurophysiological Study," *Experimental Brain Research* 91, no. 1 (1992): 176–180; G. Rizzolatti and L. Craighero, "The Mirror-Neuron System," *Annual Review of Neuroscience* 27 (2004): 169–192.

7. Kiehl and Buckholtz, "Inside the Mind of a Psychopath."

8. Kiehl and Buckholtz, "Inside the Mind of a Psychopath."

9. Kiehl and Buckholtz, "Inside the Mind of a Psychopath"; S. Williamson, T. J. Harpur, and R. D. Hare, "Abnormal Processing of Affective Words in Psychopaths," *Psychophysiology* 28, no. 3 (1991): 260–273.

10. J. T. Hancock, M. T. Woodworth, and S. Porter, "Hungry Like the Wolf: A Word-Pattern Analysis of the Language of Psychopaths," *Legal and Criminological Psychology* 18, no. 1 (2013), doi:10.1111/j.2044-8333.2011.02025.

11. P. D. Sylvers, P. A. Brennan, and S. O. Lilienfeld, "Psychopathic Traits and Preattentive Threat Processing in Children: A Novel Test of the Fearlessness Hypothesis," *Psychological Science* 22, no. 10 (2011): 1280–1287; K. A. Kiehl, "A Cognitive Neuroscience Perspective on Psychopathy: Evidence for Paralimbic System Dysfunction," *Psychiatry Research* 142, nos. 2–3 (2006): 107–128.

12. N. J. Weinshenker and A. Siegel, "Bimodal Classification of Aggression: Affective Defense and Predatory Attack."

13. J. W. Buckholtz et al., "Mesolimbic Dopamine Reward System Hypersensitivity in Individuals with Psychopathic Traits," *Nature Neuroscience* 13, no. 4 (2010): 419–421.

14. P. E. Mullen et al., "Study of Stalkers," *American Journal of Psychiatry* 156, no. 8 (1999): 1244–1249.

15. P. Babiak and R. D. Hare, *Snakes in Suits: When Psychopaths Go to Work* (New York: HarperBusiness, 2007).

16. P. Babiak, C. S. Neumann, and R. D. Hare, "Corporate Psychopathy: Talking the Walk," *Behavioral Sciences and the Law* 28, no. 2 (2010): 174–193.

17. Joshua Buckholtz, interview by Guy Raz, "Study: Psychopaths' Brains Wired to Seek Rewards," *All Things Considered*, National Public Radio, March 27, 2010.

18. J. P. Newman et al., "Attention Moderates the Fearlessness of Psychopathic Offenders," *Biological Psychiatry* 67, no. 1 (2010): 66–70; A. R. Baskin-Sommers, J. J. Curtin, and J. P. Newman, "Specifying the Attentional Selection That Moderates the Fearlessness of Psychopathic Offenders," *Psychological Science* 22, no. 2 (2011): 226–234.

19. R. Hare, "This Charming Psychopath," *Psychology Today*, January 1, 1994.

20. Kiehl and Buckholtz, "Inside the Mind of a Psychopath."

21. R. J. Blair, "Neurocognitive Models of Aggression, the Antisocial Personality Disorders, and Psychopathy," *Journal of Neurology, Neurosurgery, and Psychiatry* 71, no. 6 (2001): 727–731.

22. Y. Yang et al., "Localization of Deformations Within the Amygdala in Individuals with Psychopathy," *Archives of General Psychiatry* 66, no. 9 (2009): 986–994.

23. A. Raine et al., "Reduced Prefrontal Gray Matter Volume and Reduced Autonomic Activity in Antisocial Personality Disorder," *Archives of General Psychiatry* 57, no. 2 (2000): 119–127.

24. D. J. Stein and F. G. Moeller, "The Man Who Turned Bad," *CNS Spectrums* 10, no. 2 (2005): 88–90.

25. Blair, "The Amygdala and Ventromedial Prefrontal Cortex: Functional Contributions and Dysfunction in Psychopathy."; Birbaumer et al., "Deficient Fear Conditioning in Psychopathy."

26. Kiehl, "A Cognitive Neuroscience Perspective on Psychopathy."

27. V. Hughes, "Science in Court: Head Case," *Nature* 464, no. 7287 (2010): 340–342.

28. M. Cima, F. Tonnaer, and M. D. Hauser, "Psychopaths Know Right from Wrong but Don't Care," *Social Cognitive and Affective Neuroscience* 5, no. 1 (2010): 59–67.

Chapter 9: Held Hostage by Trauma

1. S. D. Norrholm and T. Jovanovic, "Tailoring Therapeutic Strategies for Treating Posttraumatic Stress Disorder Symptom Clusters," *Neuropsychiatric Disease and Treatment* 6 (2010): 517–532.

2. A. Hartocollis, "10 Years and a Diagnosis Later, 9/11 Demons Haunt Thousands," *New York Times*, August 9, 2011.

3. R. Yehuda and J. LeDoux, "Response Variation Following Trauma: A Translational Neuroscience Approach to Understanding PTSD," *Neuron* 56, no. 1 (2007): 19–32.

4. "Domestic Violence Facts," National Coalition Against Domestic Violence. www.ncadv.org/resources/FactSheet.php.

5. A. Flynn and K. Graham, "'Why Did It Happen?' A Review and Conceptual Framework for the Research on Perpetrators' and Victims' Explanations for Intimate Partner Violence," *Aggression and Violent Behavior* 15, no. 3 (2010): 239–251.

6. R. Yehuda et al., "Putative Biological Mechanisms for the Association Between Early Life Adversity and the Subsequent Development of PTSD," *Psychopharmacology* 212, no. 3 (2010): 405–417.

7. A. Caspi et al., "Genetic Sensitivity to the Environment: The Case of the Serotonin Transporter Gene and Its Implications for Studying Complex Diseases and Traits," *American Journal of Psychiatry* 167, no. 5 (2010): 509–527.

8. K. Thomaes et al., "Reduced Anterior Cingulate and Orbitofrontal Volumes in Child Abuse–Related Complex PTSD," *Journal of Clinical Psychiatry* 71, no. 12 (2010): 1636–1644.

9. "Posttraumatic Stress Disorder," in *Diagnostic and Statistical Manual of Mental Disorders,* 4th ed., http://psycho.silverchair.com/content.aspx?aID=295433&searchStr=post-traumatic+stress+disorder.

10. P. O. McGowan et al., "Epigenetic Regulation of the Glucocorticoid Receptor in Human Brain Associates with Childhood Abuse," *Nature Neuroscience* 12, no. 3 (2009): 342–348.

11. R. Yehuda et al., "Maternal, Not Paternal, PTSD Is Related to Increased Risk for PTSD in Offspring of Holocaust Survivors," *Journal of Psychiatric Research* 42, no. 13 (2008): 1104–1111.

12. R. P. Kluft, "Ramifications of Incest," *Psychiatric Times* 27, no. 12 (2011).

13. J. C. Derrick, "What Joe Paterno Taught Me: It's Time to Stop Keeping Secrets," *Washington Post,* November 11, 2011.

14. N. H. Naqvi and A. Bechara, "The Insula and Drug Addiction: An Interoceptive View of Pleasure, Urges, and Decision-Making," *Brain Structure and Function* 214, nos. 5–6 (2010): 435–450.

15. J. Schaich Borg, D. Lieberman, and K. A. Kiehl, "Infection, Incest and Iniquity: Investigating the Neural Correlates of Disgust and Morality," *Journal of Cognitive Neuroscience* 20, no. 9 (2008): 1529–1546.

16. K. S. Kendler, J. W. Kuhn, and C. A. Prescott, "Childhood Sexual Abuse, Stressful Life Events and Risk for Major Depression in Women," *Psychological Medicine* 34, no. 8 (2004): 1475–1482.

17. J. D. Bremner et al., "Childhood Physical Abuse and Combat-Related Posttraumatic Stress Disorder in Vietnam Veterans," *American Journal of Psychiatry* 150, no. 2 (1993): 235–239.

18. K. A. Peace, S. Porter, and L. ten Brinke, "Are Memories for Sexually Traumatic Events 'Special'? A Within-Subjects Investigation of Trauma and Memory in a Clinical Sample," *Memory* 16, no. 1 (2008): 10–21.

19. A. S. New et al., "A Functional Magnetic Resonance Imaging Study of Deliberate Emotion Regulation in Resilience and Posttraumatic Stress Disorder," *Biological Psychiatry* 66, no. 7 (2009): 656–664.

20. Yehuda and LeDoux, "Response Variation Following Trauma: A Translational Neuroscience Approach to Understanding PTSD."

21. Norrholm and Jovanovic, "Tailoring Therapeutic Strategies for Treating Posttraumatic Stress Disorder Symptom Clusters."

22. M. Altemus, F. S. Dhabhar, and R. Yang, "Immune Function in PTSD," *Annals of the New York Academy of Sciences* 1071 (2006): 167–183.

23. L. M. Shin, S. L. Rauch, and R. K. Pitman, "Amygdala, Medial Prefrontal Cortex, and Hippocampal Function in PTSD," *Annals of the New York Academy of Science* 1071 (2006): 67–79; S. L. Rauch, L. M. Shin, and

E. A. Phelps, "Neurocircuitry Models of Posttraumatic Stress Disorder and Extinction: Human Neuroimaging Research—Past, Present, and Future," *Biological Psychiatry* 60, no. 4 (2006): 376–382.

24. K. C. Koenen et al., "Persisting Posttraumatic Stress Disorder Symptoms and Their Relationship to Functioning in Vietnam Veterans: A 14-Year Follow-Up," *Journal of Traumatic Stress* 21, no. 1 (2008): 49–57; E. Geuze et al., "Neural Correlates of Associative Learning and Memory in Veterans with Posttraumatic Stress Disorder," *Journal of Psychiatric Research* 42, no. 8 (2008): 659–669.

25. J. D. Bremner et al., "Neural Correlates of Exposure to Traumatic Pictures and Sound in Vietnam Combat Veterans with and Without Posttraumatic Stress Disorder: A Positron Emission Tomography Study," *Biological Psychiatry* 45, no. 7 (1999): 806–816.

26. E. B. Binder et al., "Association of FKBP5 Polymorphisms and Childhood Abuse with Risk of Posttraumatic Stress Disorder Symptoms in Adults," *Journal of the American Medical Association* 299, no. 11 (2008): 1291–1305.

27. M. J. Meaney and M. Szyf, "Maternal Care as a Model for Experience-Dependent Chromatin Plasticity?," *Trends in Neurosciences* 28, no. 9 (2005): 456–463.

28. K. Skelton et al., "PTSD and Gene Variants: New Pathways and New Thinking," *Neuropharmacology* 62, no. 2 (2012): 628–637.

29. R. Yehuda and L. M. Bierer, "The Relevance of Epigenetics to PTSD: Implications for the DSM-V," *Journal of Traumatic Stress* 22, no. 5 (2009): 427–434.

30. K. Skelton et al., "PTSD and Gene Variants: New Pathways and New Thinking."

31. Hartocollis, "10 Years and a Diagnosis Later."

32. A. Holmes et al., "Chronic Alcohol Remodels Prefrontal Neurons and Disrupts NMDAR-Mediated Fear Extinction Encoding," *Nature Neuroscience* 15, no. 10 (2012): 1359–1361.

Chapter 10: Another Route to Survival or Sickness: The Reward Pathway

1. M. A. Gray and H. D. Critchley, "Interoceptive Basis to Craving," *Neuron* 54, no. 2 (2007): 183–186.

2. "Alcohol Dependence," in *Diagnostic and Statistical Manual of Mental Disorders*, 4th ed., http://psycho.silverchair.com/content.aspx?aID=949&searchStr=alcohol+dependence.

3. D. M. Small et al., "Changes in Brain Activity Related to Eating Chocolate: From Pleasure to Aversion," *Brain* 124 (2001): 1720–1733.

4. T. C. Adam and E. S. Epel, "Stress, Eating and the Reward System," *Physiology and Behavior* 91, no. 4 (2007): 449–458.

5. A. R. Childress et al., "Prelude to Passion: Limbic Activation by 'Unseen' Drug and Sexual Cues," *PLOS One* 3, no. 1 (2008): e1506.

6. J. M. Gilman et al., "Why We Like to Drink: A Functional Magnetic Resonance Imaging Study of the Rewarding and Anxiolytic Effects of Alcohol," *Journal of Neuroscience* 28, no. 18 (2008): 4583–4591; P. Amorapanth, J. E. LeDoux, and K. Nader, "Different Lateral Amygdala Outputs Mediate Reactions and Actions Elicited by a Fear-Arousing Stimulus," *Nature Neuroscience* 3, no. 1 (2000): 74–79.

7. G. F. Koob and M. Le Moal, "Plasticity of Reward Neurocircuitry and the 'Dark Side' of Drug Addiction," *Nature Neuroscience* 8, no. 11 (2005): 1442–1444; G. F. Koob and M. Le Moal, "Addiction and the Brain Antireward System," *Annual Review of Psychology* 59 (2008): 29–53.

8. A. D. Craig, "How Do You Feel—Now? The Anterior Insula and Human Awareness," *Nature Reviews: Neuroscience* 10, no. 1 (2009): 59–70; H. Garavan, "Insula and Drug Cravings," *Brain Structure and Function* 214, nos. 5–6 (2010): 593–601.

9. A. Frankort et al., "Reward Activity in Satiated Overweight Women Is Decreased During Unbiased Viewing but Increased when Imagining Taste: An Event-Related fMRI Study," *International Journal of Obesity* 36, no. 5 (2012): 627–637.

10. N. H. Naqvi and A. Bechara, "The Hidden Island of Addiction: The Insula," *Trends in Neuroscience* 32, no. 1 (2009): 56–67.

11. N. H. Naqvi et al., "Damage to the Insula Disrupts Addiction to Cigarette Smoking," *Science* 315, no. 5811 (2007): 531–534.

12. B. Knutson and J. C. Cooper, "Functional Magnetic Resonance Imaging of Reward Prediction," *Current Opinion in Neurology* 18, no. 4 (2005): 411–417.

13. E. S. Bromberg-Martin, M. Matsumoto, and O. Hikosaka, "Dopamine in Motivational Control: Rewarding, Aversive, and Alerting," *Neuron* 68, no. 5 (2010): 815–834.

14. G. F. Koob and N. D. Volkow, "Neurocircuitry of Addiction," *Neuropsychopharmacology* 35, no. 1 (2010): 217–238.

15. Small et al., "Changes in Brain Activity Related to Eating Chocolate."

16. Koob and Volkow, "Neurocircuitry of Addiction."

17. A. Bechara, "Decision Making, Impulse Control and Loss of Willpower to Resist Drugs: A Neurocognitive Perspective," *Nature Neuroscience* 8, no. 11 (2005): 1458–1463.

18. A. R. Damásio, *Descartes' Error: Emotion, Reason, and the Human Brain* (New York: Putnam, 1994).

19. Bechara, "Decision Making, Impulse Control and Loss of Willpower to Resist Drugs"; X. Noël et al., "Alcoholism and the Loss of Willpower: A Neurocognitive Perspective," *Journal of Psychophysiology* 24, no. 4 (2010): 240–248.

20. E. V. Sullivan and A. Pfefferbaum, "Neurocircuitry in Alcoholism: A Substrate of Disruption and Repair," *Psychopharmacology* 180, no. 4 (2005): 583–594.

21. R. Gilbertson, R. Prather, and S. J. Nixon, "The Role of Selected Factors in the Development and Consequences of Alcohol Dependence," *Alcohol Research and Health* 31, no. 4 (2008): 389–399; M. Oscar-Berman and A. Bowirrat, "Genetic Influences in Emotional Dysfunction and Alcoholism-Related Brain Damage," *Neuropsychiatric Disease and Treatment* 1, no. 3 (2005): 211–229.

22. H. Scholz, M. Franz, and U. Heberlein, "The Hangover Gene Defines a Stress Pathway Required for Ethanol Tolerance Development," *Nature* 436, no. 7052 (2005): 845–847.

23. "The Fruit Fly in You," *Science News*, NASA Science, February 3, 2004.

24. A. Z. Pietrzykowski and S. N. Treistman, "The Molecular Basis of Tolerance." *Alcohol Research and Health* 31, no. 4 (2008): 298–309.

25. Oscar-Berman and Bowirrat, "Genetic Influences in Emotional Dysfunction."

26. A. J. Robison and E. J. Nestler, "Transcriptional and Epigenetic Mechanisms of Addiction," *Nature Reviews: Neuroscience* 12, no. 11 (2011): 623–637.

27. R. Z. Goldstein et al., "The Neurocircuitry of Impaired Insight in Drug Addiction," *Trends in Cognitive Sciences* 13, no. 9 (2009): 372–380.

28. C. Kornreich et al., "Impaired Emotional Facial Expression Recognition in Alcoholism Compared with Obsessive-Compulsive Disorder and Normal Controls," *Psychiatry Research* 102, no. 3 (2001): 235–248.

Chapter 11: Smothering the Fire: Treatment

1. Adapted from Don and Sally Meredith, *Two Becoming One: Experiencing the Power of Oneness in Your Marriage* (Chicago: Moody Publishers, 1999.

Index

About the Authors

Ted George is an associate clinical director at the National Institutes of Health in Bethesda, Maryland. He holds the position of Associate Clinical Director for the National Institute on Alcohol Abuse and Alcoholism and is a clinical professor of psychiatry at George Washington University School of Medicine. He is board-certified in psychiatry and internal medicine and is a Captain in the U.S. Public Health Service. Dr. George has been published extensively in scientific medical journals and has presented before numerous professional groups, including the American Psychiatric Association, American Neuropsychiatric Association, Research Society on Alcoholism, and the American College of Neuropsychopharmacology.

Lisa Berger has written numerous popular nonfiction books, most of which deal with psychiatry, mental illness, and neuroscience. She has written about manic depression, chronic pain, and memory. *Untangling the Mind* is her eleventh book.